LANDMARKS IN DELHI ADMINISTRATION

LANDMARKS IN DELHI ADMINISTRATION
(Post-Independence Era) 1947-97

Editors:
S.C. Vajpeyi
Prof. S.P. Verma

Foreword by:
Tejendra Khanna
(Lieutenant Governor, Delhi)

GYAN PUBLISHING HOUSE
New Delhi-110002

on behalf of:
INDIAN INSTITUTE OF PUBLIC ADMINISTRATION
New Delhi-110002

LANDMARKS IN DELHI ADMINISTRATION
(Post-Independence Era)
1947-97
(Public Administration, Education, Environment, Health, Industry, Law, Management, Political Science, Rural Development, Sociology)

ISBN : 81-212-0568-9

Published in 1998 by
Gyan Publishing House,
5, Ansari Road, Darya Ganj
New Delhi-110002

Laser Typesetting at A.S. Printers, Delhi.
Printed at Mehra Offset Press, Delhi.

CONTENTS

FOREWORD

Governance of the National Capital Territory of Delhi has gone through a considerable evolution in the past decades. Within the overall umbrella of the final responsibility for governance being vested in the Union Government, it is only natural that powers for the day to day administration in a number of areas have been decentralised to the elected representatives. It has been suggested that if a unified control mechanism had remained in place, as was the case during the tenure of the former Chief Commissioners and Lieutenant Governors, the responsibility would have been more specifically located and problems of coordination between different tiers of authority would not have been as arduous as have been found to be the case under the present constitutional arrangements.

On the physical side, the multifarious problems that the city has to cope with including the imbalance between demand for and supply of housing, water supply, electricity, waste disposal facilities, health care, education, sports and recreation, etc., are getting more accentuated because of the mounting population pressure arising both from continued inward migration as well as natural growth. The National Capital Territory has also to cope with law and order problems which not only cover normal crime which is endemic to all societies but also those arising from antiestablishment movements surfacing from time to time in different parts of the country. It is felt by the protagonists of such movements that if they are able to create law & order disturbances in the National Capital, they can get greater exposure for their causes, however well or poorly they may be justified. There is also the paucity of financial resources common to developing societies, which is further compounded by inefficiency and low productivity of resource utilisation. A substantial part of the responsibility for such low productivity arises from failure by persons holding positions of public authority to observe the code of conduct of honesty and complete integrity in pecuniary matters.

The National Capital Territory of Delhi is a city of global importance keeping in view its history and its multi-ethnic, religious, linguistic and cultural composition reflecting in a cameo form, the vast variety of our unique country. In such a situation, the values of mutual tolerance, respect for all sections of the people and commitment to peaceful co-existence become essential attributes for the residents of our capital city.

Late Shri S.C. Vajpeyi, IAS (Retd.) who had spent many valuable years of his professional life as a senior civil servant of the Union Territory of Delhi and held the position of Chief Secretary, has rendered a great service to practitioners and thinkers in the field of administration of the National Capital Territory of Delhi, by editing this volume being published under the auspices of the IIPA, containing contributions by a number of distinguished personalities. Shri Vajpeyi was a dedicated civil servant of great intellectual and personal integrity and it is a matter of regret that he is no longer with us to witness the publication of the book which he had compiled and edited with such distinction.

(Tejendra Khanna)
Lieutenant Governor, Delhi

PREFACE

To celebrate completion of four decades of the Indian Institute of Public Administration (IIPA) it was decided to plan studies on "Landmarks in State Public Administration Since Independence." In response to this initiative, it was decided to undertake a study, in accordance with the broad guideline issued by the Institute, in respect of the National Capital Territory of Delhi. It took some time for the Delhi Branch to muster resources both financial and academic—to undertake such a study.

The guideline emphasized that focus in the study should be on the legacies inherited by the States on the date of their formations. It was also suggested that an account of both the history and background of the administrative set-up as also description of the existing administrative set-up and immediate challenges and opportunities before the State public administration may be outlined.

The first two chapters of the volume deal with the legacy inherited by the Union Territory of Delhi with a historical survey of the administrative set-up. Its administrative set-up has naturally gone through kaleidoscopic changes which has been brought out in these chapters.

The next two chapters deal with the issues of democracy, decentralization and development with reference to the constitutional arrangement in regard to the governance of the NCT of Delhi. It is axiomatic to say that because of Delhi's status being 'the Capital of the country' its constitutional and administrative arrangements have consistently been receiving attention of the Constituent Assembly before the independence and the Parliament thereafter. One of the unique features of Delhi, as in respect of Capitals of other countries as well, is related to the relationship between the Council of Ministers (previously the

Executive Council) and the Lt. Governor (previously the administrator) of the Union Territory appointed by the President/Central Government under Article 239 of the Constitution as amended from time to time. This relationship has been riddled with controversy, more particularly, in relation to the powers reserved to be exercised in his discretion by the Lt. Governor. This aspect has been discussed in considerable detail with reference to historical perspective in Chapter 4.

Law and Order under the present arrangement has to be dealt with by the Lt. Governor. How far these functions are to be exercised by the Lt. Governor, with or without consultation with the Council of Ministers, has been discussed in Chapter 5 relating to Law and Order Management and Institution of District Magistrate and Police Commissioner.

The next chapter deals with the welfare programmes launched by the Delhi Government relating to Women and Children. DDA deals with the acquisition, development and disposal of land which again is dealt with directly by the Lt. Governor and the Ministry of Urban Development. Various issues and controversies have arisen in respect of the functioning of the DDA. These have been briefly touched upon in Chapter 7.

Chapters 8 and 9 relate to the setting-up of Training Institutions in Delhi and the Landmarks in Delhi Legislation.

The next four chapters relate to the administration of needs of common man, i.e., the arrangement for transport, electricity supply, safe drinking water supply to the metropolis and policies and programmes dealing with the migration of persons residing in the surrounding areas outside Delhi in search of employment opportunities. The authors have respectively dealt with these problems with thoroughness both in historical and futuristic perspective. After an analytical survey of the existing and proposed arrangements, the authors of these respective chapters have raised important issues and outlined an agenda for the next decade or so. In their own ways they have focused on both the challenges and opportunities ahead, the unfinished task and the initiatives which need to be taken up in future. These points are only suggestive in nature. They could at best form the theme for debate and discussion in respect of these areas for future initiatives.

From the olden times, Delhi has been the Capital town and was famous for its products, improved communications, higher level of education, transport, availability of materials, etc., were quite sufficient for industrial growth in Delhi. Delhi has been leading in country in manufacturing and exports of ready-made garments. Delhi has become the home town for manufacturing of domestic appliances, electrical devices, automobile parts, sport goods, etc. But in Second Master Plan it was observed that industrial units using acids, chemical and inflamable materials which are noxious and hazardous. So it was decided to shift the industries to industrial area.

During the past decade or more, seemingly, there has been a conflict between the environmental conservation and development. This problem has been discussed at various fora at both micro and macro levels. Recently there has been judicial intervention in this area through judgments of courts, mainly the Apex Court. Chapter 15 delineates the problems faced by the capital and how the conflict between environmental conservation and sustainable development could be resolved.

Education is the backbone of any nation. Delhi occupies a unique position which makes education as the centre of activities, growth, programmes and different types of experiments. The population of Delhi has grown just double in fifty years and in the same ratio educational institutions started. In 1988 under the Societies Registration Act, SCERT was set-up and it started functioning in 1989. There was a good cooperation of NCERT with SCERT. Vocational programmes are also introduced. However some educationists do say that poor results in schools due to underutilised and even misutilised of available resources.

Chapter 17 deals with the progress made in the field of Technical Education. In this study a number of major points on development of technical education have been raised and suggestions made for discussion.

Redressal of Grievances is a core issue which has so far defied an effective solution. In the first part of this chapter, the problem of redressal of grievances has been dealt with both at the macro and micro levels. This part contains some tentative suggestions for action. Part II of this chapter, however, is important from two angles. First, it brings out in no uncertain terms a frank appraisal of the redressal machinery seen through the eyes of the former chief executive of the Delhi Government. And more importantly, it depicts both the pain and anguish, as also the determined will of the former chief executive to deal with this problem as effectively as the system and the constitutional arrangements would permit. The impediments—constitutional, systemic and human—find mention in Lt. Governor's address reproduced in this part. Our note at the end marked as 'Editors' Note' indicates that determined efforts made in this direction, have borne fruit, at least in some fields.

We would wish to add that the views expressed in various chapters are those of the authors and the IIPA or the editors do not necessarily subscribe to these. We are conscious of the fact that the present effort suffers from inadequacies and gaps but for that the editors take the responsibility. Finally, before we offer the volume to our readers, perhaps we owe them an explanation. Delhi has gone through a number of changes in its administrative set-up during the last hundred years or so. These changes have been brought about by different legislations from time to time. In several chapters, a historical survey of such developments finds mention. Some authors have given more details than others. That naturally sounds repetitive. We are conscious of this fact. However, we have more or less left those portions as they were, lest the thread of continuity running through the essay gets disturbed. The readers may, therefore, overlook this.

We would wish to thank mainly the Delhi Government, as also the IIPA, who have given the necessary financial support for this effort. We are grateful to the authors who have contributed to this venture, though some of them took quite some time in 'perfecting' their contributions.

We are indeed indebted to Shri P.K. Dave, ex-Lt. Governor, Delhi, for permitting us to include the text of his address regarding redressal of public grievances in this volume.

On the operative side Shri S.S. Gigoo and Paul Satyanathan gave us invaluable support for which we owe them thanks.

S.C. Vajpeyi
S.P. Verma

INTRODUCTION

During the last fifty years those who governed Delhi may not have found lasting and real solutions to the myriad problems encountered in different fields of administration. Yet, considerable progress has been made in the traditional functions discharged by the State as also multifarious and expanding welfare activities which the State has gradually undertaken during the last few decades. The progress made in diverse fields is depicted in the different chapters included in this volume. What is more important, however, is that during the struggle by the successive governments to cope with the problem of better performance in different spheres many profound (and not so profound) questions that face the administration in respect of policy formulation and its implementation have been posed by them. Many ticklish policy issues have perforce been formulated for debate and discussion. The solution of some of these, particularly in the area of infrastructural development or administration of law and order or in the area of environment and pollution control or migration of rural population to the metropolis will perhaps need to be intensively discussed and debated beyond the din and controversies and hustle and bustle of party politics. An effort has been made in some of these articles to identify some such major issues, and wherever feasible, to indicate possible policy options. It is felt that due to various constraints (not excluding the occasional subjective approach of scholarly contributors) there are some gaps in analysis and discussion of some topics. The true worth of this effort, however, lies in raising some of these issues even though the authors could not provide complete answers. Hopefully, they have been successful in highlighting these issues cogently.

T.N. Chaturvedi
Chairman
Delhi Regional Branch,
I.I.P.A.

1 LEGACY INHERITED BY UNION TERRITORY OF DELHI

S.C. VAJPEYI AND S.P. VERMA

Traditionally Delhi's past is linked with Mahabharata legend of the foundation of Indraprastha, the site of which is believed to be the present Purana Quila. Extensive excavations carried out at this site have yielded evidence to indicate that the earliest habitation here belonged to the *fifth* or *fourth* century B.C. According to early Pali literature the territory of Delhi formed a part of Kuru-Mahajanpada at the time of the Buddha. By about the *third* century B.C. Delhi was included in the empire of the Mauryas, and this is supported by discovery of a Minor Rock Edict of Ashoka on a rocky outcrop near Kalkaji in South Delhi.[1]

The origin of the name of Delhi is lost in antiquity. The name 'Delhi' seems to have made its appearance for the first time during the first and second centuries A.D. Ptolemy, the Alexandrine Geographer has marked "Daidala" in his map of India close to Indraprastha and midway between Mathura and Thaneshwar. Cunninghum, the eminent archaeologist, concurs with the tradition accepted by "Firishta, author of *Tarikh-i-Firishta*" that Delhi derives its name from Raja Dhilu of early times whose date is not definitely known. According to another and more reliable tradition, Delhi was founded in 736 A.D. by the Tomars, a Rajput clan which ruled over the Haryana country with

Dhilliba as their capital. The name of Delhi seems to have finally evolved from "Daidala", "Dhillika", and "Dilli".[2]

In the Rajput period, the Tomars ruled the Haryana country from their capital Dhillika (present Delhi). The tradition runs that Taurs (a contraction of Tomara), founded Delhi in 736 A.D. of the important Tomar rulers of Delhi, mention may be made of Ananga Pala whose name is also inscribed in the old iron pillar which formed originally, as early as the fourth century, the standard of an unidentified Vishnu temple. He is said to have constructed the Anangapur Dam. Another ruler, Surajpal was the founder of Suraj Kund. Anangapala is said to have also built the Lalkot at Mehrauli which is the first known regular defence work in Delhi and may be regarded as the core of the so-called first city of Delhi. The Tomars were defeated by Vigraharaja (1153-63) of Chauhana dynasty, and therefore, Delhi became a part of their dominion.[3]

An inscription on the Ashokan pillar of the year 1163 or 1164 now, in Kotla Firoz Shah, refers to Vigraharaja's conquest of the land between the Vindhyas and Himalaya. His capture of Delhi is mentioned in an inscription from Bijolia in Udaipur District, while other inscriptions refer to Delhi having been ruled successively by the Tomars and Chauhans. Vigraharaja's grandson Prithviraja III, also known as Rai Pithora, the popular hero of stories of Hindu resistance against the Muslim invaders, was ruling over Delhi, when Muhmmad Gauri led his incursions into India. The latter was repulsed at least once by a confederacy of the Rajputs under Prithviraja on the battlefield was inflated on Prithviraja and he was killed. Thereafter Muhmmad Gauri returned to his native land, leaving Qutb-ud-din-Aibak, his slave and general, as his Viceroy in India. In 1193, Qutb-ud-din-Aibak captured Delhi which was still in the hands of the Chauhans. Later, after the death of Muhmmad Gauri in 1206, Aibak enthroned himself at Lahore as the first Sultan of Delhi. Delhi, thus became the capital of the slave dynasty, the first dynasty of the Muslim Sultan to rule over northern India.[4] Five dynasties ruled with Delhi as their capital from the assumption of power by Qutb-ud-din-Aibak in 1206, till its conquest by the Mughals in 1526.

The decline of the Mughal Empire became visible in the latter part of Aurangzeb's reign. Its collapss was brought about by mutual dissensions, the growing entrenchment of foreign power and repeated blows dealt by Nadir Shah and his successor Ahmad Shah Durrani from Afghanistan on the one hand and the Marathas on the other. In 1788, Delhi was occupied by a Maratha garrison. In 1803, the British entered the city after defeating the Marathas in the battle of Patparganj. Delhi's political scene changed with its conquest by the British. A new system of government with alien traditions was established. The Resident Agent was in charge of the city government of Delhi and its surrounding areas. The Mughal king enjoyed more respect than obedience. In 1819, the Delhi District was constituted. Thirteen years later in 1832, the Resident Agent was replaced by the Commissioner and the city came under the control of the Government of North-Western Province.[5]

With the defeat of the Nationalist forces in 1857, the First War of Independence, the District of Delhi was transferred to Punjab. It was made the Headquarters of the Eastern Division comprising of seven districts. In 1862, the Delhi Municipal Committee—the premier local self-governing body of the capital—came into existence but it failed to satisfy the local populace which was demanding elected legislature.[6] Participating in the fourth session of the Indian National Congress at Allahabad in 1888, in which the delegates from Delhi participated for the first time, Umrao Mirza Hairat of Delhi supported the elected legislative councils with more powers.

Under the Government of India Act of 1919, Indian Legislature had the power to enact laws for the province of Delhi. However, for so small an area as Delhi, whose life was indistinguishable from that of the surrounding territories, the best mode of legislation was considered to be an extension of the laws of the neighbouring provinces.

By notifications issued under the Delhi Laws Act of 1912 and 1915, provision was made that the enactments in force in other territories could be extended to Delhi. This enabled the Governor-General in Council to ensure, so far as possible, uniformity of laws with Punjab since a substantial part of Delhi had originally formed an administrative part of that province. The Government of India Act, 1935, did not effect any substantial change and it continued to be a province directly administered by the Chief Commissioner appointed by the Governor-General.

Position during 1947 to 1950

After India attained independence in 1947, Delhi continued to be administered directly by the Government of India and different departments of the Central Government began to deal directly with the corresponding department in the Chief Commissioner's office. This arrangement continued till the commencement of the Constitution.

Pattabhi Sitaramayya Committee

On July 31, 1947, in response to the suggestion made in the Constituent Assembly, a Committee under the Chairmanship of Dr. Pattabhi Sitaramayya, was set up to study and report on the constitutional changes required in the governmental set up of the Chief Commissioner's provinces to give them a due place in the democratic government of free India. To work out an appropriate setup for Delhi, the committee had before it, notes and memoranda describing the administrative arrangements obtaining in some federal capitals like Washington D.C. and Canberra. Mr. N. Gopalswami Ayyangar had also furnished a memorandum to the Committee on the future constitution of the Chief Commissioner's Provinces. The Committee formally recommended that, while the Chief Commissioner's Province of Delhi might be kept intact it might be provided with a responsible government, subject to certain limitations.

The salient recommendations of the committee were as follows:

(1) The province should function under an Administrator to be appointed by the President.

(2) There should be a Council of Ministers with Chief Minister at the head to aid and advise the Lt. Governor in the exercise of his functions. The Council of Ministers should be responsible to the Provincial Legislature. Any difference on any important matter arising between the Lt. Governor and the Ministry should be referred to the President for a final decision.

(3) The number of Ministers should not exceed three, except with the approval of the President.

(4) The Province of Delhi should also have an elected legislature consisting of not more than fifty members which might function like other Provincial Legislatures except that

  (a) The Union Legislature should have concurrent powers of legislation even in respect of matters included in the "provincial list".

  (b) All laws passed by the provincial legislature would require the assent of the President.

  (c) The budget, after being voted by the provincial legislature, would require the approval of the President before it becomes operative.

(5) The Centre must have special responsibility for the good governance and financial solvency of the province.

(6) Delhi's area being small and resources limited, the need for Central assistances would continue for maintaining the standard of administration at the same level and in the major provinces.[7]

Drafting Committee's Reservations

The Drafting Committee of the Constitution did not agree with the recommendations of the Pattabhi Sitaramayya Committee as it felt that Delhi, being the capital of India, could not be placed under a local administration. It pointed out that in the U.S.A. and

Australia, their respective federal legislatures exercised exclusive power in respect of the seat of the federal government. It suggested, however, that while Delhi should be directly administered by the President through a Lt. Governor, powers should be available to the President to create by an order a local legislature with such duties and functions as may be specified therein.[8]

The decision finally taken was that the provision of legislatures and Council of Ministers to centrally administered areas these territories should be left to the discretion of the Parliament for which an enabling provision should be made in the Constitution. A specific provision was made that, Delhi being one of the Part "C" states, shall be administered by the President acting to such an extent as he thinks fit, through a Chief Commissioner or a Lt. Governor to be appointed by him or through the Governor of a neighbouring state, subject to certain procedural requirements, Articles 239 and 240 were accordingly added.[9]

Position after the Promulgation of the Constitution

Under the provisions in Article 240 (as it stood at the commencement of the Constitution) the Parliament was authorized to create or continue, for any Part "C" state, a body whether nominated, elected or partly nominated or partly elected, to function as a legislature for the state, or a council of advisors or ministers or both, with such constitutional powers and functions, as may be specified in the law. The then Prime Minister Jawaharlal Nehru gave an assurance in the Constituent Assembly that an enactment in this behalf would be undertaken very soon.

Consequent to this assurance given by the then Prime Minister and in pursuance of the power under Article 240 (as it stood then), the Parliament passed on 6 September, 1951, the Government of Part C States Act, 1951, under which provision was made for a Council of Ministers in Delhi. The state was provided with a Legislative Assembly and popular ministry but, in view of Delhi being the Capital of India, the powers delegated had to be circumscribed.

Thus what was given to Delhi was a form of diarchal government seeking to counsel Central control over the federal capital with autonomy at the state level.[10]

The Legislative Assembly of Delhi

The Legislative Assembly had 48 seats, of which 6 were reserved for the Scheduled Castes. Its life was five years, unless dissolved earlier. In the matter of franchise, qualifications of voters and members and legislative privileges, the rules were similar to those in respect of the legislatures of Part A states. For the purposes of elections, the state was divided into 36 single-member constituencies and six double-member constituencies with reservation in each of them for a member of Scheduled Castes. Voting was distributive, the voters having as many votes as there were candidates to be elected.[11]

Under the Act of 1951, the legislatures of Part C states were empowered to enact laws in respect of any matter enumerated in the State List or the Concurrent List of the Constitution, just as in Part A and B states. The sources of revenue, enumerated in the list, were the same for both. The administration of these states was, however, vested by the Constitution in the Parliament. Its authority was preserved by providing that in case of repugnance, the law made by Parliament shall prevail over that of the state legislature. The Parliament was normally expected to interfere in purely local matters. The position allotted to Delhi was the same as that of the other Part C states except that, in view of its being the capital of India, the following subjects and connected matters were excluded from the purview of its Legislative Assembly :

(a) Public Order.

(b) Police, including railway police.

(c) The Constitution and powers of Municipal Corporation and other local authorities of improvement trusts, water supply, drainage, electricity, transport and other public utility authorities in Delhi or New Delhi.

(d) Lands and buildings vested in or in the possession of the Union which were situated in Delhi or New Delhi.

(e) Incidental matters such as offences, fee and jurisdiction in respect of the above.[12]

The Chief Commissioner and the Council of Ministers

The executive authority for administration of Delhi state was vested in the President of the Union who exercised it through a Chief Commissioner. The Chief Commissioner was, for all practical purposes, the head of the administration. The Ministry consisted of the Chief Minister, the Health Minister, the Development Minister and two Deputy Ministers. The President, not the Chief Commissioner, appointed the Chief Minister. The other Ministers were also appointed by the President on the advice of the Chief Minister.[13]

The Council of Ministers was to meet at such time and place as the Chief Commissioner directed and he himself presided over the meeting. While the ministers ran the departments and worked on the principle of joint responsibility, there was provision for all important matters being referred through the Chief Minister to the Chief Commissioner before issuing final orders. While the Chief Commissioner was expected to act normally on the advice of his ministers on all matters within their purview, he was empowered to overrule them and act in his discretion on matters concerning New Delhi. The authority of the President was fully secured by the provision. Notwithstanding anything in the provisions of the Act, the Chief Commissioner and his Council of Ministers were to be under the general control of President and bound to comply with such particular direction, if any, as may from time to time be given by the President. In case of failure of the Constitutional machinery, the President could suspend the operation of the Act and make such other arrangements for its administration as he thought fit. (The Government of Part C States Act, 1951.[14]

In 1956, the status of statehood for Delhi came to an abrupt lend. The States Reorganization Commission (SRC) attached great importance to the needs of the national capital. It favoured its direct administration. It argued, "If it is conceded that national capital has to be under the effective control of national Government and both New Delhi and Old Delhi have to be treated as a single unit for administrative purposes, there will be little scope for difference of opinion on its future administrative pattern". The Commission also found that this democratic experiment had proved costly and this was not compensated by increased administrative eficiency or rapid economic or social progress. The SRC emphasized that these states could not subsist as separate administrative units without excessive dependence on the Centre and had no alternative but to either remain a centrally administered territory or become a part of a neighbouring state. But, in the case of Delhi, while making a choice between the two alternatives, the following special factors were to be taken into consideration:

(a) "Delhi is the seat of national government;

(b) It is basically a city unit; 82 per cent of its total population being resident in urban areas".

The Commission felt that if Delhi was to continue as Union Capital, it could not be made part of any state. National capitals are usually placed under special dispensation even in case of unitary systems. So far as federal capitals are concerned, any constitutional division of powers in case of units functioning in the seats of national Government, is bound to give rise to embarrassing situations. In order to avoid conflicting jurisdictions, there is need for effective control by national Government over federal capital.[15] The Commission recommended that "Democracy in these areas should take the form of the people being associated with administration in an advisory rather than in directive capacity". The Commission further held: "We are definitely of the view that municipal autonomy in the form of Corporation, which will provide greater local autonomy than is the case in some of the important federal capitals, is the right and, in fact, the only solution of the problem of Delhi State".

Hence, on the recommendation of the Commission, statehood was done away with, and Delhi became the direct responsibility of the Central Government. Vide Seventh Amendment Act, 1956, it was constituted as Union Territory under the Constitution of India. A Municipal Corporation covering almost the entire area of Delhi State (excluding NDMC, Delhi Cantonment Board and some areas of Red Fort) was constituted in April 1958, under the provisions of Delhi Municipal Corporation Act, 1957. It was hoped that "autonomous Corporation would satisfy the requirements of the cosmopolitan character of Delhi city and would strike a balance between local needs and political aspirations of the people".

After becoming a Union Territory, Delhi was given an Advisory Council at the Central level and a Corporation to fulfil the needs of people at the territorial level. The Council consisted of Home Minister, Delhi's MPs, the Mayor, the Vice-Chancellor of Delhi University, the President of New Delhi Municipal Committee, the Inspector-General of Police and two Advisers—the Chairman, Public Relations Committee and the Chairman, Industrial Advisory Board. At the territorial level the Chief Commissioner, as the Administrator of Delhi, was directly responsible to the Union Government. Thus, the formal head of state became an effective ruler of Union Territory. For the next ten years the only popularly elected body in Delhi was Delhi Municipal Corporation.[16]

Delhi Municipal Corporation

The Delhi Municipal Corporation was governed by the Delhi Municipal Act, 1957. The Act was devised on the pattern of Bombay Corporation.

The Corporation was a representative body consisting of 100 Councillors elected directly by the people on the basis of adult sufferage in single member constituencies but 13 seats were reserved for Scheduled Castes. In addition to Councillors, there were six Elderman who were elected by the Councillors in accordance with the system of proportional representation by means of single transferable vote. The term of office was four years but it might be extended by the Central Government in special circumstances for a period not exceeding one year".[17]

Mayor and Deputy Mayor were elected at the first meeting of the Corporation. The Mayor was the Presiding Officer of the Corporation with no executive authority vested in him. The tenure of his office was one year but he was entitled for reelection for subsequent term.[18]

Functions

The functions of the Corporation were enumerated in Chapter 3 of the Delhi Corporation Act, 1957. A long list of functions was mentioned under Sections 42, 43 of the Act. These were divided into two categories—obligatory or compulsory and discretionary or optional.[19]

The obligatory functions were construction, maintenance and cleaning of drains, public latrines and urinals; construction and maintenance of works and means for water supply; removal and disposal of filth and rubbish materials; construction, maintenance, extension, management and conduct of electricity generation and distribution; road transport systems; registration of births and deaths; public vaccination and innoculation, construction of public streets, bridges and culverts, maintenance of fire brigade; establishment and maintenance of hospitals, dispensaries and maternity and child welfare, etc.

The discretionary functions comprised the responsibilities like furtherance of cultural and physical education, maintenance of libraries, museums, art galleries, organization and management of chemical or bacteriological laboratories for examination of water, food and drugs, organization and management of cottage industries, distribution and processing of milk, provision for unfiltered water supply, housing accommodation, etc.

The following Statutory Committees under-took the obligatory functions of the Corporation :

1. Standing Committee.
2. Delhi Electric Supply Committee.
3. Rural Areas Committee.
4. Delhi Water Supply and Sewage Disposal Committee.
5. Education Committee.
6. Delhi Transport Committee.

These Committees consisted of elected representatives as well as official nominees numbering between 7-12 members. Amongst all, the Standing Committee was the most important and has been called centre of gravity in the Corporation set up. The Committee consisted 14 members elected by Councillors and Eldermen from amongst themselves at the first meetting of the Corporation after each election.[20]

Dissatisfaction with Corporation

The Corporation could not succeed in fulfilling the aspirations of the people and failed to deliver the goods it was entrusted with under the Delhi Municipal Corporation Act. One big corporation for a metropolitan town could not look after the vastly diverse needs and requirements of various areas which were themselves not less than a small town. The pattern of economic development of each area was largely different than the other. With the growth of population the size of voters in each Constituency proportionately increased. Consequently, the interest of the people in Municipal policies and affairs and in Municipal elections dwindled. Another point regarding the failure of Corporation is that its deliberative wing had greater say in the promotion and appointment of bureaucrats. The Corporation had the power to appoint officers as it deemed fit at such monthly salaries and such allowances, if any, as may be fixed by it. This provision, in consonance with Section 91 of the Act, conferred more power on the Corporation. According to Section 91 of the Delhi Corporation Act, "no permanent officer or other employee shall be entertained in any department of municipal administration unless he has been appointed under Section 89." This leads to unhealthy political patronage by political elites causing embarrassment to all those concerned. The bureaucrats channelised their energies to win their favour which had a demoralizing effect on the conscientious officers. These practices rendered the corporation incompetent and ineffective in dealing with the day to day problems of the people and continue to do so. The citizens of Delhi became fed up with the bickering and dissensions which had marked the debates in the corporation meetings.[21]

Demand for Future Set-up

With the dissatisfaction from the corporation the demand for the new democratic set-up for Delhi was raised. It was supported by all political parties. The demand for it got intensified when five Union Territories, i.e., Himachal Pradesh, Manipur, Tripura, Goa, Daman and Diu and Pondicherry were given responsible government in substantial measure. The political parties of the capital clamoured for the Statehood. In 1954, a memorandum was submitted by the Delhi State Government to States Reorganization Commission which stated;

"Formation of a corporation of elected members will not and cannot satisfy the political aspirations of the people of Delhi as the corporation will be concerned only with Civic affairs. Over the vast field of State Administration, Delhi people will have no effective voice. There can be more retrograde step, politically speaking than to replace democratic government by bureaucratize administration in Delhi State.[22]

Seven-day debate was held by Delhi State Legislative Assembly on report of State Re-organization Commission. The main points emerging out of this debate were :

(1) The Municipal Corporation was no substitute to a State Legislature.

(2) An Advisory Council of Chief Commissioner or appointment of Deputy Minister at Centre to administer Delhi would not solve any problem.

(3) The future setup of Delhi was to be democratic with maximum powers of self-government.[23]

Memorandum of MPs

Radha Raman, Naval Prabhakar, C. Krishna Nair, the three Congress MPs of Delhi sent a memorandum to Joint Select Committee of State Re-organization Bill in 1955 in which they proposed the following guidelines for the set up of Delhi:

(1) The representatives of the people were to be chosen by direct election.

(2) The representatives thus chosen should have the power to legislate on local matters within the limits imposed by the Parliament.

(3) The responsibility of day to day administration should be effectively shared with the popular representatives.

(4) Delhi's representation in the Union Parliament should be increased.

Their suggestions for having a territorial council, a Council of Ministers and the President's power to make regulations for Delhi resembled to Dr. Jajoria's scheme.[24]

J.N. Sahani's Scheme

The scheme of G.N. Singh, Dr. Jajoria and J.N. Sahani were half-way house proposal between State Legislature and a Municipal body. They saw Delhi as an urban unit. County council pattern of London inspired Singh, while Sahani was impressed by Metropolitan Government in Kenya. The elected Governor of Shri Sahni's scheme will not act as constitutional head, but will look for real power. How is it possible that two persons of similar rank can enjoy equal status when one is elected and other is nominated?

Following the discussion with various political parties and public fora demanding democratic administration—a limited democracy was conceded to Delhi through the reforms of 1966. The Central Government prepared a Delhi

Administration Bill which was introduced in the Parliament on November 18, 1965 and thereafter it was referred to Joint Select Committee of both the Houses of Parliament on May 19, 1966. The Report of Joint Select Committee was presented to the Parliament and it was passed as Delhi Administration Act, 1966 on November 18, 1966. The administrative set-up provided by Delhi Administration Act, 1966, was introduced on September 7, 1966 which gave birth to Metropolitan Council with the object to meet half-way the popular demand for Assembly.[25]

The Delhi Administration Act, 1966

The 1966 Act provided for the establishment of a Metropolitan Council and an executive council which together with the Administrator had been given certain specific functions in relation to Delhi.

Composition

The Metropolitan Council of Delhi consisted of 56 members chosen by direct election and not more than five non-official persons nominated by the Central Government. Seats were reserved for Scheduled Castes, as in the case of a Legislative Assembly of a state. The qualification for membership to fill a seat in the Metropolitan Council was the same as for a member of a state Legislative Assembly of a state. The qualification for membership to fill a seat in the Metropolitan Council was to be held in accordance with the provisions of the Representation of the People Act, 1951, as in the case of a state Legislative Assembly.[26] The term of the Metropolitan Council was five years which could be extended.

Summoning Prorogation and Dissolution

The Metropolitan Council could be summoned by the Administrator to meet at such time and place as it thought fit, subject to statutory restrictions. The administrator had the power to prorogue the Metropolitan Council. He could also, with the approval of the President dissolve it. The administrator had also the right to attend and address any meeting of the Council.

The Chairman and Deputy Chairman of the Metropolitan Council were to be elected by the Council from amongst the members under the provisions of Section 12(1) of the 1966 Act. In all such matters, the provisions of the Act, 1966, were analogous to those applicable to state legislature.[27]

Power and Jurisdiction of the Metropolitan Council

The Metropolitan Council had the right to discuss and make recommendations on proposals for undertaking legislation, budget of Delhi and the DDA. The Metropolitan Council did not have any power to pass legislation including any law for appropriating money from the consolidated fund of India. Under the Act of 1966, the Metropolitan Council also did not have any power with regard to what were called the "reserve subjects" on which the administrator acted according to his discretion. In this field were also included matters relating to law and order which includes the organization and discipline of the police force and such other matters as the President was from time to time to specify. Under the last mentioned category, excluding the Metropolitan Council's jurisdiction, the President had specified matters dealt with by the Home Department, Services Department and Land and Building Department of Delhi Administration as well as matters concerning the New Delhi Municipal Committee. In practice, however, matters relating to the reserved subject had also sometimes been allowed to be raised and discussed in the council through questions, calling attention motions and short duration discussions. The recommendations made by the Council could be considered by the Executive Council and forwarded to the Central Government through the Lt. Governor.

The forum of the Metropolitan Council was intended to serve the purpose of associating the people's representatives with the administration to enable them to highlight the problems of the people of Delhi and their grievances for redressal by the administrator and the Central Government.

The councillors under Section 20 of Delhi Administration Act enjoyed the various privileges and powers.[28]

The functions of the Metropolitan Council are enumerated under Section 22 of the Delhi Administration Act, 1966.[29]

The interim Metropolitan Council came into being in September, 1966 and its term ended just after a period of six months in February, 1967, after the holding of elections for the first Metropolitan Council (1966-72). The term of the second council (1972-77) was intended by the Central Government for one year by Delhi Administration (Amendment) Ordinance, 1977, by invoking the emergency provisions contained in Section 10 of the Delhi Administration Act. But there was a change of government at the Centre which affected Delhi also. The aforesaid ordinance was subsequently withdrawn vide a Presidential order and the second Metropolitan Council was dissolved after one month on April 20, 1977. The third council which was set-up in 1977, was dissolved in 1980, by virtue of powers conferred under Section 31 of the Delhi Administration Act, consequent to a change of government at the Centre after the seventh general elections. During the tenure of the fourth council, Section 10 of the Delhi Administration Act, was amended by the Delhi Administration (Amendment) Act 1988, so as to provide that the central gazette, extended the said period of five years by such period not exceeding one year at a time, as it thinks fit, the total period, however, was not to exceed three years. The fourth Metropolitan Council was constituted on February 8, 1983. Its term was to expire on March 16, 1988. Since the government was considering the question of re organizing the set-up of thc Union Territory of Delhi, the term of the fourth council was extended twice by Government of India notifications for a period of one year each upto March 16, 1990. Meanwhile, the ninth general elections led to a change in the Central Government. The fourth council, which had functioned beyond its normal time schedule, was dissolved on January

13, 1990, by the President, who exercised the powers conferred on him by Section 31 of the Delhi Administration Act. Thereafter, the period for which the council was to remain under dissolution was extended from time to time by the order of the President dated September 12, 1991 and December 6, 1991.

Executive Council

According to Delhi Administration Act, 1966 there should be an Executive Council consisting of not more than four members, one of whom was to be designated as a Chief Executive Councillor and others as Executive Councillors. They were appointed by the President of India and held office during his pleasure.

The function of Executive Councillors was to assist and advise the Administrator in exercise of his functions in relation to matters enumerated in the State List or in the Concurrent List, excepting where he was required by law to act in his discretion. In case of differences of opinion between Administrator and Executive Council, the Administrator was required to refer the matter to the President for decision and acts according to the decision given by the President. The Administrator functioned in his discretion with regard to law and order of Delhi, including the organization and discipline of Police force, and with respect to such other matters as were specified by the President of India from time to time.

The Administrator and Members of the Executive Council were under general control of the President of India and function according to the directions and orders given by him from time to time.[30]

Assessment

The whole gamut of legislative and executive wings created under the provisions of the Delhi Administration Act, 1966 for Delhi reflected the mockery of it. The Metropolitan Council was created on the lines of the State Legislative Assembly with elected representatives to associate the will of the people with the administration.

But it was not an assembly as the Constitution of India does not recognize it. The Parliament enjoyed absolute power to frame laws regarding Union Territory in accordance with the provisions of Articles 246 and 248. It recalls that the Central Government has an effective control on the working of the Council.

The Executive Council looked like Council of Ministers but it was not responsible to the Metropolitan Council. It could not be removed by no confidence vote. The Executive Council was nominated, while the Metropolitan Council was an elected body. The latter, had been made advisory and the former wielded the executive authority. It reflected the undemocratic nature of the entire concept of the Metropolitan Council and the Executive Council set-up under the Act. The function of the Executive Council was to advise the Lt. Governor, who was the real executive head and nominee of the Central Government, but was not binding. Although the Executive Council was in charge of certain "transferred" subjects, yet in case of differences of opinion, the Administrator could refer it to the President for decision under Section 27 of the Delhi Administration Act, 1966.

Sometimes the differences between the Lt. Governor and the Executive Councillors have been aired in the public. For example, the first Lt. Governor A.N. Jha and V.K. Malhotra, Chief Executive Councillor, in the second council Lt. Governor Jag Mohan and Chief Executive Councillor, Radha Raman and also in the third council, there had been rift over the exercise of powers. During the emergency period, ironically there was perfect cooperation between Lt. Governor Kishan Chand and the Executive Council.[31]

Administrative Reforms Commission and the Set-up

The reforms introduced in 1966 could not satisfy the aspirations of the citizens of Delhi, but it was too early to scrap the system without giving a fair trial to it. The Administrative Reforms Commissions (ARC) examined at considerable length the peculiar features of the administrative set-up. It pointed out that Central Government was finding it difficult to discharge their consitutional responsibility to ensure the proper administration of the national capital. The ARC had further observed that the "Two institutions which have been created at this level viz—the Metropolitan Council and the Executive Council, are not substitutes for Legislatures and Council of Ministers, for the former has no legislative power and the latter is not subject to control of representative body, the Metropolitan council".

The ARC in order to give respectability to the Metropolitan Council suggested that :

(a) The recommendations of the Metropolitan Council on legislative matters must, as a general rule, be accepted by the Central Government and acted upon accordingly.

(b) The prohibitions which existed in the Rules of Business regarding initiation of legislation by the territorial administration without prior approval of Central Government may be removed.

ARC further said that the guiding principle which should govern the relations of Central Government with the Delhi Administration is that in respect of "transferred subjects", irrespective of legal position, the Central Government must treat the Delhi Administration in a manner similar to any state government, particularly in matters of day to day administration. In regard to "reserved" subjects, however, where the Central Government's responsibility is directly related to administration of national capitals, it will have to take detailed interest in their administration.[32]

In order to raise the status of the Executive Council and to arm it with some real authority, ARC made certain recommendations so as to make it function on the lines of a Cabinet :

(a) The Executive Council should consist of the Chief Executive Councillor and two Executive Councillors.

(b) The Chief Executive Councillor be appointed by the Administrator. He should select the persons commanding majority in the Metropolitan Council. The two executive councillors be appointed by Administrator on the advice of the Chief Executive Councillor.

(c) The Executive Council be collectively responsible to the Metropolitan Council.

(d) In the exercise of his function under "transferred" field the Administrator be advised by the Executive Council.

ARC's recommendations were mainly by four considerations namely, first, to reduce the multiplicity of authorities, secondly, concrete steps to be taken to give metropolitan Administration a free hand in the "transferred" subjects, thirdly it should have defacto status of State Government and, lastly, to give more representative character to the government. The ARC study team had no illusions about the ills of such dual control. It suggested continuance of this system not because it found the set-up efficient, but because it felt that it was too early to reject it. The period of its trial revealed its shortcoming. Its inefficiency renewed the cry for statehood and change in the Administrative set-up by all political parties. This culminated in the setting up a high powered committee headed by Justice R.S. Sarkaria for reorganizing the administrative set-up of the Union Territory. The overlapping of functions and responsibilities had been a perennial problem and almost all the parties which matter in Delhi have been seeking solution.

Main Recommendations of the Committee

In its report submitted to the Government of India in December, 1989, the Balakrishnan (Sarkaria) Committee concluded that most of the difficulties encountered by the common man, as well as by the Delhi Administration were due to certain functional and structural deficiencies and drawbacks in the existing system.

On the basis of its exhaustive studies and

deliberations, the Committee mentioned that the National Government ought to have adequate control and authority over the affairs of the national capital. It accepted the principle of associating the people in the capital with sectors of administration affecting them by means of a representative body. The structure of administration to be devised for Delhi should, therefore, secure a balance between an adequate control by the Centre over the affairs of Delhi for discharging its national and international affairs of Delhi for discharging its national and international responsibilities, and the need to satisfy the democratic aspirations of the people.[33]

The Committee was of the view that the existing structure of the administration for Delhi under the 1966 Act had not proved to be effective and was responsible for many of the difficulties faced by the common man and the administration. A restructuring of the system had, therefore, become imperative. Delhi could not be placed under the direct charge of the Central Government for being administered through officials.[34]

The other recommendations of this Committee, with regard to some important aspects, are as follows :

(a) *Statehood for Delhi.* The case for granting statehood to Delhi with a Legislative Assembly and a Council of Ministers answerable to it in order to provide a democratic and responsive government at the local level, had been supported by a number of arguments. At the same time contrary views that Delhi should not be made a state of the union were also supported by a number of arguments.

The Committee after an objective appraisal, felt that most of the arguments presented against making Delhi a state of the Union are substantial, sound and valid and deserve acceptance. In case Delhi becomes a State, there would be a constitutional division of sovereign legislative and executive powers and functions between the

Union and Delhi state which would make it virtually impossible for the Union to discharge its special national and international duties. Therefore, it was in the national interest that the control of the Centre over the affairs of the national capital should be all pervasive, irrespective of whether the subject matter of control was in the state field or in the Union field and this could not be secured if Delhi becomes a fullfledged state. Secondly, if Delhi becomes a state it would also face constant financial constrainsts because the difference between the resources it can raise and the expenditure would always be high. Further, being the Capital, it may have to meet sudden demands for funds which may be beyond the capacity of the state government. The normal mode and volume of financing the deficits followed by the special category of states may also prove inadequate to meet the deficits in the case of Delhi and the centre would have to make major innovations and departures from the accepted norms and financial procedures applicable to other states which would not be feasible on a permanent basis.[34]

(b) *Legislature for Delhi.* A good case was been made out for providing Delhi with a Legislative Assembly having a Council of Ministers responsible to the Assembly with adequate powers to deal with matters concerning the common man. The provision of a Legislative Assembly and a Council of Ministers for Delhi would not hamper the Union from discharging its own special responsibilities in relation to the Capital and to the country. The only way of ensuring this was to keep Delhi as a Union Territory for the purposes of the Constitution even after the establishment of a Legislative Assembly and a Council of Ministers. The Union Territory of Delhi could be called the National

Capital Territory in recognition of its special status.[35]

Ideally, the Legislative Assembly should have the full legislative powers in relation to matters in the State List and the Concurrent List of the Constitution in matters applicable to Union Territories. However, certain specific exceptions were to be made keeping in view the special responsibilities of the Union in relation to the capital. The subjects to be excluded from the purview of the Legislative Assembly should preferably be public order, the police and matters relating to land.

REFERENCES

1. Thapar, Romila, *A History of India*, Vol. I, Penguin, 1968, p. 229.
2. Chopra, P., Delhi : *History and Places*, Delhi Administration, Delhi, 1970, p. 5.
3. Frybenberg, R.E., *Delhi through The Ages*, Oxford University Press, Bombay, 1986, p. 4.
4. Sharan, Parmatma, *Delhi Ki Kahani Aur Uska Smaraka*, Delhi, 1964, p. 11.
5. Chopra, P., op.cit., 1970, pp. 20-28.
6. *Delhi Gazetteer*, Delhi Administration, Delhi, 1976, p. 711.
7. Dr. Pattabhi Sitaramayya Committee : Report on Centrally Administered Areas, Constituent Assembly Debates, Vol. VII, Lok Sabha Secretariat, 1949, pp. 49-51.
8. Dr. B.R. Ambedkar's letter dated 21-2-1948 written to President of the Constituent Assembly, Draft Constitution of India, Govt. of India Press, 1948, p. viii.
9. Kilwant, C.S., *The Government of the Federal Capital of India (Delhi)*, Publication Scheme, Jaipur, 1986, p. 47.
10. *The Statesman*, 7th September, 1951, Delhi, p. 1.
11. Government of Part 'C' States Act, 1951, Govt. of India Publication, Delhi, 6th September, 1951.
12. *Ibid.*, Section 21(1).
13. *Ibid.*, Section 24(3).
14. *Ibid.*, Section 36.

15. Report of the States Reorganisation Commission, 1955, Govt. of India Press, New Delhi, pp. 197-98.
16. Kumar, Sudhir, *Political and Administrative Set-up of Union Territories of India*, Mittal Publication, New Delhi, 1991, pp. 72-73.
17. Delhi Municipal Corporation Act, 1957, Section 3, Govt. of India, Ministry of Law, 1962, p. 7.
18. *Ibid.*, Section 35.
19. *Ibid.*, Sections 42-43.
20. *Ibid.*, Section 65.
21. Chandra, Jag Pravesh, *Delhi : A Political Study*, Metropolitan Book Co., New Delhi, 1969, pp. 54-55.
22. *Ibid.*, p. 59.
23. Pandit, V.L., *Elites and Urban Politics*, Inter-India Publications, New Delhi, 1984, p. 53.
24. *Ibid.*, p. 53.
25. *Ibid.*, pp. 54-56.
26. Lok Sabha Debates, 1966, Vol. 56, Dated 18-5-1966, Column 17529, The Original Bill provided 42 elected members. The Joint Select Committee raised it to 49 and after the discussion and various suggestions given by the members the Government agreed to increase the number to 56.
27. Delhi Administration Act, 1966, Section 12.
28. *Ibid.*, Section 20.
29. *Ibid.*, Section 22.
30. *Ibid.*, Section 27.
31. *Ibid.*, p. 66.
32. Report of the Administrative Reforms Commission, Vol. I, September 1968, pp. 302-3.
33. Committee on Reorganisation of Delhi Set-up, Govt. of India, Ministry of Home Affairs, 1989, p. 26.
34. *Ibid.*, p. 27.
35. *Ibid.*, p. 82.

2

ADMINISTRATIVE SET-UP OF DELHI

S.C. VAJPEYI AND S.P. VERMA

In 1803, the Marathas were defeated by Lord Lake in the battle of Patparganj on the outskirts of Delhi, and the Mughal Emperor, Shah Alam, came under British protection. When the Marathas had the Emperor under their control, they had allowed him certain Jagirs for his maintenance. These were continued by Lord Welleseley and were known as the "Assigned Tract", and later as "the Delhi Territory". This tract was much greater in size than the present Union Territory of Delhi. It comprised roughly of the districts of Hisar, Rohtak, Gurgaon and Karnal and the Old Delhi District.[1]

Shah Alam was allowed civil and criminal jurisdiction within the precincts of the place. For the rest, the administration was in the hands of an officer of the East India Company, the Resident and the Chief Commissioner of Delhi. The latter was charged as the designation of the post shows, with both political and administrative duties and acted under the direction and control of the Governor-General in Council. By Section 4 of Bengal Regulation VIII of 1805, the "Assigned Tract" was specifically excluded from the purview of the General-Regulations in force in the old presidency areas and was administered in the name of the Mughal Emperor according to the Mohammadan Law. This arrangement continued upto 1832, when the nominal but anomalous authority of the Mughal Emperor was put to an end and the administration of the Delhi Territory was placed, both in law and in fact, in the hands of the officers of the East India Company. By Regulation V of 1832, the office of the Resident and Chief Commissioner of Delhi were abolished and the administration of Revenue, police, civil and criminal justice in the territory were vested in the Board of Revenue and High (Sadar) Court at Agra, the Sadar/Dewani Adalat and the Sadar Nizamat Adalat at Allahabad. The Commissioner who was in immediate charge of the Territory and all the officers working under him were required to act under the order of the Sadar Court and the Revenue Board. The Governor-General in Council was empowered to introduce in the Territory, the whole or any part the Regulations in force in the Bengal Presidency. Delhi was a part of the upper provinces of Bengal Presidency which came to constitute the "North West Provinces" under a Lt. Governor in 1835. During the rebellion of 1857, the administration of Delhi passed into the hands of the army. With the return of peace and the re-establishment of civil government, there was re-adjustment of provincial boundaries. Delhi Territory was transferred from the North-West Provinces to the Punjab under Act XXXVIII of 1858. With this accession of territory, the Punjab which was till then administered by a Chief Commissioner, became a Lt. Governor's Province. Delhi was one of the five divisions of the Punjab, comprising the districts of Hisar, Rohtak, Gurgaon, Karnal, Ambala, Simla and Delhi.[2]

Establishment of Delhi Province

On 12 December, 1911, at the Darbar held in Delhi, King George V announced the transfer of the seat of the Government of India from Calcutta to Delhi. Right from the days of Lord William Bentick, there had been continuous demand for completely dissociating the Central Government from the administration of any of the Provincial Governments. The present occasion provided a fitting opportunity. According to the India Statutory Commission 1927 the creation of the Delhi Province was, with the sole object of providing the Government of India, with a seat free from the dominant influence of any Provincial

Government. But political considerations greatly influenced the decision. The city of Delhi and such of the surrounding area as could be conveniently served, were detached from the Delhi Division of the Punjab and constituted as a separate province known as "The Delhi Province" with effect from 1 October, 1912. This was followed by a Government Notification No. 911 dated 17th September, 1912.[3]

In 1912, when it was decided to make Delhi the Capital of India, the city of Delhi and its immediate environs were separated from the Punjab and constituted to form a separate and independent province under a Chief Commissioner. When it was first constituted, the total area of the Delhi Province was 547 sq. miles. In 1915, the Shahdara Pargana and a few more villages were transferred to it from the Ghaziabad Tehsil in the Meerut District of the United Provinces. This was necessitated by consideration of health, expansion and other interests attaching to the surrounding areas of the New Capital. It was also considered desirable and convenient to vest the control of the river channel in a single authority. Three more villages were transferred to it from the Meerut District in 1925-26. For the rest, there were only slight changes in the boundary of the province due to river action from time to time. According to 1917 census, the present area was 1485 sq. kms.[4]

Place of Delhi under British Indian Constitutional System

The separation of Delhi from the Punjab had and adverse effect on its constitutional position. In 1912, when the province was formed. It lost the benefits derived from its representation on the Punjab Legislative Council — two, out of fourteen non-official seats - and no local legislature was set-up either under the Montagu—Chelmsford Reforms of 1919 or under the Constitutional changes of 1935. Indeed at the time the Government of India was opposed to devolution of authority to the Delhi Administration in any form. It did not favour the setting-up of a local legislature, since the existing system of extending the laws of the neighbouring provinces prevented diversity in legislation, when there was no natural diversity of condition. It doubted the wisdom of financial devolution because the province could not meet its needs and had to depend on Central grants, and it opposed administrative devolution, because the development and efficient administration of the seat of imperial Government were the intimate concern of that Government. Under the Government of India Act, 1935, however, Delhi figured as a "transferred" subject to be placed under the control of one popular minister at the Centre. If the federal part of the scheme had come into force, there was a possibility of some constitutional advance in the province. Thus, except for a few changes in the representation of the province in the Central Legislature, its position remained the same between 1912 and 1947. It was administered by the Chief Commissioner as an agent of the Government of India. The whole of its administration and finance was a Central charge and there were no limits to the power and control vested in the Governor-General in Council. Its annual estimates of revenue and expenditure formed part of the budget of the Central Government and its legislative needs were met by the Central legislation. After Independence this arrangement continued till 1951, when the administration was completely reorganized.[5]

Executive Government And Administration

The Chief Commissioner, who was the executive and administrative head of the Delhi Administration acted under the control of the Government of India in the Home Department, and was vested with the powers of a local Government. While Delhi Administration was under the over-all supervision of the Home Department of the Government of India. Under the proviso to Section 3 of the Delhi Laws Act of 1912, the Governor-General in Council was given the authority to reserve to himself or to delegate to another authority such powers or duties to the local government under existing enactments as he was to specify. Accordingly, the powers of the Chief Commissioner were limited by notification issued from time to time. In the case of certain measures such as the Administrator

General's Act, 1913, the powers of the local Government in respect of Delhi were vested in the Punjab Government and in the case of certain other measures such as the Indian Extradition Act, 1903, Chapter II, the India Press Act, 1910 and the Local Authorities Loans Act of 1879, the powers were reserved by the Governor-General in Council to himself.[6]

At the time the Indian Statutory Commission reported (1927), the ministerial and lower subordinate establishments were borne on local cadres and were recruited by the Chief Commissioner. There were, however, no local cadres for other services. Generally speaking, all posts were borne on the Punjab cadres, but the posts of Chief Commissioner, Deputy Commissioner, Civil Surgeon and some others were borne on the imperial establishment. Irrigation remained with the irrigation branch of the Public Works Department of the Punjab, and technical assistance of other officers of the Punjab Government was also availed of. However, the Chief Commissioner discharged the function of the Inspector-General of Police in the matter of control of the Police personnel in Delhi, and the province was a separate police district. The High Court at Lahore exercised jurisdiction over the Delhi Courts. The judicial officers presiding over the courts established in the province were obtained from the Punjab. The principal officers of the Delhi Administration in 1939-40 were the Chief Commissioner, the Deputy Commissioner, the Senior Superintendent of Police, the Superintending Engineer, the Chief Medical Officer and Civil Surgeon, the Superintendent of Education and the Chief Health Officer, Delhi.[7]

Legislative Arrangements and Policy

With the passing of the province under the direct administration of the Government of India in 1912, the Central Legislature became also the local Legislature for Delhi. For so small an area as Delhi, whose life was indistinguishable from that of the surrounding areas, the best mode of legislation was considered to be extension of the laws of the neighbouring provinces. Section 7 of the

Delhi Laws Act, 1912 provided that the Governor-General in Council might extend to the Delhi province or any part thereof, any enactment which was in force at the time in any part of British India, with such restrictions and modifications as he thought fit. This provision prevented unnecessary resort to legislation in cases where suitable laws were already in existence and, by this simple method, uniformity was maintained between the laws of Delhi and those of the Punjab, of which Delhi was formerly a part. Thus, the province got its laws from two sources, the Indian Legislature and the Governor-General in Council in his executive capacity. The Indian Legislature passed some important laws specifically for Delhi, namely the Delhi University Act of 1922 and Delhi Joint Water Board Act of 1926. But the Governor-General in Council in his executive capacity was the main source of local legislation. Mostly the laws of the Punjab were adopted and extended to the province. For instance, under the Delhi Code of 1939, of the 54 laws extended to it, 48 were those of the Punjab, 3 of the United Province, 2 of Bombay and 1 of Bengal.[8]

Representation of Delhi in the Indian Legislature

Since the India Legislature was also the local Legislature for Delhi, the representation of the province on that body was of paramount importance. On the creation of the province, the Chief Commissioner for Delhi was invariably appointed a member of the Imperial Legislative Council but no non-official representative was added. Under the constitutional reform of 1919, one elective seat, open to all communities, was allotted to Delhi in the Lower House, namely, the Legislative Assembly. Delhi had no seat in the Council of State, but the Chief Commissioner was in practice nominated to it. Franchise was highly restricted, the electoral qualifications in respect of the Lower House being generally the same as those in the Punjab. In 1926, there were only 5,551 electors on roll although Delhi had on population basis, a larger representation than any other province. It was considered quite inadequate since the Central Legislature was also the local legislature for Delhi and also the body which had to provide money for Delhi's needs. The Indian Statutory Commission recommended two elective seats for the province, one in the Upper House and another in the Lower House. Under the Government of India Act, 1935, Delhi was allotted two seats, one general and one Muslim in the Federal Assembly, and one general seat in the Council of State. The provision in this respect did not, however, take effect.[9]

The Montague-Chelmsford Report recommended the setting-up of an advisory council attached to the Chief Commissioner. This recommendation was not implemented, since the Government felt that Delhi's normal interests were municipal and municipal bodies and the District Board, which were in existence, provided adequate scope for the expressionof the wishes of the people.

The Pre-Independence Administrative Set-up of Delhi

As a part of the Punjab, the Delhi division was in the charge of a Commissioner, who had, in addition to his general administrative duties, control over the protected State of Sirpur, Kalsia, Dujana, Pataudi and Laharu. The Deputy Commissioner was assisted by 8 Assistant or Extra-Assistant Commissioners, and each of the Tahsil was under a Tahsildar and Naib Tahsildar. These officers performed both revenue and judicial duties. Kanungos and Patwaris constituted the subordinate revenue staff and Zaildars and Lambardars (Chief and Headman) rendered general assistance in revenue matters. There were magistrates, stipendiary and honorary, to assist in the administration of criminal justice. The Deputy Commissioner was the Registrar for the whole district and supervised the work of Sub-Registrar located at four different towns. He was the ex-officio-President of both the District Board and the Delhi Municipality. There were other District officers too. The Civil Judiciary was under a District Judge, who was subject to the supervisory control of the Divisional and Session Judge of the Delhi Civil Division. The public works of the District were under the Sub-Divisional Officer, who worked under the Executive Engineer in charge of the Delhi Provincial Division of the Public Works Department. The District Police was under a Superintendent and the Delhi District formed part of the eastern range under the Deputy Inspector-General of Police with headquarters at Ambala. There was also the Civil Surgeon who exercised control over all the official medical institutions, excluding military hospital; Delhi, Sonepat, Ballabgarh and Faridabad had Municipal Committees to administer them and Mehrauli and Najafgarh had Notified Area Committees. There was also a District Board.[10]

Departmental Layout

The Commissioner was assisted by three Deputy Commissioners, three Assistant Commissioners and other principal statutory officers and heads of departments. The number of officers and departments had been gradually increasing from year to year to cope with additional duties and functions.[11]

Report of the States Reorganization Commission

In December 1953, the States Reorganization Commission was set-up to study the working of the units of the union. It took up the functioning of Part "C" States for separate examination. In its report (1955), the Commission expressed its opinion that Part "C" States were neither financially viable nor functionally efficient and recommended that each of them should either be amalgamated with a neighbouring state or made a centrally administered territory.

The Commission devoted special attention to the needs of the national capital. It observed that the position in Delhi was more anomalous than other Part "C" States because of the special restrictions placed on its powers by Section 21 of the Government of Part "C" States Act, 1951, and concluded that there was no justification for making it a constituent State of the Union. While arriving at this conclusion, the Commission was primarily influenced by the following two factors;

(1) That Delhi was the seat of the Union government.

(2) That it was basically an urban unit with 82% of its total population residing in urban areas.[12]

A view was expressed before the Commission that the dual control arising out of the division of responsibility between the Centre and State Government of Delhi had not only hampered the development of the Capital but also resulted in a marked deterioration of administrative standards in Delhi. With regard to the suggestion that New Delhi could be regarded as the National Capital under the full control of the Union Government while the rest of Delhi could have a separate administration.[13] The Commission felt that it was wholly unrealistic to draw a line between these two parts of the territory of Delhi due to their close interdependence on each other in the spheres of law and order, social life of the people, commerce and trade and public utility services, pointing out the need for effective control of the national government over the federal capital.

It is hardly necessary to discuss in any detail the reasons why Delhi, if it is to continue as the Union capital, cannot be made part of fully-fledged constituent unit of the Indian Union. Even under a unitary system of government, the normal practice is to place national capitals under a special dispensation. In France, for example, there is a greater degree of central control over Paris than over other municipalities. In England, the police, administration of the metropolitan areas is directly under the control of the Home Secretary, who does not exercise similar powers in respect of other municipal areas. Apart from reasons, which are peculiar to each country or city, there are some general considerations necessitating special arrangements in respect of national capitals. Capital cities possess or come to possess, some degree of political and social predominance. They are seats of National Governments with considerable property belonging to these governments. Foreign diplomatic missions and international agencies are located in these capitals. They also become centre of national culture and art. So far as federal capitals are concerned, there is also an additional consideration.

Any constitutional division of powers, if it is applicable to units functioning in the seats of national governments, is bound to give rise to embarrassing situations. Practice in other countries, administrative necessity and the desirability of avoiding conflicting jurisdictions, all points to the need for effective control by national governments over federal capitals.

With references to the plea for a popular municipal autonomy in the form of a corporation which will provide greater local autonomy than is the case in some of the important federal capitals is the right and, infact, the only solution of the problem of Delhi State. Such an arrangement, the Commission observed, would reconcile the broader requirements of the National Government as well as the local needs and wishes of the people.

The recommendation of the States Reorganization Commission with regard to the autonomy in the form of Municipal Corporation was accepted by the government and implemented by the enactment of the Constitution (seventh) Amendment Act, 1956. Among the other far-reaching changes, the Commission recommended the remaining of Part "C" States as Union Territories and omitted Article 240, as it then stood, which enabled the Parliament to create legislatures and Council of Ministers.[14]

Delhi : Directly Administered Union Territory 1956-66

Consequent to the acceptance by the Government of the recommendations of the States Reorganization Commission, Delhi ceased to be a Part "C" State and became a Union Territory under the direct administration of the President. The Legislative Assembly and Council of Ministers for Delhi also ceased to exist with effect from 1st November, 1956.[15]

In accordance with another recommendation of the Commission, the Delhi Municipal Corporation Act, 1957, was enacted comprising of members elected on the basis of adult franchise, with jurisdiction over almost the entire Union Territory of Delhi, including both the urban and the rural areas. The areas within the limits of the N.D.M.C. and the Delhi Cantonment Board were kept outside the jurisdiction of the Delhi Municipal Corporation, but the territotrial jurisdiction of the N.D.M.C. was limited to 42.73 kms. The Corporation took over the functions previously entrusted to ten local bodies and three statutory boards.

Scheme for Decentralization

In 1962, an ad hoc committee was appointed by the Municipal Corporation to study the whole question of administrative set-up with particular reference to decentralization of the executive wing. The Committee in its report observed that there was over centralization in the administrative set-up and also noted a good deal of confusion about the sphere of duties and responsibilities of the Zonal Officers, Assistant Assessors and Collectors therein, and made certain recommendations for decentralizing the work of the executive.[16]

REFERENCES

1. Delhi Gazetteer, Delhi Administration, Delhi, 1976, p. 548.
2. *Ibid.* p. 549.
3. *Ibid.* p. 551.
4. *Ibid.* p. 3.
5. Kumar Sudhir, *Political and Administrative set-up of Union Territories in India*, Mittal Publication, New Delhi, 1991, p. 67.
6. Sharma, Sudesh, *Union Territory Administration in India : An Analysis of Constitutional Administrative and Political Trends*, Gandhi, Publications, Patiala, 1968, p. 117.
7. Delhi Gazetteer, Delhi Administration, Delhi, 1976, p. 552.
8. Mathur, P.N., *Political and Administrative set-up of Part "C" States*, Agra, 1972, p. 213.
9. *Ibid*, p. 170.
10. Awasthi, A, *Municipal Administration in India*, Agra, 1972, p. 164.
11. *Ibid*, p. 167.

12. Report of the State Re-organisation Commission, Delhi, 1966, para- 583, p. 158.
13. Case for Greater Delhi: A Memorandum Submitted to the State Re-organisation Commission on Behalf of the Delhi State Government, dated 1.5.1954, p. 14.
14. Goyal, P, Delhi's March Towards Statehood, UBS Publications, New Delhi, 1993, p. 25.
15. *The Hindustan Times*, dated 2.11.1956, Delhi, p. 1.
16. Awasthi, A. *Municipal Administration in India*, Agra, 1972, p.179.

3 GOVERNANCE OF THE NCT OF DELHI: ISSUES OF DEMOCRACY, DECENTRALIZATION AND DEVELOPMENT

NOORJAHAN BAVA

In a short time from now the city of Delhi, one of the most beautiful historic capitals of the world, will complete half a century of its glorious history as the National Capital of the Sovereign, Democratic, Socialist, Secular Republic of India. Does the chequered history of governance and administration of Delhi from 1947-97 contain empirical evidence to conclude that it has met the requirements and parameters of good governance? Can the diverse political models and administrative innovations and experiments that were tried out during this last 50 years in the city's governing pattern claim that they have succeeded in fulfilling the genuine aspirations of Delhictes for democratic government— a representative, responsible, responsive, clean and people friendly administration? Or, one that readily responded to the genuine needs and demands of the citizens? Or, has the governance of the Capital ensured national security and protection from criminals, terrorists and anti-social elements? Did Delhi Administration provide protection of life, liberty and right of the citizens which their brethren elsewhere in the country enjoy? Can the government of Delhi or municipal authorities in the city take pride in providing civic amenities to the people in a smooth and satisfactory manner? Can the law and order machinery of the Capital prove its concern for human rights and dignity of the citizens of the metropolis?

PART I
CONCEPTUAL FRAMEWORK OF THE STUDY

Before one finds answers to these questions and others it is imperative to have clear theoretical perspective on good governance in the light of which the empirical data relating to the governance of Delhi, in the past 50 years can be examined, analyzed and used for drawing inferences and conclusions.

The twentieth century will go down in human history as the age of Democracy, Decentralization and Development— the three essential ingredients of Good Governance. These concepts their values, norms, goals, means, contents, structures, institutions and processes have dominated the Post World War II literature in all social sciences and public administration. Today, democracy enjoys unprecedented global popularity but faces problems[1] also. According to one estimate 107 out of 186 countries had competitive elections and some guarantees of civil and political rights.[2] The democratization process is sweeping the lands of former authoritarian regimes in Eastern Europe and erstwhile Soviet Union. There is renewed interest amongst scholars and statesmen in the connection between active citizen participation required for flourishing civil society and the process of democratization.

The twin goals of socio-economic development and nation-building, which are at the centre-stage of all public policies and administration in the developing nations call for total involvement of the public which is facilitated by decentralized administration and devolution of political authority from the national to sub-national and from the latter to the local Government in both rural and urban areas. Decentralization is as much an essential prerequisite for successful democracy as for socio-economic development since it paves the way for citizens participation channeling local people's support, involvement, cooperation and resources into the structures of local level democracy and in the decision-making process for development[3]. A triangular relationship thus exists among democracy, decentralization and development.[4]

What is Good Governance?

The concept of good governance signifies many things to many people. To some, it implies a democratic polity characterized by rule of law, safeguarding of human rights, presence of honest and efficient government, accountability transparence and openness.[5] To others, it connotes purposive and development-oriented administration committed to improvement of quality of life of the masses without necessarily being democratic.[6] The World Bank associates good governance with capacity building and the exercise of political power needed for efficient and effective management of national programmes, whether the political system is democratic or not.[7]

The concept of decentralization connotes dispersal of authority and power away from the top or the centre of an organization/government to the people at the periphery or field offices or government at the grassroots level. Decentralization is a centrifugal force in society that aims at transfer of as much authority and responsibility for performance of as many functions of the community as possible to people or government as far away as the centre. In contrast, centralization is a centripetal force that concentrates authority and responsibility for as many functions as possible at the Centre. While there are several approaches to decentralization, the doctrinal, political, administrative, dualistic (James Fesler)[8], decentralization takes four major types, that is, (1) Deconcentration (2) Delegation (3) Devolution and (4) Debureaucratization.[9] Of these devolution of authority (political, administrative and financial) by the government is the only method which permits maximum participation of the people at the local levels in the process of governance, administration and decision-making for development.

The concept of democratisation as a political process implies democratically elected, responsible and responsive government with maximum freedom for the citizens. It is opposed to authoritarian rule by individuals or a single political party. It signifies orderly succession/political change/governance by two or more political parties, a viable opposition, free and fair elections at regular intervals, accountability of the government and bureaucrats for acts of omission and commission, recognition of the democratic rights of people including equality, freedom of speech, and expression, freedom to form associations or unions, and to choose and change government by exercising their sovereign power as citizens by adult franchise, rule of law, active citizen participation in government and administration, and a flourishing civil society.[10]

A good government always works for the promotion of welfare and development of its people and the nation. The concept of development which is an integral part of good governance is multi-dimensional and multi-faceted. It is normative and empirical, it has political, economic, social, cultural personality, environmental, individual-group, spatial, temporal, local, national, international, global, material, and spiritual aspects. It is not just economic growth measured by gross national product per capita. Development means human ascent, improvement in the quality of life and standard of living and well-being of people. Development demands social and gender justice within a nation and between nations. It means eradication of poverty, unemployment and inequality from society at national and international levels.

PART II

GOVERNANCE OF DELHI (1947-1997)

The political and administrative profile of Delhi in the last fifty years which has undergone significant changes reveals the constant tug-of-war between the two opposite principles— centralization and decentralization. The pattern of governance of the Capital city has been largely determined by two important considerations— national interest and democratization. The national and international responsibility of the Central Government towards the nation as a whole has sealed the political status of Delhi as an Union Territory and given the Centre a comprehensive control over the affairs of the capital to secure a high degree of security and a high level of administrative efficiency and effectiveness. The genuine concern for national interest, and security and need for efficient and effective administration from the seat of the Central Government has resulted in the adoption of the principal of centralization as the overriding principle of determination of Delhi's political and administrative status as an Union Territory.

The second principle at work in the determination of Delhi's set-up has been the growing demand for democratic participation of the citizens of the city in its governance and administration. The demand for democratization of government of Delhi was not easily acceded to by the Central Government.

This explains why Delhi was provided with a Metropolitan Council and an Executive Council under the Metropolitan Council Act, 1966. The Metropolitan Council (consisting of 56 elected and 5 nominated members) was not a Legislative Assembly but only an advisory and recommendatory body with no powers to enact laws or control the government or to appropriate money from the Consolidated Fund of India. The Executive Council was not collectively responsible to the Metropolitan Council either. Thus for more than 20 years (1966-1988), the Delhi Administration was under the constant control and vigilance of the Central Government Ministries on the one hand and of the Lt. Governor of Delhi on the other. The recommendations made by the Metropolitan Council were considered by the E.C. and forwarded to the Central Government and the Administration. The principle of democratization which was upper-most in the minds of the founding fathers of the Constitution was mainly responsible for their decision to make Delhi, a Part "C" State in 1950, with a full-fledged Legislative Assembly and a Council of Ministers headed by a Chief Minister[12] to "aid and advise" the Governor and to be collectively responsible to the Assembly in accordance with the requirement of parliamentary form of government.

Delhi ceased to be a State (Part C) under the States Reorganization Act, 1956 and the Constitution (seventh) Amendment Act of 1956 and became a Union Territory under the direct responsibility of the President of India acting through an Administrator, designated as the Chief Commissioner (later designated Lt. Governor) and appointed by him.

The years 1988 to 1991 left the citizens of Delhi with no elected or nominated representatives to agitate, articulate and place their problems and needs before the Lt. Governor or the Central Government. They had to be satisfied with few MPs from the capital. Delhi was under the bureaucratic Raj during this period. The evils of bureaucratic government came to the fore with mounting problems, grievances and difficulties of the Delhi citizens including multiplicity of authorities, lack of coordination, increasing urbanization, industrialization, population explosion, and its attendant problems of growing encroachment on government land, spurt in unauthorized colonies, J.J. clusters, slums and increasing rate of crimes. Delhiites were completely at the mercy of the bureaucrats of Delhi Administration on the one hand and the Central Government on the other. The vociferous demand for Delhi Statehood made by citizens, political parties, like the BJP and some Congressmen compelled the Centre to get the status paper on Delhi set-up prepared by the Delhi Administration and finally refer the issue of Delhi's governance to the Sarkaria Commission, which became Balakrishnan Committee on Reorganization of Delhi Set-up. The report of this committee submitted in 1989 to the Central Government became the basis of the Constitution (69th) Amendment Act, 1991 and Government of National Capital Territory of Delhi Act, 1991 under which Delhi continues to be an Union Territory but rechristened as

National Capital Territory of Delhi to indicate the national importance vis-a-vis other Union Territories.

The present reorganized set-up of Delhi as Government of NCT of Delhi is based on the acceptance of the recommendation of the Balakrishnan Committee by the Central Government that :

"Delhi as the capital of the Union occupies a unique position for the nation as a whole and it has also certain special features inherent in national interest that the Central Government should have a comprehensive control over the affairs of the capital to secure a high degree of security and a high level of administrative efficiency and effectiveness. At the same time the demand of the large and articulate population for the democratic right of participation in the government is too important to be ignored. The structure of administration to be devised for Delhi should, therefore, be such as to secure a balance between the need to retain with Centre adequate control over the affairs of Delhi for discharging its national and international responsibilities and the need to satisfy the democratic aspirations of the people."[13]

With effect from 1.2.1992, the Government of the National Capital Territory of Delhi is carried on, in the name of the Lt. Governor of Delhi appointed by the President, by a Council of Ministers headed by a Chief Minister to aid and advise the Lt. Governor in the exercise of his functions. Under the Act the Chief Minister and the Council of Ministers are collectively responsible to the Legislative Assembly which is elected directly by the citizens of the city from territorial single member. The Assembly consists of seventy elected members and it enjoys full power to make laws for the NCT with respect to any of the matters enumerated in the State and Concurrent Lists in so far as any such matter is applicable to Union Territory except matters relating to public order, Police and Land Management. These subjects have been retained as reserved subjects the administration of which is vested directly in the Central Government through the Lt. Governor.[14]

The administration of NCT of Delhi which implements the decisions and policies of the Government consists of the Secretariat headed by the Chief Secretary and comprising several Secretaries of the Administrative Departments. These departments of Delhi Administration—Home, Law, Finance, Planning, Food Supplies, Agriculture, Horticulture, Forestry, Wildlife, Animal Husbandry, Poultry, Fisheries, Rural Development, Irrigation and Flood Control, Agricultural Marketing, Energy Development, Cooperative Societies, Industries, Labour, Education, Delhi Archives, Archaeology, Social Welfare, Transport, Tourism, Health and Family Welfare. The administration of NCT of Delhi is carried on by civil servants belonging to various cadres such as IAS, IPS, DANICS, DANIPS, DASSS and others.

The Government of Delhi has to closely coordinate its activities and those of its local bodies like the Municipal Corporation of Delhi, as well as those agencies/ corporations established by the Central Government, such as Delhi Development Authority, Delhi Milk Scheme, Delhi Transport Corporation, etc. In order to achieve the desired level of coordination which was lacking in the previous regime, there exists a Standing Committee headed by the Chief Secretary, Vice-Chairman, DDA, Commissioner MCD, General Manager DESU and the Administrator NDMC with Secretary (Local Self-Government) as Member Secretary.[15]

Conclusion and Suggestion

The BJP Government of NCT of Delhi headed by Chief Minister (Mr. Madan Lal Khurana first, now by Mr. Sahib Singh Verma) has taken a number of decisions to promote the welfare of the people and to respond to their needs and demands. The fledging government has decided to increase the districts of Delhi to nine, each headed by a Deputy Commissioner for more efficient and effective district administration. It has been holding People's Courts and Consumer Courts. The Rent Control Act for Delhi has sown seeds of conflict between the Centre and NCT Delhi's mounting problems of population explosion (10 million people according to a latest estimate), law and order problems, lack of water-supply, power breakdowns in summer, inadequate transport, housing, health, educational facilities, and increasing environmental pollution (the recent Supreme Court order to the authorities to control pollution). The Delhi Government must work very hard to reach the goal of good governance— a responsible, responsive, clean, efficient and good administration of public services and security of life, liberty and property to its citizens. The quality of life of the people of this Metropolis has been adversely affected by galloping rate of urbanization, industrialization, unplanned growth of the city aggravated by population growth, increasing pollution of air, water, land encroachment, growing slums, uncontrolled migratory labour, falling standards in the provision of civic amenities and facilities and increasing crime rate, corruption in political and administrative echelons and failure of the city's police and land administration. The administration of reserved subjects is far from satisfactory. These and other problems call for strong political will, concerted administrative action and increased participation of citizens in Delhi Government and administration to realise the letter and spirit of the 74th Constitutional Amendment Act.

REFERENCES

1. Pattman Carole "Democracy and Democratization" *International Political Science Review*, Vol, 17, 1996. p. 5-6.

2. Lipset, S.M., "The Social Requisite of Democracy Revisited" American Sociological Review, 59. 1-22, 1994.

3. Bava Noorjahan, *People's Participation in Development Administration in India*, New Delhi, Uppal Book Publ., 1984.

4. Maddick Henry, *Democracy, Decentralisation and Development*, Bombay, Asia Publishing House, 1993.

5. A Etouga— Mangnella, Democratization and Good Governance, The Hague, Ministry of Foreign Affairs, June, 1993.

6. Jeffries Richard, "Urban Population Attitudes Towards the Economic Recovery Programme and the PNDC Government in Ghana, Journal of African Affaris. Vol. 91, 1992 pp 307-26.

7. Quoted in H.K. Asmerom, K. Borgman and R. Hope, *Good Governance Decentralization and Democratisational in Post-Colonial States*: A

Comparative Study of Ghana, Indonesia and Surinam", Indian Journal of Public Administration, October-December 1995, Vol. XII, No. 4, pp.736.

8. Fesler J.W., "Approaches to the understanding of Decentralization" paper present at the 6th IPSA World Congress, Geneva, 1964 and also see B.C. Smith Decentralization: The Territorial Dimensions of the State, London, George Allen and Unwin, 1985.

9. United Nations. Decentralisation for National and Local Development, U.N. Technical Assistance Programme, New York, 1962. Also see G.S. Cheema and D.A. Rondinelli (Eds). Decentralisation and Development: Policy Implementation in Developing Countries, London, Sage Publication, 1983.

10. For a complete appraisal of meaning of civil society see Adma B. Saligman, The Idea of Civil Society, New York, The Free Press, 1992.

11. Bava Noorjahan, *Development and the Social Science Method*, Uppal Book Publ., New Delhi 1994.

12. The only Chief Minister of Delhi State, Brahm Prakash, who addressed the members of the Delhi Regional Branch of the Indian Institute of Public Administration in 1987 in the seminar on Indian "Multiplicity of Authorities in Delhi."

13. Committee on Reorganisation of Delhi Set-up Report, December 1989 (Balkrishna Committee).

14. *Ibid.* pp. 81.

15 Delhi Admn., Annual Administration Report 1992-93, pp.1-2.

4 RELATIONSHIP BETWEEN LT. GOVERNOR AND COUNCIL OF MINISTERS

S.C. VAJPEYI

Consequent to the passing of the Constitution (Sixty-ninth Amendment Act, 1991) the Delhi Administration Act, 1966 has been replaced by a new Act, namely "The Government of National Capital Territory of Delhi Act, 1991" (hereinafter called 1991 Act) vide notification No. 1 of 1992 published in the Gazette of India Extraordinary Part-II Section 1 of 3-1-1992.

The Genesis

Clause (4) of Article 239 AA, *inter alia* provides for the setting up a Council of Ministers to aid and advise the Lt. Governor in the exercise of his functions except in so far as he is, by or under any law, required to act in his discretion. And the clause stipulates the manner in which the Lt. Governor shall act.

Section 27(3) of Delhi Administration Act, 1966, provides that the functions of the Administrator with respect to law and order in Delhi including the organization and discipline of police force, land and with respect to such other matters as the President may from time to time specify in this behalf, shall be exercised by him in his discretion. Sub-sections (4), (5) and (6) provide for the manner in which the Administrator shall deal with the matter.

Section 41(1) of the new Act 1991 is an analogous provision requiring the Lt. Governor to act in his discretion in matters which fall outside the purview of the powers conferred on the Legislative Assembly but in respect of which powers or functions are entrusted or delegated to him by the President.

These functions will relate to law and order, including the organization and discipline of Police force, land, New Delhi Municipal Committee and other matters in respect of which the President may delegate the powers.

Due to the changes in the constitutional provisions and conferment of more powers on the Legislative Assembly and Council of Ministers, under the 1991 Act how such matters would be dealt with by the Lt. Governor vis-a-vis the Council of Ministers has to be determined with due care and circumspection so as to ensure smooth conduct of official business and avoid friction amongst various authorities.

Rules of Business

Rules of Business are to be framed with a view to ensure systematic, smooth and orderly transaction of business in accordance with a pre-determined system. The purpose is to avoid any confusion about or overlap in respect of the responsibilities of the respective parties and to ensure that each one is fully cognisant of its functions and plays its assigned role in a constructive and positive manner both under the law and the Rules framed thereunder as also established conventions.

The objective of such Rules is to regulate the relationship of the following namely:

(a) Process of consultation and relationship between Lt. Governor and the Chief Minister and his Council of Ministers, both collectively and individually;

(b) Responsibilities and the relationship of the Chief Minister with the Ministers and consultation process amongst themselves;

(c) Relationship between the Council of Ministers and

the Chief Secretary and other Secretaries and the responsibilities of the latter in ensuring that the Rules of Business are followed;

(d) Relationship between Ministers and the Secretaries and to regulate the manner in which the Ministers are to be consulted and classification of matters which the Secretaries could dispose of on their own without reference to Ministers;

(e) Relationship amongst the Secretaries and more particularly in respect of such matters where they are required to consult the Law Department and the Finance Department or matters which they are required to bring to the notice of the Lt. Governor as provided for in the Rules of Business.

Matters in which Lt. Governor has to Act in his Discretion

Section 41(1) of Govt. of National Capital Territory of Delhi Act 1991 provides as follows:

"The Lt. Governor shall act in his discretion in a matter:

(a) Which falls outside the purview of the powers conferred by the Legislative Assembly but in respect of which powers and functions are entrusted or delegated to him by President,

(b) In which he is required by or under any law to act in his discretion or to exercise any judicial or quasi-judicial functions.

It may appear ironical, but it is true, that after independence, the British made Constitution of 1935 has been transplanted under National Capital Territory of Delhi Act, 1991. And one need not be surprised if similar assurances are being demanded by the newly constituted Government.

It is interesting to note that each of the ancient and medieval empires of India had the institution of the Governor, but it was more a centre of disintegration, rather than of integration a fact which should disprove the claims of the champions of Centrally-appointed Governors. Although nominally functioning as appointees of the Central Government, the Governors under the ancient and medieval empires of India functioned in reality as mini-emperors who subsequently revolted against their overlords. It was under the British that the Governors became not merely the appointees but subordinates of the Central Government. This new tradition of the Governor being subordinate to the Centre was incorporated in every constitutional reform planned by the British rulers for India, including the last of these the 1935 Government of India Act. It will be recalled that in 1937, when the Congress secured majority in seven State Legislatures under the 1935 Act, it laid down as a condition for the formation of the Ministry that the Governor's special powers would not be used.[1]

In order to appreciate how the Lt. Governor may exercise his powers in respect of reserved subjects it may initially be useful to note the difference between the powers of the President and those of the Governors under the Constitution. Of course, there are certain special features in respect of the administration of the National Capital Territory of Delhi which will be dealt with separately.

(a) Articles 74 and 103 and Powers of the President

Under the express terms of Article 74 of the Constitution, as amended, the President is bound to act in accordance with the advice of the Council of Ministers. There are no express constitutional provisions which enable or empower the President to act in his discretion or in exercise of his individual judgment, except Article 217(3) which states: "If any question arises as to the age of a judge of a High Court, the question shall be dicided by the President after consultation with the Chief Justice of India and the decision of the President shall be final".

Under Article 103(1) any question about the disqualification of a member of either House of Parliament is left to the final decision of the President. However, Article 103(2) provides that "before giving any decision on any such question, the President shall obtain the opinion of the Election Commission and shall act according to such opinion." Strictly speaking, there is no exercise of individual judgment or descretion in such a case because the President is required to act according to the opinion of the Election Commission.

(b) Article 239 and 371 and Powers of Governor

On the other hand, there are several constitutional provisions under which the Governor can act independently of the Council of Ministers, or act in his own discretion irrespective of— or even contrary to— their advice. For example :

— **Article 239 (2)** provides that the President may appoint the Governor of a State as the Administrator of an adjoining Union Territory, and where a Governor is so appointed, he shall exercise his functions as such Administrator.

— **Article 371** contemplates a Presidential order with respect to the State of Maharashtra or Gujarat which may provide for any special responsibility of the Governor for the matter mentioned therein. The details of these are, however, not material for present discussion.

— **Article 371-C** makes special provision with respect to the State of Manipur and contemplates a Presidential order which may provide for special responsibility of the Governor in order to secure the proper functioning of a Committee of the Legislative Assembly of that State consisting of members of that Assembly elected from the Hill Areas of that State.

— **Article 371-A** speaks of the special responsibility of the Governor of Nagaland with respect to law and order in that State and exercise of his individual judgment as to the action to be taken. The provision states that the decision of the Governor in his discretion shall be final.

— **Article 371-A (1) (d)** states that the Governor shall

in his discretion make Rules providing for the composition of the regional council for the Tuensang District.

— **Article 371-A (2) (b)** states that for specific periods the Governor shall in his discretion arrange for an equitable allocation of certain funds between the Tuensang District and the rest of the State.

— **Article 371-A (2) (f)** states that the final decision on all matters relating to the Tuensang District shall be made by the Governor in his discretion.

— **Article 371-F** makes provisions with respect to the State of Sikkim, and under Clause (g), the Governor of Sikkim is entrusted with special responsibility and 'subject to such directions as the President may, from time to time, deem fit to issue, act in his discretion'.

— **Schedule VI** of the Constitution makes provisions for the administration of tribal areas in the States of Assam, Meghalaya and the Mizoram.

— **Paras 18 (2) and (3) of the Sixth Schedule** provide that the administration of the areas mentioned therein would be carried on by the President through the Governor of Assam as his agent, and that in the discharge of these functions, the Governor shall act in his discretion.

Definition and Scope of Discretion

Above list is illustrative and not exhaustive. The scope of expressions 'discretion', 'special responsibility' and 'individual judgment' as they are used in the Constitution, and also in the Constitution Act 1991 and by implication in the government of National Capital Territory of Delhi Act 1991 has been explained by the Committee of Governors appointed by the President on 20th November, 1970. This may perhaps be quoted for the sake of clarity:

"Discretion" relates to functions which were outside the areas of ministerial responsibility and where the administration was exclusively vested in the Governor aided by his own secretarial staff. So far as the term "special responsibility" is concerned, the declaration of a special responsibility with respect to a particular matter was never intended to mean or even to suggest that when a question relating to that matter comes up for consideration, the decision is to be that of the Governor to the exclusion of his Ministers. In no sense does it define a sphere from which the action of Ministers is excluded. It does no more than indicate a sphere of action in which it will be constitutionally proper for the Governor after receiving Ministerial advice, to signify his dissent from it and even to act in opposition to it if, in his own unfettered judgment, he is of opinion that the circumstances of the case so require. The term "individual judgment" is necessarily linked with the exercise of a special responsibility. When a Governor acts against the advice of the Council of Ministers in relation to a matter which involves special responsibility, he exercises his individual judgment as to the action to be taken.[2]

Apart from the above constitutional provisions, there are other Articles where the exercise of discretion by the Governor is implicit and inherent in the situation. These provisions, *inter alia*, are Article 213 relating to promulgation of ordinances, Article 200 where the Governor can withhold his assent to a Bill or reserve a Bill for consideration of the President and, of course, Article 356 which provides for the imposition of Presidential Rule in a State.

(c) Position of the Governor Prior to 1950

The Process of Constitutional interaction between the bureaucracy and democracy began with the introduction of Dyarchy— Division of power as transferred and restricted in 1921 based on the provisions of 1919 Act. This interaction was, however, partial, for it was limited to transferred subjects and was further reduced by the absence of joint ministerial responsibility and the powers of the Governor to appoint ministers and keep them in office during his pleasure inspite of an adverse vote in the legislature. Key officers like Secretaries were also appointed and transferred at Governor's pleasure. The reports of the provincial Government on the working of reforms made it clear that there had been no want of loyal cooperation on the part of the service or of cordial appreciation on the part of the ministers.[3]

Some progress in regard to advance of democracy, however, was registered with the enactment of Government of India Act of 1935. Even under this law there were three types of reservations namely, statutory restrictions, special financial safeguards and discretionary powers of the Governor General and Governors. The Governor of Assam had some special powers. The ministerial responsibility provided under the Government of India Act, 1935 was doubtless based on principles of parliamentary democracy, especially in the provinces.[4]

In the political situation then prevailing, the completion of parliamentary evolution was obstructed by provision for the reservations and safeguards which expressly laid down that in certain specified situations the Governor might act without the advice of his Ministers, or even contrary to their advice. That became the cause of serious confrontation with the democratic forces emerging under the leadership of Indian National Congress with the General Elections held under the 1935 Act in 1937 and constituted a challenge to the bureaucracy. The public services sought protection under the constitutional safeguards which politicians viewed as blocking the road to a full-fledged Dominion Constitution. While the bureaucracy regarded these safeguards as essential for a transition from an administrative government to a democratic one, the politicians insisted that they should proceed straight to full democracy without any intervening period of transition. Except for the safeguards which caused considerable irritation and misunderstanding, British policy was to sincerely seek the cooperation of Congress leaders to work the Act. Writing to Governor on the subject, it is pertinent to refer to what the Viceroy (Lord Linlithgow) said in 1937.[5] Neither wanted to leave the relations between the Governor and his Ministers to develop through the evolution of constitutional practices or conventions on the lines of the Dominion Constitution Acts of other countries. The rigidity of Indian Society and its colonial politics were, perhaps, both responsible for an emphasis on the written word, though, both Governors and Ministers used restraint to avoid any resort to the safeguards on which so much heat had been generated in the course of constitution-making and thereafter.

Interaction Under 1935 Act

The interaction that took place between bureaucracy (headed by the Governor) and democracy (represented by the Council of Ministers) was chiefly in the provinces. For purposes of guiding and regulating the subsisting relationship between the Lt. Governor and his Council of Ministers (under the Govt. of National Capital Territory of Delhi Act, 1991 and the Constitution (69th Amendment Act) a discussion of this interaction is particularly relevant. This discussion will help in appreciating the peculiar position of Lt. Governor vis-a-vis his Council of Ministers and the Central Government Unlike the present position obtaining in the States and other Union Territories, the Lieutenant Governor, Delhi in his relationship with the Council of Ministers is placed in a state of two-tier relationship, or to use a rather odd phrase, dichotomy and dyarchy more particularly in view of the provisions contained in Clause 3 (a) of Article 239 AA read with Section 41 of the 1991 Act which effectively provides that the matters relating to Public order, police and land will be dealt with by Lt. Governor in his discretion i.e. without necessarily and compulsorily consulting the Council of Ministers.

It would be interesting to note that even in 1937 senior Congress leaders like Gandhiji and C Rajagopalachari demanded from British Government a public and/or written assurance that Governors would govern constitutionally and would not use safeguards in the ordinary course of government business except on specific instructions from the Viceroy or the Secretary of

State.[6] After 55 years or so, echoing the same sentiments one of the former Chief Executive Counsellors of Delhi gave detailed advice on the same lines in a discussion organised by IIPA (Delhi Chapter)[7] on 22nd July, 1992 when the new set-up for Delhi was being discussed. Lt. Governor Mr. P.K. Dave inaugurated the conference and Mr. MMK Wali, former Lt. Governor and Mr. Balakrishnan and Mr. Ramesh Chandra, authors of what is now known as Balakrishnan Committee Report were also present. Mr. Jag Pravesh Chandra then said:

> "Mr. Dave, the dyarchy to which you referred is to be introduced to three subjects— police, public order and land. Let me make it very clear, Sir, to you in particular, because you are the Lt. Governor, whether reservation or no reservation, the future Chief Minister will be responsible for everything that happens in Delhi, you should bear in mind— it is very respectfully I am saying, not arrogantly— and things will move very well. Therefore, I request, you that the Lt. Governor should consult the Chief Minister regularly, otherwise, administrative complications are bound to arise."[7]

British Government's general attitude in 1937 was to somehow bridge the gap created by mutual suspicion and social barriers through the expediency of social and personal contacts and to promote cooperation. General advice of Viceroy to the Governors was couched in the vein. Two examples from Orissa and UP will perhaps suffice to illustrate that politics reigned higher than the rigid, administrative propriety or strictly legalistic approach. The trouble in Orissa was about Dhenkanal State where the Praja Mandal was agitating for abolition of forced labour and introduction of democracy. Kanungo, the premier sought to lend his support to the Praja mandal while the Governor wanted to protect the ruler. JA Hubbak, the Governor was advised by the Viceroy not to get involved in any major crisis with Ministers over the Princes Protection Act in Orissa, at a time when political authority did not regard its application essential.[8]

The political situation in U.P. which led its Governor, Sir Harry Haig to refuse the request of Pandit G.B. Pant's Ministry to release certain ex-terrorist leaders created a serious problem. There were repeated secret reports from various Districts both by the Intelligence Bureau and other agencies that the released ex-terrorist prisoners were encouraging revolution, preaching di-affection against the police and impressed on the audience that with Congress Government in power the Police were entirely under the control of the local Congress leaders who could dismiss or transfer any police officer at will.[9]

Such speeches were being made at that time in various Districts of U.P. including those by Bal Krishna Sharma at Kanpur. The situation so created led to a confrontation between the Governor and his Ministry. As directed by the Premier, the Chief Secretary U.P. in a circular letter of 15 September, 1937 instructed the heads of concerned departments that "speeches of ordinary public meetings be no longer reported. The Hon'ble Premier has promised to discontinue the practice of reporting political speeches and order should be issued accordingly."[10] The Governor's advice to the Premier, both oral and written to check and restrain the incitement to revolution and violence was not needed. Here it may be relevant to give *in extenso* the substance of a note from the Governor which said that such speeches and activities were undermining the morale of the police force and weakening its authority to control crime. The authority of the provincial Government, the Note added, 'is exercised through the Government services, the machinery of which was at their disposal. Party organizations and machinery have their own functions, but they are quite distinct, and it seems to me exceedingly important that they should not appear to be usurping the functions of the Government services'. The Governor went on to say that relations between landlords and tenants might shortly become 'very strained', while relations between Hindus and Muslims were already becoming 'more strained'. He, therefore, warned that 'there must be some limit to this policy of tolerance' and that 'the Government may be foreced by the essential nature of its responsibilities to the province as a whole to action'. Through his Note to the Premier he thus invited the attention of the Council of Ministers 'most seriously to the situation' and suggested that immediate steps be taken to check open incitement to revolution and violence, to check attacks on the police, and to announce that the Ministry would maintain the authority of their own Services, more particularly of the police. The Governors of Bihar and U.P., Hallett and Haig, supported by the Viceroy refused to act in accordance of the advice of their ministeries and declined to order general release of ex-terrorist prisoners in the interest of the maintenance of public order.[11] The Premiers offered their resignations. The Viceroy and the two Governors took a hard and inflexible attitude. However, bowing down to the reactions in the British press, the Secretary of State took the view that the risk which the release of political prisoners in U.P. and Bihar involved was not so great as to justify causing a Constitutional crisis. Finally on the suggestion from the Secretary of State a compromise was arrived at about the release of prisoners. This ultimately proved that the consideration of political expediency led to this decision and established the supremacy of "politics" over the "Constitution". The former determined the content of the latter.[12]

Under dyarchy, as under 1935 Act, the Governor was in a strong position. As the actual administrative head, all the matters of importance in the reserved Departments came to him. A Secretary was under the then rules of executive business, as in the Delhi Govt. Rules of Business, required in the "transferred" Departments to bring certain classes of cases to the Governor's notice. Under 1919 Act all Secretaries except those for Public Works were taken from the Indian Civil Service. The appointee's position was that of a Secretary to the Government, not to a Department, the obligation of every Secretary was, therefore, to see that the Governor's rules of executive business were carried out in his Department. Those rules provided for regulating consultation with other Departments, the reporting to the Governor of cases where the Head of a Department was to be overruled, and reference to him of major matters which in the opinion of the Secretary were to be brought to his notice. This was the basis of what was known as the 'right of access', which meant a regular interview the Secretary had with the Governor, even on matters which fell within the purview of a Minister. He was also to send to the Governor a weekly list of all cases in which orders had been passed by the Minister.[13]

Under the new Act of 1935, however, the position changed. The Governor could make rules of executive business, but not without consulting council of Ministers (as under the present 1991 Act). As suggested by Sir Malcolm Hailey, the Governor could under his Instrument of Instructions, demand information on orders passed in various Departments on certain classes of cases relating for instance, to communal riots, outbreak of violence or disorder. He claimed in addition a definite 'right of access' to make personal contact with high officials, and take over exclusive control of the information collected by his special Branch or Intelligence Bureau. These powers already existed with the Governors of U.P. and Bihar. They made use of them, and yet could not force their Ministers to act as they wished. This has been referred to earlier with reference to the two specific cases of U.P. and Bihar. As in politics, the dice had been cast in favour of democracy at the Government level also.[14]

Under the 1935 Act, at both administrative and secretarial levels, the Minister, whatever his political ideology, could not but depend upon the civil servant's cooperation to secure the execution of policy. Various studies reveal that inspite of acute political differences the Ministers in various provinces in 1937 freely interacted with the Governors and readily accepted the Governors' advice on all but very controversial matters. The relations of Ministers with the Secretaries to the government were based on cooperation, understanding and mutual respect. This has been testified by the Viceroy Lord Linlithgow in his letters to Zetland in a reference to C. Rajagopalachari and B.G. Kher and to other Prime Ministers in his letter of August 2, 1937.[15]

With a view to work out organisational arrangements the Viceroy Linlithgow appointed a committee of Secretaries under the Chairmanship of Maxwell, then Home Members mainly to define the functions and status of the Secretaries of the Government in relation to his Minister. The Committee took into account mainly three factors; namely:

(a) The Ministers were essentially politicians and in no sense officials. In addition to their ministerial duties, they would, therefore, have to nurse their constituencies, justify the policy of their party through public speeches, tour with a view to keeping in touch with areas of electoral importance, and finally, devote considerable time to their parliamentary duties when the Legislature happened to be in session. This clearly meant that the demands upon their time would be substantial and their dependence on the bureaucracy correspondingly great.

(b) The Minister was neither concerned with the departmental discussions nor interested in knowing the details of the original files, norms and procedures that form part of a final decision. All that he needed to know was the result which emerged from departmental discussions or from an expression of information on a case by different officers. This involved summing-up of a case in the form of a concise, self-contained and objective statement of its history, of the issues raised of the arguments on both sides, and the sepecific points on which orders were called for.

(c) Duc to the possibility of frequent changes in the ministerial field arising from the democratic set-up there was need to have a separate and continuous existence of administrative and secretarial staff to carry out the policy of the Government.[16]

The committee made the following important

recommendations which are equally valid today and in fact many of our present Rules of Business draw inspiration from these principles. Main recommendations were:

(a) The principle of collective ministerial responsibility has for its administrative counterpart the individual responsibility of one departmental head to the Ministry and the Minister. Other departmental officers had to speak or give their opinion only through their departmental head. A Minister was of course not to be precluded from consulting experts or other Department Officers on questions of technical or even administrative importance. But it was considered essential that the Secretary should invariably be associated with such consultations and that in any event final decisions on matters so discussed were not to be taken without giving him an opportunity of expressing his own views.

(b) In view of the Minister's inability to attend to the details of administration, the Committee suggested a classification of the business that ought to be submitted to him. The principle of this classification was that, while it ensured a reference to the Minister on all matters of major importance, it left the secretary free to deputize for him in other matters.

(c) The power of disposal of business in the secretariat to be exercised by Secretaries to the Government was thus in a strict constitutional sense a delegation from the Minister. It was nevertheless essential; without such delegation the joint pressure of parliamentary and administrative duties would be too heavy for any Minister to carry for long. The added responsibility of Minister for management of party affairs and intra-party rivalries and differences further leaves less time to devote to details of administrative and Secretarial work.

(d) The Committee felt that the Ministers need not issue orders to subordinate officers direct. The question of confidence and trust, however, depended more on the calibre, quality and character of individuals than the rules governing their relationship. For example, in Madhya Pradesh on objections being raised by the Governor in some cases, a Minister assured that this practice of issuing orders over the head of the Secretary to the Government would cease and they would in future conform to the rules of business in this connection. In Bihar the Governor countered a move on the part of his ministers to side-track the official Secretary and bring the Parliamentary Secretaries more in forefront. The 1935 Act recognised provision for permanent Secretaries but not Parliamentary Secretaries.[17]

Let us pause here for a while and ponder over the position under Constitutional (69th Amendment) 1991 and provisions contained in Clause IV of Article 239 AA of the Constitution and Section 41 of the Delhi Administration Act 1991. These provisions are comparable to the situation that prevailed under the 1935 Act when the Congress ministries functioned in seven provinces in 1937. And that is where, the relevance of the above discussion bringing out these problems faced by the Governors, the Ministers and the officers at that time, lies.

Even under the Delhi Administration Act 1966, the Lt. Governor was required to discharge certain functions in his discretion and there was an analogous provision in the Rules of Business applicable thereto. The subjects excluded from the purview of the Council of Ministers under the 1991 Act are almost the same as in the 1966 Act. Standing orders regulating the discretion and disposal of the business relating to such functions, have not been so far framed and perhaps it may be difficult to do so in the present context. Previous experience both under the 1935 Act and also more recent experience in Delhi under the 1966 Act, and the experience of the working of present Government however, does indicate that there are likely to be increasing pressures on the Lt. Governor. He is likely to discover that discharge of his functions in respect of such subjects will not be a bed of roses. He is also likely to encounter thorns irrespective of whether the Chief Minister of the Capital belongs to the ruling party at the Centre or otherwise. Only the nature of his difficulties and the pressures and the counter pressures may be different. This aspect has been discussed in the last part of this chapter with reference to same specific issues.

Law and order, police and land, touch, directly or indirectly, most of the citizens and it is natural that the elected representatives would like to not only know as to how the Lt. Governor deals with these subjects but also to discuss them with him and the concerned officers dealing with concerned Departments. The Council of Ministers also wants to take part in decision-making process whether directly and/or even indirectly. These matters figure in the Legislative Assembly either in response to questions or call attention notices or otherwise. And as in the past, Secretaries in charge of Land, Home and officers of the DDA and Police are expected to remain present in the official gallery of Legislative Assembly to assist the Minister-in-charge.

Let me add that the above proposition is not a mere theoretical assumption. Successively both the Chief Executive Councillor under the Delhi Administration Act and the Chief Ministers under the NCT Act have expressed themselves strongly for participation in the decision-making process in regard to the reserved subjects. In fact they have taken up this question repeatedly with the government of India seeking suitable modification in the Rules of Business. (*The Times of India*, dated 8-3-1995).

There is yet another point which must be referred to. The scope of expressions and the connotation of 'Law and Order' and 'land' is not easy to define and encompass. For example, while 'public land' will be a reserved subject, removal of encroachment thereon by the Municipal

Corporation of Delhi or DDA or NDMC or Cantt. Board could be stretched to fall within the purview of Local Self Government Department which is a transferred subject; allotment of houses was, under the 1966 Act, being dealt with by Secretary Lands and Buildings (who was also Secretary P.W.D.) without consulting the Executive Consellor in charge (who would now be the Minister). The point to note is that there is adequate scope for doubts, genuine or otherwise, in similar situations.

The competence of the Legislative Assembly is restricted in regard to entries 1, 2 and 18 of the State List and entries 64, 65 and 66 of the Concurrent List which are related to those entries. In regard to entry 18, the State List says "Land, that is to say, rights in or over land, land tenures, including relation of landlord and tenants and collection of rents; transfer and alienation of agricultural land; land improvement and agricultural loans; colonisation". This is too large an entry and its wide scope is likely to raise difficulties. It may be noted that as far as this provision is concerned, it does represent stepping down even from the position under the 1951 Act where the barred entry was "Lands and buildings vested or in the possession of Union of India or New Delhi including all ancillary rights, transfer of land etc." Again in the 1966 Act "Land and Building Department" was a subject which was excluded from the purview of the functioning of the Metropolitan Council. No previous statute had such a large exclusion of land. In regard to land administration, therefore, the uncertainty will continue. The Land and Development Officer (L & D O) would continue to discharge his responsibility. There is no indication whether his jurisdiction would come under Lt. Governor, or the Lt. Governor will be delegated those powers. Various difficulties, referred to elsewhere, regarding the functioning of DDA in land settlement will remain. Another point which seems to have been missed is entry 35, "Works, lands and buildings vested in or in possession of the State". This is outside the purview of the Delhi Legislature.

There have been suggestions that there should be a

convention that the Lt. Governor should act in consultation with the Chief Minister in regard to public order and police. In regard to police, in the Balakrishnan Committee Report, suggestions have been made that Deputy Commissioner should exercise the powers under Sections 108, 109 and 110 of Criminal Procedure Code. But the basic problem in Delhi is that we have Police Commissioner System. Where the Police Commissioner System exists in Metropolitan Cities, over the Police Commissioner there is the Home Secretary, the Chief Secretary, the Home Minister and the Chief Minister. In the present Delhi set-up, some of these links do not exist.

Shri Ramesh Chandra, Member of the Balakrishnan Committee, in a Seminar on 23-7-1992 had made very pertinent observations both in regard to the Police and also the Services. Perhaps they could be quoted so as to appreciate how far conventions in regard to consultation by Lt. Governor in respect of these subjects could successfully be evolved and implemented. He said:

> "..... In the case of Delhi, the difficulty is that the police remains as an island in the air, except that the Lt. Governor has some semblance of control with the power delegated to him from the President.

"In regard to services, again, I think that position has been made clear. Entry 41 of the State List, that is, State Public Service and State Public Service Commission will fall outside the purview of Delhi Legislature. In the case of Pondicherry, under Rule 47 of the Rules of Business of the Government of Pondicherry, 1963, there is provision for consultation with the Chief Minister. Actually, it is stated that the Administrator shall, while exercising his discretion, consult the Chief Minister. Here the suggestion is that there should be a convention of consultation with the Chief Minister. Well, I do not know how it will function. Firstly, the system of convention is something alien to India, because ours is a written Constitution. I do not think the conventions so far have played any part, except in the sense of precedents for deciding cases in various fora."

Yet another factor needs to be noticed. In spite of the new dispensation, NCT of Delhi would continue to be a Union Territory and consequently it cannot have its own Cadre for the IAS and IPS Ministry of Home Affairs would continue to be the controlling authority for these cadres as also in the case of DANI. The Home Ministry thus, continues to control the postings and transfers unless a workable and firm arrangement is arrived at with them. Otherwise the Lt. Governor's authority and control over the concerned departments and officers posted therein will be proportionately diluted. Similarly, the present position is that the nodal Ministries in the Central Government are controlling the postings and transfers in the DDA, and NDMC, and Central Health Services. In fact, over the past several years, the powers of Delhi Government over the posting of officers in the DDA, NDMC and CHS gradually have been taken away and are now being exercised by the Ministry of Urban Development. There have been no protests from Delhi Government Reference in this behalf may be made to the following general orders issued by the Ministry of Home Affairs or Ministry of Urban Development undermining the authority of Lt. Governor. These, *interalia* include:

(a) Discretionary allotment of flats in DDA on compassionate groups;

(b) Appointment of Principal Commissioner and Commissioners in DDA and other specific directives issued under Section 41(1) of DDA, Act in individual cases. (It is felt that issue of directives in individual cases is against the spirit of the Act. Number of such directives issued during the past two years is more than 12).

(c) Posting and transfer of officers of IPS, Central Health Service and IAS without consulting the Lt. Governor.

If the Lt. Governor is to exercise desired control over

the affairs of the NDMC, DDA and the police how far this situation would need to be remedied needs to be considered seriously. The remote control by the Central Government makes the position of the Lt. Governor much more difficult and unenviable when, directly or indirectly, the state of affairs comes under discussion or review in the Legislative Assembly either at the time of budget discussion of the Government or the DDA or otherwise and the Council of Ministers would quite understandably press for being consulted or at least being kept informed. In fact several such situations have arisen during the last three years but for the understanding and patience remedies to such a situation, however cannot be found either in Statues or in Rules framed thereunder but only when healthy conventions are established. Situations become far more difficult to manage when on occasions a Minister of Central Government chooses to deal with an issue directly with concerned officers of the Delhi Government (in violation of the age-old principle expounded by the Maxwell Committee of 1937 referred to above) or the directions of one Minister are contrary to or at variance with those of the other Minister in the same Ministry or of another Ministry in the Central Government.

While discussing the powers of the Lt. Governor where he is supposed to exercise his discretion or individual judgment in regard to certain subjects, it must be appreciated that while the Lt. Governor is not expected to run a parallel government relating to subjects falling in the jurisdiction of the Council of Ministers, he is not supposed to be a mere sleeping partner in the affairs of the Government of National Capital either. it would be a gross fallacy to regard the institution of the Governor as a faint presence like a full moon at midday. The Governor is not a glorified cipher. With the change in the political map of India where ruling parties in States are different from the party at the Centre the Governor's role is crucial for the proper functioning of the federation and maintenance of healthy Centre State relations. More so in Delhi for reasons which are too obvious and wellknown to need elaboration. His vigilant presence could be useful if only he uses what Bagehot described as "the right to be consulted, to warn and to encourage."[18]

Lt. Governor is also an essential part of the Legislative Assembly as no bill passed by Legislative Assembly can become law unless assented to by the Lt. Governor (Section 24).

This is not a mere routine affair. Where the Lt. Governor is vigilant, he can certainly act as a moderating influence on the legislative functions of the Government of the National Capital Territory. There have been cases in the past where the Governor was able to persuade the Chief Minister of a State to modify a Bill passed by both Houses of the Legislature, disproportionately raising the emoluments and allowances of the members of the Legislative Assembly Legislative Council, of the Speaker and the Deputy Speaker of the Assembly and of the Chairman and Deputy Chairman of the Legislative Council.

The peculiar position in which the Lt. Governor finds himself in regard to subjects expressly provided under Section 41 of the 1991 Act to be dealt with by him in his discretion and in respect of allied matters in which various Ministries will directly or indirectly, exercise authority, power and influence on the Lt. Governor have been brought out in the preceding paragraphs. On occasions he finds himself in a rather difficult position to choose his course of action in regard to particular matter whether it relates to law and order, police, land or postings and transfers of higher officers or other matters. In case of clash of views or differences of opinion, he will have to choose the middle way between the dictates of his conscience based on his own judgement, advice or indication from one of the Ministries and local pulls and pressures either of the Council of Ministers or other informal public opinion. Perhaps one way could be to work out a regular, informed channel of communication and discussion with the nodal Ministries where the Secretaries of the concerned Ministries with a clear mandate and authority from their respective Ministers could have discussion at Raj Niwas to which the Chief Minister could be invited depending on the need for a free and frank discussion and exchange of views. This could well be the way out of resolving such differences of opinion on sensitive issues as are at present taken outside the corridors of power and finding their way in the press causing embarrassment to all concerned and making it difficult to reconcile the difference. One has to recognise, however, that such suggestions are easy to make but difficult to practice or implement. Whether, how and when such an informal system can be devised and worked, only the future can tell.

Other Matters where the Lt. Governor Exercises his Discretion

Apart from the subject expressly excluded from the purview of the Council of Ministers under Section 41 of the 1991 Act or such other subject which the President may so exclude, there are certain other matters in which Lt. Governor is required to exercise his discretion or individual judgment and need not consult the Council of Ministers. It may be useful to mention some of these provisions. This list obviously is only illustrative and not exhaustive. These are:

(1) The Governor's right to appoint the Chief Minister in a State is provided for under Article 164 (1). The other ministers have to be appointed by the Governor on the advice of the Chief Minister. Taking note of Article 164(2) of the Constitution which provides for the collective responsibility of the Council of Ministers to the Legislative Assembly of the State. Before appointing a Chief Minister, the Governor has to make sure that he commands a majority in the Legislative Assembly of the State. Here there is a distinction between the powers of a Governor in a State and those of the Lt. Governor in the National Capital Territory of Delhi. Under Clause (5) of Article 239 AA the Chief Minister is to be appointed by the President and thereafter the Ministers are to be appointed by the President on the advice of the Chief Minister. The law is silent as to how the Chief Minister is to be appointed by the President and

whether he is necessarily to be leader of the majority party. However, from the scheme of the Act this is obvious. And here perhaps the Lt. Governor may have to play a role and ascertain as to which political party is in majority in the Legislative Assembly and may, formally or informally, ascertain the wishes of the majority party in regard to its choice of leader. Such a leader theoretically could be an outsider also. The position becomes sensitive to handle if there is a hung Legislative Assembly. The procedure which, however, is to be decided by him in his discretion taking into account various conventions established so far in various States. But Presidential guidance in this behalf will perhaps be necessary. Explicit written guidance may not, however, be consistent with the laid down position in the 1991 Constitutional Amendment, and yet perhaps the Lt. Governor may have to fill in this gap informally. Alternatively instructions can be issued under Section 49 or 53 of the 1991 Act.

(2) Article 356 of the Constitution which provides for the imposition of Presidential rule contemplates a report from the Governor with regard to the failure of the constitutional machinery. In this regard the analogous provisions in respect of Delhi is Clause 239 AB of the Constitution (69th) Amendment Act, 1991. The Lt. Governor will be justified in exercising his discretion even against the aid and advice of his Council of Ministers as such failures of the constitutional machinery may be because of the conduct of the Council of Ministers itself.

(3) As regards summoning of the Legislative Assembly or its prorogation or dissolution the current view expressed by a committee of Governors appointed by the President is that a Governor should exercise this power on the advice of Council of Ministers. The same situation obtains in regard to the powers of Lt. Governor vis-a-vis the Legislative Assembly in the National Capital Territory of Delhi.[19] However, in

some extreme cases the Lt. Governor need not accept ministerial advice. For example, if there is a no-confidence motion against a Ministry, and the Chief Minister, instead of facing the Assembly, advises the Governor to dissolve the Assembly, the Lt. Governor need not accept such advice, but should ask the Chief Minister to get the verdict of the Assembly on the no-confidence motion. This was the situation which Mr. Dharma Vira had to face as Governor in West Bengal and had to exercise his discretion in dismissing Ajoy Mookerji's Government.[20]

(4) One of the important functions of the Lt. Governor is to ensure that healthy harmonious and proper relations are maintained between the Centre and the government of National Capital Territory. He could play the role of competent intermediary, pleading with the Union Government where he feels that the National Capital's case is not adequately considered or in other matters he could prevail upon the Council of Ministers to show reasonableness and fall in line with the Centre's point of view.

(5) The Constitution specifically provides that Judges of the High Court will be appointed after Chief Minister and the Governor have been consulted. Although there is no express analogous provision in the 1991 Act it would well nigh be impossible to deprive the Chief Minister of the National Capital his right to be consulted in this matter. Hopefully the Lt. Governor will, therefore, have a further role to play vis-a-vis the appointments of Judges in the Delhi High Court. There have been cases in various States, more particularly in the case of Karnataka where the then Governor, Mr. Govind Narain, played this role constructively.[21]

(6) Under Article 200 (Section 24 of 1991 Act) the Lt. Governor can withhold his assent to a Bill or reserve the Bill for consideration of the President. The crucial question is as to what are the norms and criteria that the Lt. Governor should follow in reserving Bills

for consideration. It is suggested that the Lt. Governor should exercise the function of reserving a Bill for Presidential consideration if

(a) The Bill is patently unconstitutional or

(b) It is palpably against the larger interests of the country from the point of view of its unity and integrity, or

(c) It is in direct opposition to the Directive Principles of State policy enshrined in the Constitution; or

(d) The Bill passed by the Legislative Assembly is of grave national importance, and especially in a case where it is apparent to him that the reconsideration of the Bill in the light of the amendments recommended in message by the House or Houses would be an idle formality.[22] Here it may not be inappropriate to underline the advantage of earliest intervention by Lt. Governor before a Bill of the above nature is introduced in the Legislative Assembly or at the time of its consideration by the Council of Ministers.

In matters in which the Constitution specifically requires the Governor to act in his discretion, it is again doubtful if the Constitution would permit the Governor's discretion to be fettered by any Instrument of Instructions or any guidelines.[23]

In case of Lt. Governor, however, in view of Section 41 and the power of the President to reserve other subjects for being dealt with by Lt. Governor in his discretion, it is doubtful if he will have the same freedom of action as the Governors in view of the position outlined above. This view finds further confirmation from the fact that in case of Lt. Governor's difference of opinion with his Council of Ministers even in respect of subjects within the latters competence he is required to make a reference to the President and thereafter abide by the latter's decision.

Before we take leave of the discussion regarding

reserved subjects it may make for some clarity if we could encapsulate what the Balakrishnan Committee had in mind. Not that those observations are binding on either the Central Government or the Lt. Governor or the Council of Ministers. But one could look for some guidance. And in regard to this we may perhaps quote in extenso what Mr. Balakrishnan himself said in a Seminar held on July 22, 1992. He said,

> "The Report itself has stated that the police function requires not only the force but also the cooperation of the public, feed back from the public. These are factors which only associated representatives can reflect to the Governor. So, the idea is that the Governor, acting as the representative of the Central Government, in the discharge of his constitutional function of law and order as well as land, has to take note of the fact that he cannot just afford to act in his own discretion in the matter. He has to take note of the feelings, the information and the feedback received by him from the Ministry. Actually, this is the very function of the Lt. Governor. To a Governor of the calibre of Shri Dave, the problem will not arise at all, because it is a question of harmonious working and understanding with each other. The Lt. Governor and the Ministry have to bear in mind that they are not hostile to each other, they form part of the same mechanism of the Government of Delhi. In certain matters, he has certain special responsibility to the Centre. But most of the time he will have to get on with the Ministry, as every Governor does. In that way, there is no risk, there need not be any unnecessary fear, that there will be constant friction between the Governor and the Council of Ministers, whenever it is a problem dealing with law and order or land. He has all the powers delegated to him from the Centre. I am not speaking as a Government representative, but it is expected that the full responsibility, the field functions, will be discharged not by the Centre, but by the Lt. Governor. He will have informal consultations with the Council of

Ministers; and that is the way the Government will have to function, not always by rules and all that."[24]

It has been urged in certain quarters that the process of consultation, which is considered politically necessary and administratively desirable, can be provided in the Rules of Business. In support of this view Article 258 of the Constitution has been quoted, which reads: "Notwithstanding anything in this Constitution, the President may, with the consent of the Government of a State, entrust either conditionally or unconditionally to that Government or to its officers functions in relation to any matter to which the executive power of the Union extends."

Shri Balakrishnan has confirmed that "as suggested in the Report, in regard to land there may be a provision in the Rules of Business that the Lt. Governor will act "in consultation with the Council of Ministers" not "aid and advise". This is the scope of arrangement at the top level between the Lt. Governor and the Council of Ministers".[25]

One view is that in regard to public order and police there should be a convention that Lt. Governor should act in consultation with Chief Minister, whenever possible. Mr. Ramesh Chandra, a member of the Committee, however, thought differently, and said:

> "In certain matters, it is recommended that there should be a convention of consultation with the Chief Minister. In a particular case, it is said that he should act in consultation. My possible objections are, firstly, there are difficulties in regard to consultation being binding, or how far the consultation is effective. Of course, given the goodwill, it should be effective. The other thing is, to provide consultation when the Chief Minister goes against the principles of collective joint responsibility of the Cabinet. This is some sort of contradiction. How is this going to be resolved?"
>
> "In the case of Delhi, the difficulty is that the police remains as an island in the air, except that Lt. Governor has some semblance of control with the

power delegated to him from the President. At the lower level— I am talking legally— under the system, there is no relationship. It has to be built up, which is essential for the maintenance of law and order, and how the representatives of public order, this is again an issue which has to be resolved."

The other view is that in regard to land, the consultation should be provided for in the Rules of Business, but regarding Police and law and order, to begin with, the consultation should be governed more by convention. More so when Home Ministry's say or interference in this field is considerable. One can do no better than give the perception of a former Chairman of DESU Mr. KS Gujral in his own words:

"The police is not brought under the Delhi Administration. I may be execused irrelevance for something I am going to say. I do not know what is written in the Report, but in practice the police is directly under the Home Ministry. Even the Lt. Governor of Delhi is by-passed, he is not even consulted. It is often after the appointment is made that the Lt. Governor of Delhi is informed. In that case, even the Lt. Governor does not play any part in it. This is a police system in which the ordinary citizen cannot go to the local representative to voice his grievances, to speak against the high-handedness of the police.

These observations do find an echo in a news item captioned "Delhi Police forced to induct official" in *Pioneer* dated 23rd April, 1992. Only the Delhi Government or Ministry of Home Affairs, would however, know how far it reflects the true situation on the ground.

General Observations

The effectiveness of the Lt. Governor's advice to the Ministers and the exercise of his discretionary powers in certain cases will primarily depend upon his impartiality and sense of fairness. It is of utmost importance that he should not only be scrupulously fair but be manifestly seen and known to be fair. It is only by such actions that he will inspire confidence in all the political parties in the Legislative Assembly and also win the respect and admiration of the people of the National Capital and the country at large. He can, by the imprint of his personality, impart the right moral tone to the administration of the National Capital. BG Kher put the matter in the proper perspective in the Constituent Assembly when he said,

> "I do not agree with the comment that he is a mere figurehead... A Governor can do a great deal of good if he is a good Governor... We have found in actual practice that if he is an active Governor, a good man, he can, by means of getting into (*sic*) touch with the opponents of the party which is in power, reconcile them to a good number of measures, and generally by tours and other means make the administration run smoothly. Similarly he can do a great deal of mischief".[26]

> And BG Kher as Premier of Bombay maintained the best of relations with the Governor and the Chief Secretary, as testified by himself to the Viceroy.[27]

A word of caution may perhaps not be out of place. In case of the Lt. Governor of the National Capital, however, he must have the Administrative background and experience of having dealt with Law and Order, Police and Land as under the 'Scheme of the 1991 Act, he will have to deal with these subjects in his discretion, without the aid and advice of his Council of Ministers and will have to constantly walk on razor's edge between the dictates of his conscience, the indications of the Central Government and the local pressures of his Council of Ministers.

Similarly, in regard to the removal of a Lt. Governor there have been several cases in Delhi where the Lt. Governors have been pursuaded to resign or removed on almost 24 hours or even shorter notice. We may perhaps note that the discussions in the Constituent Assembly were very pertinent and pointed in regard to the removal of a Governor. It is best to quote Dr. Ambedkar who did not envisage the possibility of a Governor being removed arbitrarily by the President. To quote him:

> "...certain grounds should be stated in the Constitution itself for the removal of the Governor. It seems to me that when you have given the general power, you also give the power to the President to remove the Governor for corruption for bribery, for violation of the Constitution or for any other reason which the President, no doubt, feels is legitimate ground for the removal of the Governor. It seems, therefore, quite unnecessary to burden the Constitution with all these limitations stated in express terms when it is perfectly possible for the President to act upon the very same ground under the formula that the Governor shall hold office during his pleasure."[28]

In the Constitution (Sixty-Ninth Amendment) Act 1991 and Delhi Act 1991, some provisions have been made for the exercise of the function of the Lt. Governor, but the written word is not the last word. In a democracy, particularly in the present experiment which is being tried in the Capital, the written word is supplemented by tradition, conventions and practices established and to be established in course of time. These traditions, conventions and practices will hopefully be healthy ones. In the words of John Stuart Mill "Political institutions are the work of men and owe their origin and their whole existence to human will. Men did not wake on a summer morning and find them spring up. Neither do they resemble trees, which once planted, are growing, while men are sleeping. In every stage they are made what they are by human voluntary agency."

Relationship between Chief Minister and Lt. Governor 1994-96

We have, after giving a historical backdrop of the constitutional set-up of the Government of Delhi, briefly indicated with reference to the past experience the problems that could arise taking into account both the legal provisions as also the different nuances and innuendos arising out of the implementation process of the government set-up. Let us now briefly look at the working of the set-up during the past three years or so, so as to test the theorctical framework developed in the preceding paragraphs. Contentious issue between the Chief Minister and the Lt. Governor has been the status of Delhi as a full State. The Chief Minister has on occasions more than one said and has, in fact, written to the Government of India that Delhi should be treated as a full-fledged State. (*Times of India 8.3.95*). The answer to this given by the Central Government and the Lt. Governor was that under Article 239 A of the Constitution Delhi is "a Union territory with some special powers" (Issues that turned LG-CM's relations sour— *Indian Express - 9.7.1994).*

Illustratively, the differences between the Lt. Governor and the Chief Minister which have cropped up from time to time related to the Sales Tax bill, the 1984 riot cases, the abattoir issue, the demolition at Majnu Ka Tilla Gurudwara and last, but not the least, the Rules of Business laid down for Delhi Government (*Indian Express 9.7.1994*). Some of the commentators after making a critical survey of Delhi affairs have said, "Old writ runs in New Delhi and Delhi's affairs are subject to the tender mercies of the Centre and this is hampering Government (*BS 24.6.1995*) or have dubbed the system as 'One City many governments' (MN Buch in *Hindustan Times 28.8.1995*) and others have quoted the CM as saying "We could do better with full powers" (*Hindustan Times 3.12.1994*) or "Unhappy CM says Centre ignoring constitutional powers of Delhi".

Here we may, for the sake of clarity, note that the question of functional difference between the powers and position of Administrator and Governors was conclusively laid down by the Supreme Court in a case— *Devji Vallbhabhai Tandel* vs. *Administrator of Goa, Daman and Diu* (1982-2 SCC - 222). This question has been raised time and again. To put this controversy at rest it may be worthwhile to quote from the Supreme Court judgement as follows:

"There are basic functional differences in the powers and position enjoyed by the Administrator of a Union Territory on the one hand and the President or Governor on the other. The first difference is that the Administrator is similarly situated with the Governor but not with the President when he is to act in his discretion under the Act. Further, the Administrator has to act on his own unaided by the Council of Ministers when he is to exercise any judicial or quasi-judicial functions. It is manifest from the proviso to Section 44 (1) of the Government of Union Territories Act that even in matters where he is not required to exercise such functions, he is not bound to act according to the advise of the Council of Ministers. In the event of a difference of opinion between Council of Ministers of the Union Territory and the Administrator, the right to decide would vest in the Union Government and the Council of Ministers of the Union Territory would be bound by the view taken by the Union Government. The Administrator can completely override the advice of the Council of Ministers and act according to his right. Neither the Governor nor the President enjoys any such power.

Laying aside the question of Statehood for Delhi, on which the Central Government both of the Congress as also of the Janata Party during 1977-1979 held similar views, it is the issue of the Rules of Business that lies, as some critics say, at the heart of the problem. This, however, as our earlier detailed analysis will show, is not the real problem, because if the Rules of Business turn out to be an obstacle they could, and should be, changed as per the present Statute with the approval of the President. The heart of the problem lies in subjects which have been excluded from the purview of the Council of Ministers and are reserved to be dealt with by the LG in his discretion or individual judgment. This would remain as long as the constitutional status of this provision is not reversed. What, however, is important is to evolve a workable mechanism so as to enable the elected Government to influence the policies and implementation process relating to reserved subjects as well. And this is where the Central Government must play the game properly, fairly and in accordance with the spirit with which the present constitutional set-up was evolved through a consensus in the Parliament. During the discussion in the Lok Sabha the then Home Minister, SB Chavan, had assured the nation that irrespective of the legal provisions, the Centre would extend all support— financial and administrative— to enable the Council of Ministers to effectively discharge their functions. Unfortunately, the field implementation of the aforesaid assurance has been halting and wanting. One of the issues related to the cut of Rs. 54 crores to pay DESU's arrears and attempts to cut another Rs.130 crores from Plan Assistances (*Times of India 8.3.1995*). Another sensitive issue has been the hiatus between the administration of law and order and the Council of Ministers. The Home Ministry continues to have remote control (and also immediate control as Cadre Controlling Authority) in respect of the law and order administration. In fact, the apprehensions expressed by public men in a seminar (referred to earlier) have proved to be true. It is after a three-year long effort that the Lt. Governor, has been successful in getting his proposal regarding setting up a Police Complaint Authority approved. Again, 'land' being a reserved subject, DDA has been functioning almost as an island so far as its administration is concerned. Instead of evolving as a via media to involve the Council of Ministers in its administration the Ministry of Urban Affairs has gradually, but deliberately, centralized certain powers with the Ministry, that were earlier available with the Lt. Governor. Lastly, while the Ministry of Urban Development enjoys powers without responsibility, the Lt. Governor is in an unenviable position of having to own responsibility without power.

These are some of the issues which constitute the core of the present constitutional set-up and its functioning. It is not enough for the then Chief Minister

Madan Lal Khurana to say that "he had very cordial relationship with the Lt. Governor and consulted him as a senior colleague even in matters in which he was fully competent to deal with". (*The Hindustan Times 13.12.1994*). To this club of cordial relationship must be invited the Central Government and if problems of the citizens of Delhi are to be resolved the three must functions without political bias and with a view to speedily resolve the problems of Delhi arising largely out of the "one city—many Governments" syndrome. But that would need statesmanship of the first order which, unfortunately, is a rare commodity today.

REFERENCES

1. The Governor '*Sage or Saboteur*; Roli Books International, New Delhi, 1985, pp. 99-100.
2. Report of the Committee of Governors (1971) President's Secretariat, New Delhi.
3. Reports on the Working of Reformed Constitution, 1927, pp. 246.
4. Hoare to Freeman Jan. 1935, Templewood Papers IO MSS Eur. E240/4 pp.218-220, 8 March, 1937, p. 34.
5. *From Viceroy to Secretary*. In Barbourne papers 10 MSS F97/7 at 91B 8-3-1937. p. 34
6. *Ibid.*
7. Verbatim record of proceedings of the Seminar on Administrative Implication of New Political set-up of Delhi held on July 22, 1992 at IIPA (Delhi Chapter).
8. Zetland Papers IO MSS EurD 609/9p. p.9125.
9. Haig Papers IO MSS Eur p.115/12.
10. *Ibid.* the Chief Secretary's (C.W.G. Wynne's) Confidential Do No. 504-P/VIII dated 15 Sept. 1937.
11. Secret Reports (No. 8/28/32 dt. 27.10.1937 and another dt. 25.10.1935) from Lansdown on Congress activity
12. Hailey Papers IO MSS Eur E 220/32 pp. 28-45 (It see con. papers Vol. I). p. 356.
13. B.B. Misra, the Bureaucracy in India, Oxford University Press, 1977, p. 357.
14. *Ibid.*

15. Linlithgow to Zetland 2 Aug. 1937 IO MSS D609/14, p.107.
16. B.B. Misra, *The Bureaucracy in India*, Oxford University Press, 1987, pp. 358-59.
17. Zetland Papers IO MSS D 609/14 Sept. 1937, p.313.
18. Soli J. Sorabjee, in *The Governor : 'Sage or Saboteur'* Roli Books International, New Delhi, 1985, p.30.
19. Report of the Committee of Governors on Role of the Governor (1971) President's Sectt., New Delhi.
20. (a) See Note 21, *Ibid* pp. 84-85.

    (b) Also Dharma Vira 'The Exercise of Discretion in *'The Governor-Sage or Saboteur'* pp. 84-85.
21. Govind Narain "Constitutional Obligation" in *The Governor : 'Sage or Saboteur'*, Roli Books International, New Delhi, 1985, pp. 68-69.
22. Soli J. Sorabji, in *The Governor : 'Sage or Saboteur'*, Roli Books International, New Delhi, 1985, p. 25.
23. *The Governor : 'Sage or Saboteur'*, Roli Books International, New Delhi 1985, pp. 77-78.
24. Balakrishnan, See note 7.
25. *Ibid.*
26. Constituent Assembly Debates, Vol. VIII, Lok Sabha Secretariat, p. 435.
27. Zetland Papers IO MSS Eur D 609/4, p. 313.
28. Constituent Assembly Debates, Vol. VIII, p. 474.

5 LAW AND ORDER MANAGEMENT AND INSTITUTION OF DISTRICT MAGISTRATE AND POLICE COMMISSIONER

JAYTILAK GUHA ROY AND YATISH MISHRA

The district-oriented police system in India is the heritage of colonial legacy. It was the creation of the Police Act of 1861 which continues to regulate our police system till today. It was framed in an altogether different context of colonial rule under which law and order management and revenue collection were the main objectives of the government. Accordingly, the District Magistrate (DM) was the head of both law and order and revenue management. He was a district collector as well as a magistrate performing three roles of judiciary, executive (including police) and revenue collection.[1]

The amended Criminal Procedure Code (Cr PC), 1973 has brought about a significant change in the district administrative system. In pursuance with the doctrine of 'separation of powers' the judiciary has been separated from the executive. The Executive Magistrates no longer decide criminal cases as they used to. The DM continues to be the district collector, but he has also been entrusted with the responsibility of development and welfare work of the government at the district level. As regards the law and order management, his powers are now confined primarily to the preventive sections of law and promulgation and enforcement of regulatory order and also executive processes for the supervision of police work through the executive magistrates.

Another significant change is the separation of the prosecution wing of the criminal justice administration from both the magistrate and the police. It now functions as a separate entity under the Law or Prosecution Department. Hence, as a logical outcome of the separation policy, all wings of the criminal justice administration are now working as separate entities.

However, "the umbilical chord of the DM with the SP (Superintendent of Police) continues as a legacy of the Act of 1861"[2] which stipulates u/s 4 the administration of police by a district SP 'under the general control and direction' of the DM. Unfortunately, any discussion of the Act of 1861 revolves round a very trivial issue of this control of DM over police, ignoring the real issue. The real issue is to consider whether this Act is capable of giving right type of direction to the police force in the context of our constitutional mandate for democratic and secular values, fundamental rights, directive principles and fundamental duties. As the National Police Commission has observed very poignantly :

"It appears to us that even in the existing legal set-up considerable amount of operational independence in matters relating to the internal management of the force is vested in the Superintendent of Police. The general control and direction of the District Magistrate cannot be construed as warranting any interference by that authority in the internal management of the police force."[3]

Surprisingly, in several State Police regulations and manuals the DM is still referred to as the Head of the Criminal Administration although neither the Police Act of 1861 nor the CrPC, 1973 has conferred upon him such a position. Discarding this position, the National Police Commission has made the following observation: "Legally the District Magistrate's capability to control and direct the Superintendent of Police should only be restricted to selective and individual situations and should be exercised more as an exception than as a rule. We note that the present position in several States far exceeds this legal stipulation. This, in our view, is untenable and needs to be corrected."[4]

The Commissionerate System of Policing (COP)

Unlike the district-oriented police system, in the Commissioner of Police (COP) system the responsibility for all aspects of policing vests in the Commissioner and the accountability for adequate performance also lies in him. To fulfil this responsibility the Commissioner is vested with powers of regulations, control, licensing, etc., in addition to the usual police powers. To quote the National Police Commission, "An operationally autonomous police force functioning under professional command is as responsible and accountable to the Government, the legislature, the press and the public as the District Police Force under the District Magistrate. All that happens is that the police function under their own professional leadership and this leadership is in turn accountable to the Government and the various other forums in our democratic society."[5]

The COP system owed its origin to that of the London Metropolitan Police and was first introduced more than a century ago in the erstwhile primate city of Calcutta and then, some years later in Bombay and Madras. Subsequently, it was extended to other metropolitan cities of Hyderabad, Bangalore, Ahmedabad, Pune, Nagpur and Kanpur. The distinction between the primate or London pattern and the metropolitan pattern of the COP system lies in that the former pattern means the abolition of district administration in the respective cities, whereas in the latter the COP systems co-exist with the district administration.

The COP System in Delhi

Delhi was brought under the COP system in 1978 on the recommendations of the 1966-68 Khosla Commission. While making its recommendations, the Commission noted the successful functioning of the COP system in other metropolitan cities of the country and its endorsement by the prominent citizens of Delhi. The proposal was opposed by the administrative service but strongly advocated by the police. However, "the urgency for reform", observed Professor Datta very forthrightly, "arose due to the twin needs for unification of the machinery for public order, and the separation of the executive and judicial functions in the administration of criminal justice."[6]

It would not be inappropriate to mention that the National Police Commission also recorded that the Police in Commissionerate, not only in Bombay, Madras and Calcutta but also in other cities had given "a much better account of themselves than the Police in districts." As the Commission elucidated this point further:

In large urban areas several problems arising out of social tensions, more opportunities for crime, and the occasionally spontaneous explosion of law and order situations call for an extremely quick response from the Police at the operational levels and precise, comprehensive and prompt directions from the superior levels... quick action springing from purposeful direction is called for. This can be achieved only when the police are organised in a unitary chain of command which embraces the two basic functions of decision-making and implementation. Particularly in large cities these two functions have to go together. We, therefore, recommend that in large cities, that is those with a population of 5 lakhs and above and even in places where there may be special reasons like speedy urbanisation, industrialisation etc. the system of Police Commissionerates... should be introduced.[7]

Delhi's COP system followed the metropolitan, rather than the primate pattern, presumably due to the existence of large rural tracts within the capital territory.

Under the Delhi Police Act 1978, the direction and supervision of police force vests in the Commissioner of Police. He is assisted by the Additional Commissioners in the exercise of his powers and the performance of his duties. Each police district is placed under the charge of a Deputy Commissioner of Police (DCP) who is assisted by one or more additional DCPs. The DCPs are empowered to hold externment proceeding against the habitual offenders u/s 47 and 48 of the Act. However, their action can be challenged in the higher courts of law. Likewise, each police sub-division is placed under the charge of an Assistant Commissioner of Police (ACP) and each police station under the charge of an Inspector of Police. The ACPs are empowered to conduct security proceedings u/s 107 Cr PC. The action under this head is only preventive and can be challenged in the Sessions/High Courts. The ACPs being the Special Executive Magistrates are also accountable to the Sessions Court rather than to their parent department. Thus, the Act of 1978 provides for adequate checks on the concerned police officers in the exercise of their judicial powers.

As mentioned earlier, Delhi's COP system followed the metropolitan pattern. However, with the growing urbanisation and the fast disappearance of its rural hinterland, Delhi may have to adopt in near future the primate pattern as it exists in Calcutta, Bombay and Madras. Till then, the coexistence of district administration and the COP in Delhi would leave 'a few grey areas' under the existing arrangement. Such grey areas, as have been identified by Professor Datta very poignantly, are "the unclear role of the Lt. Governor in exercising operational control over the COP; retaining the authority to call the army to assist Civil power with the district officer rather than vesting it with the Lt. Governor, concentrating both the judicial and crime prevention powers on the COP; and conferment of non-police powers on the COP under various enactments."[8]

The 1989 Sarkaria-Balakrishan Committee highlighted some of these problems with the existing COP system of Delhi and emphasised the need for its proper civilian control. The Committee considered it ideal either to abolish the COP system in Delhi or to confine its powers only to those required for maintaining public order. Commenting on this, Professor Datta has made the following observation:

"The committee thus displayed its bias in favour of reviving the colonial system of district policing and, as an after-thought, suggested an alternative method for the coexistence of the COP and district administration. The other alternative of departmentalizing the residual functions of the district officer under the Delhi Administration— an arrangement prevailing in the other three primate cities- was not considered by the committee at all."[8]

Another grey area relates to the political accountability of the COP. Although the Lt. Governor is statutorily responsible for superintedence of Police in Delhi, the Union Home Ministry often gets directly involved in the police management of Delhi in terms of its political control. This is particularly evident in the transfer and posting of police officers in Delhi. Even after the revival of statehood, the Union Home Ministry retains its political control over the COP in Delhi through the Lt. Governor. Since police is a 'State Subject' under the Constitution of India, there has been an increasing demand for the political control of the COP by the territory Government of Delhi. Even the 1989 Committee could anticipate this problem and recommended that the Lt. Governor should consult the future Chief Minister of Delhi in all matters concerning the security of the National Capital Territory.

It may be noted that Section 27(3) of the Delhi Administration Act, 1966, provides that the functions of the Administrator with respect of law and order including the organisation and discipline of the police force shall be exercised by him in his discretion. Section 41(1) of the Constitution (Sixty-ninth Amendment Act 1991, is an analogous provision.

Despite the successful functioning of the COP system in the metropolises of India, there is the strong feeling that the co-existence of the COP system with the notion of police self-regulation (excluding external review system) is not conducive to promotion of public confidence in a clean and efficient police administration. In this context, it is relevant to note that the legislative endeavour to counter police misconduct in various countries reflects the complexity of the issues and the diverse interests at stake. The crux of the problem is the perceived nature of the complaint process as a closed, secretive system and the lack of information available to a complainant or the public about the investigation and any disciplinary action taken as a result of the complaint. Increasingly there is the public belief that the police attitude towards citizens' complaints is self-protective.

The Balakrishnan Committee has suggested the establishment of an external authority which should be statutory. What form such an external review system should take is again a matter of detail and study. Three factors, however, are essential; political will to support such a change so that it has a statutory basis; the authority in question, by whatever name it is called, must be external; and thirdly, it must be assured of a functional role in the actual process of handling citizens' complaints.

Keeping these factors in view, the then Lt Governor of Delhi, PK Dave had more than two years back proposed setting-up of a Police Complaints Authority on the pattern of the one existing in UK. The Lt Governor's well-meaning initiative initially failed to evoke a positive response from the Union Home Ministry. It is, however, heartening to note that the Police Complaints Authority for dealing with public complaints against police is likely to see the light of the day. This is evident from the statement of the then Prime Minister Mr. H.D. Deve Gowda in Rajya Sabha on August 2, 1996, a part of which is reproduced below :

"There has been a general feeling among the public that complaints against police are investigated by the police themselves and, in most cases, they reach, in their original form, the very officers against whom they are made. Even though there is a Vigilance Cell in the Delhi Police, public confidence in the objectivity and impartiality of the inquiries conducted against police officials seems to be much less than what it should be. It is proposed to create an independent authority, the Police Complaints Authority, for dealing with public complaints against police. These complaints will cover, *inter alia*, police inaction, non-registration of FIR, partisan attitude on the part of the police, registration of false cases, corruption and intervention in civil disputes particularly those relating to property and tenancy, custodial torture, rape and other misbehaviour, abuse of police power, etc. We would involve eminent public men and women with this Police Complaints Authority".

As and when such authority is set up, it would hopefully minimise some of the problems relating to police misconduct and ensure cleaner and more efficient administration of law and order.

Control and Supervision of Delhi Police

The question as to whether under the present constitutional set-up of the governance of Delhi and the COP system, the Council of Ministers should or should not have a say in the administration of law and order has been a subject matter of discussion for decades. The final position taken by the Central Government is that Police and Law and Order will be a reserved subject as Delhi, like Washington, is the capital of India. While the arguments for and against the present status of control can be considered by decision-makers, we could perhaps draw on the experience of UK which has the distinction of having an efficient police force.

The outstanding feature of the British Police is that, except in London, they are not under the direct control of the Central Government, but organised in local forces maintained by local authorities. A local authority has no powers to give orders directly to local forces and the local Chief Constables (analogous to the Police Commissioners) have a high degree of independence from any kind of political control. This is a prime safeguard against the evils of a Police State.[10]

The Local Council do not, however, administer their Police forces directly but act primarily through statutory police authorities, known as Police Committees. These committees are composed of two-thirds of magistrates appointed by quarter sessions (U.K. Police Act 1964, s.2).

Chief constables and deputy and assistant chief constables are appointed by the police authorities, subject to the approval of the Home Secretary (equivalent to India's Home Minister). Controversies do arise when the Home Secretary refuses consent to the appointment of a chief constable from within the same police force so as to prevent 'inbreeding'. The 1993 White Paper envisages that Police authority would usually have sixteen members, eight of whom would be local councillors, three magistrates and what is more important, is that five local people appointed by the Home Secretary under a complicated procedure designed to ensure that the appointed members were independent.

It is important to note two factors. One that a Police officer holds a public position, that of peace officer under which he owes obedience to no executive power outside the police force.[11] The chain of command terminates at the Chief Constable, who is in effect an independent authority and must act free from all political influence, whether national or local. It was best put in by an Australian case, which said:

"The powers of a constable qua peace officer, whether conferred by common or statute law, are exercised by him by virtue of his office and cannot be exercised on the responsibility of any person but himself."[11] In fact, this legal position established by English and Australian Courts will have a bearing on the detailed supervision of investigation being presently conducted by various High Courts and the Supreme Court in our country, but let us leave this matter for a separate discussion.

The second point, which is more relevant to the present discussion, is that it has been considered necessary and expedient to associate five independent persons from the area. The case law in UK is quite clear on the subject, namely, that both the ministers and the local authorities expressly recognized the principle that the police are independent in their task of preserving law and order. No ministerial responsibility is assumed or acknowledged for specific things that the police do, except that the position is slightly different in respect of London, where the Home Secretary in practice accepts a responsibility for the metropolitan police. For purpose of legal liability the Police officer in U.K. is the servant of no one, neither of the Crown, nor of the local authority, nor of the Chief Constable.

Thus, the Police in UK have had a remarkable success in avoiding challenge in the Courts of Law, even though they often stretch their powers and risk actions for tress-pass. During the last three decades, however, even in UK, cases of malpractices, corruption, bad relations between the Police and the immigrant communities in London and other big cities have resulted in change in training, discipline and policing methods also about police community relations, which the Government accepted.[12] Police authorities now have a statutory duty to make arrangements for obtaining views of the people of the area about policing and for obtaining cooperation of the people in preventing crime.

In fact, in the context of the present political set-up of the capital territory, there has been a general feeling that the Lt. Governor should no longer be held responsible for police supervision since this arrangement conflicts with the notion of political control in democratic system as ours. In case, the Central Government is opposed to bring the COP in Delhi under total political control of the territory Government in view of the special security requirements for the capital territory, it should at least take necessary measures to formalise such dual control by the Central and territory/state Governments, as prevalent in Arunachal Pradesh vide special provision under Art. 371H of the Constitution. At the local level, in pursuance with the policy of democratic decentralisation "the logic of political control over the police," as suggested by Professor Datta, "could likewise be shared with the elected local government in Delhi (as exists in the UK) to start with, and extended elsewhere in the country in future."[13]

The same logic is equally applicable to the elected district governments under the New Panchayati Raj.

Effective Policing of Delhi

Apart from the structural reforms in Delhi's COP system as suggested in the foregoing pages, certain administrative and operational measures need also to be taken in order to make the law and order management more effective in dealing with the growing problem of organised crime and gangsterism in the National Capital Region (NCR) of Delhi.

As far as the "rising criminal behaviour" is concerned, the national capital city of Delhi, according to a report of the Voluntary Health Association of India, ranked second in the country in crime. Compared to Mumbai, Calcutta, Chennai and other metropolitan cities, Delhi "tops" in certain crimes, viz., murder, rape, kidnapping, theft and abduction.[14] Of late, sensational crimes such as extortion, kidnapping for ransom, forcible dispossession of landed property, threatening of witnesses before or during court trials, raping of minors, burglary with violence, dacoity and murder of old couples are on the rise in the National Capital.

There is no denying that the problems of policing are increasingly becoming acute and complex in this Region for varied reasons, such as recent industrial boom in the neighbouring towns of Uttar Pradesh and Haryana and involvement of persons, including youths, without any criminal antecedence in sensational crimes. Since ethnically the whole of the NCR constitutes one single cohesive area with links based on caste, marriage, etc., the gangsters and offenders after committing heinousCrime in one part of the Region take shelter in its another part. This again has posed a serious threat to effective policing in the NCR.

It was against the above backdrop that the 1994 Conference of the Director Generals of Police unanimously resolved that the forces of the different states should come together and there should be better coordination among them in tackling the problem of organised crime in the NCR. Subsequently, the Indian Institute of Public Administration (IIPA) was entrusted by the Bureau of Police

Research and Development (BPR&D) of the Union Home Ministry to undertake a short-term research project to examine the emerging problem of effective policing in the NCR, and suggest suitable measures/remedies to overcome them. The IIPA Study Team completed the project within the stipulated period of four months and submitted its report to the BPR&D in May 1995.

In order to examine the recommendations contained in the IIPA study report and formulate a Plan of Action for perusal of the Union Home Ministry, a workshop was organised by IIPA under the aegis of the BPR&D on December 19-20, 1995. The workshop was attendent by senior and middle level administrators and Police officers of Delhi, Haryana, Rajasthan and Uttar Pradesh, eminent jurists and academicians, retired IPS officers, senior officials of the Ministry of Home Affairs including the Home Secretary, Goverment of India, and the Chiefs of Central Police Organisations.

THE NCR POLICE BOARD

The Plan of Action adopted in the workshop, recommended the setting-up of the NCR Police Board on the lines of the National Capital Region Planning Board.

The Plan of Action further suggested that there should be a three-tier administrative system in the NCR as recommended by the IIPA Study Team for joint police action.

The details of the proposed three-tier system are as follows:

(a) Police Board: Composition and Function

At the highest level, a Police Board should be constituted with the Union Home Minister as Chairman, Commissioner of Police, Delhi as Member Secretary, Chief Ministers of the States of UP, Haryana, Rajasthan, Home Secretary/Special Secretary (Home), Government of India, Lt. Governor of Delhi and DGPs of UP., Rajasthan and Haryana as members. The Chief Minister of Delhi is not directly related to law and order, but his co-option may also be considered.

The main function of the proposed Board would be to formulate long-term and short-term policies/action plans for effective policing in the NCR.

(b) Core Group

The Core Group should be set up under the Chairmanship of the Commissioner of Police with Additional Commissioner of Police (Crime), Delhi Police, IG/DIG of the adjoining areas of the concerning States and representatives of CBI, NCRB, DCPW, NCB, MTNL, NDMC, etc. as members. The Core Group may co-opt any person or persons from other departments or agencies as members. The functions of this group would be coordination between concerning States and between different agencies for tackling day-to-day problems of organised and other crimes in the region.

(c) Specialised Cells

The Specialised Cells for all the districts of the adjoining areas of the concerning States should be set-up. These Cells will be manned by officers of Police and other departments such as Income Tax etc. of appropriate level. These Cells would also work under the guidance and advice of the proposed Core Group.

These apart, the Plan of Action also contains detailed recommendations pertaining to uniform personnel policy for the police personnel of the NCR, specialised training courses, community involvement, adoption of Police Commissionerate system in other parts of the NCR and technical and logistic support.

The Plan of Action is currently under the consideration of the Union Home Ministry.

REFERENCES

1. P.S. Bawa, 'Beyond the Police Act of 1861." *SVPNPA Journal*, Jan-June 1995, p. 6

2. Government of India *National Police Commission, Fifth Report*, November 1980, p. 35.

3. *Ibid.*

4. Government of India: *National Police Commission, Sixth Report*, March 1981, p.39.

5. Abhijit Datta, "Administering Delhi Police". *The Statesman*, Delhi, November 10, 1992.

6. *Ibid.*

7. *Ibid.*

8. *Ibid.*

9. White Paper, *Police Reform: A Police Service for the Twenty-first Century, UK*,

10. *Royal Commission's Report*, Comnd. 1728, para 106.

11. Griffith CJ in *Enever vs. The King* (1906) 3 CLR 969.

12. *The Brixton Disorders Report*, UK, April, 1981.

13. *Supra*, note 5.

14. "Delhi Second in Crime Rate," *The Hindustan Times*, October 16, 1993.

6 WOMEN AND CHILD DEVELOPMENT PROGRAMMES IN DELHI

INDERJEET KAUR

The culmination of freedom struggle into an independent India also heralded an era of exhilaration and well being which was expected to be free of shadows of miseries, impoverishment, exploitation, untouchability and immorality but marked by social justice, prosperity and happiness. The pronouncement made in the Preamble of Indian constitution and the agenda of programme, incorporated in Chapter fourth on the Directive Principles of State Policy and Fundamental Rights made it obligatory for the State for exploring all possible opportunities and making all possible efforts to march towards this supreme goal.

For the attainment of the goal, the process was initiated at the first stage by identifying deserving groups in the society and in the second stage by planning and directing the process of socio-eco-political development, the State endeavoured to bring them into the mainstream. The deserving groups in this context stand for a group of people living under sub-human conditions. To bring them into the mainstream a humane approach on the part of Administration envisages at the first step providing welfare services, at the second, developing them into the useful human resources and consequently transforming them into qualitatively perfect human beings. Women and children were identified as the most deserving group for this social transformation.

In Delhi, in spite of having capital status, the condition of women and children was not very different from their counterparts in the rest of the country on the basis of various indicators— rate of mortality, level of education, employment, health security etc. The Delhi Government in the State launched a multi-pronged welfare programme for women, children, old aged people and other backward classes with the establishment of social welfare department in the year 1959[1]. Its approach in this direction has been incremental in pace and humane in effect. Starting with only three institutions the Department gradually succeeded in creating 26 institutions by 1972, vis-a-vis its increasing responsibilities.

Its services have been conditioned with twin aspects of Delhi's growth namely industrialization and urbanization marked with the population growth. Juvenile delinquency, beggary, vagrancy, crime against women and unemployment are some of the major problems of Delhi. The handicapped, the destitute, the old and the infirm, the women, Scheduled Castes/Tribes and the poor children stand neglected in this environment. Basically urban in nature these problems have crept in rural Delhi as well due to obliteration of line between rural and urban under the spell of fast urbanization. The social service programmes of the Department though having urban orientation in the beginning were extended to cover rural Delhi as well.[2] The Directorate of Social Welfare is entrusted with the task of implementing the following Acts:

(1) Juvenile Justice Act, 1986.

(2) The Bombay Prevention of Begging Act, 1959 (as extended to Delhi).

(3) The Immoral Traffic (Prevention) Act 1956 (as amended upto 1986).

(4) The Probation of Offenders Act, 1958.

(5) The Women and Children Institutions (Licensing) Act, 1956.

(6) The Good Conduct Prisoners Probational Release Act, 1926 (2A).

(7) The Dowry Prohibition Act, 1961.

The Women and Children Welfare Cell within the Directorate of Social Welfare had been entrusted with the task of their welfare. The Cell has launched various services separately for women and children. However, some services are catering to the welfare of children and women simultaneously because of the natural intimate relationship between the two.

The discernible feature of the endeavour of the Directorate since its inception has been an incremental approach which has evolved from bureaucratic delivery of services to all round development. It should also be noted that programmes implemented by the Directorate for children and women are supplementary and complementary to the other general developmental programmes carried out by the departments/directorates of health, education, labour, employment, rural development and poverty alleviation programmes.

Child Development

The Directorate of Social Welfare, since its inception is implementing various welfare programmes for children which were improvised commensurating National Policy on Child, which was adopted on 22 Aug., 1974. The policy describes children of the country as 'supremely important asses'. It enjoins on the state to provide adequate services to the children both before and after birth and through the period of growth to ensure their full physical mental and social development.[3]

Statutory Institutions

The department is running many statutory institutions for children which include three Observation Homes (OH) and 11 Juvenile Homes (JH) under the Juvenile Justice Act 1986.[4] The neglected and destitute children who are brought by the police probation officers, and social workers etc., are being provided with care and protection at Observation Home for Boys-I. Whereas at Observation Home Boys-II only the delinquent boys brought by police are given care and protection. The delinquent, destitute and neglected girls are kept in OH for Girls and are produced before the Board/Court as the case may be.[5]

The inmates of the Homes are provided with free boarding, lodging, medical care, school education and vocational training.

Home/School/Institution for mentally retarded persons— girls, boys and adults are provided protection and care to the inmates. The admission to these institutions are either under the orders of Juvenile Welfare Board or orders of Department of Social Welfare.[6] In these homes all other facilities are also provided.

The Department is also having non-statutory Institutions for the care of children. These can be broadly divided in three categories:

(i) Institution for healthy children of leprosy affected patients numbering four. These institutions protect the children from infectious disease of their parents.

(ii) There are three institutions, known as Sanskar Ashram, for the children of denotified tribes. Taking care of children of a specific group these aim to bring the inmates into mainstream by providing a conducive atmosphere marked by free boarding, lodging, medical care, school education, recreation and counselling services.[7]

(iii) Three Village Cottage Homes have been created on the pattern of SOS. In these Homes the parentless, destitute children of widows/widowers and children of single parent are admitted. Children with IQ below normal or suffering from major physical disability or infectious disease are not admitted. Admission to these are on voluntary basis. Children are kept in a group of 10-12 under the care and supervision of a House Aunty. Children of both sexes are kept together upto 12 years to provide family atmosphere.[8]

After Care Home for Boys

Established in 1955, it is a non-custodial Home for male inmates of Juvenile Homes, Sanskar Ashram for Boys, Bal Sadan, where they cannot be kept after attaining the age of 18 years, yet want protective shelter to complete their education or training. These boys belonging to age group of 16-21 years of custodial and non-custodial institutions are admitted on the basis of their good performance and behaviour to complete unfinished school/ college education and vocational training. Maximum period for the stay is three years which can be extended in deserving cases for two years by the Directorate of Social Welfare. With the maximum strength of 100 the Home provides free boarding, lodging and medical care to inmates.[9]

Scheme of Drug Abuse Prevention and Co-ordination

Directorate of Social Welfare has been declared as nodal agency for this programme. On the one hand it co-ordinates all the measures and activities undertaken by various government agencies and on the other it carries out education and awareness programmes in association with NGOs.

Day Care Centres (DCC)

The Department is implementing a programme of Day Care Centres to provide care facilities to the children of working mothers during the day when they are away at work under the care of trained teachers and *ayahs*(female attendants for children). This is a common programme serving two ends— providing care to the children of working mothers and facilitating mothers to work. Healthy children in the age group of 1-5 years of working parents/mothers who are residents of Delhi, are considered for admission. Medical attention, nursery education, recreation and nutrition are also provided to the children under the care of trained teachers and ayahs.[10]

Foster Care Services

Foster care services came into existence in the year 1963 to provide placement of illegitimate and abandoned children and their supervision under Juvenile Justice Act, 1986 and provisions laid down in Delhi Foster Care Placement Rules, 1983. To foster the care of children the following conditions are satisfied about the parents:

1. They should be of 30 years of age and above.
2. They should be residents of Delhi.
3. They should be free from contagious and chronic disease.
4. They should possess proper and sufficient residential accommodation.[11]

Foster care services are presently being made available at Nirmal Chayya Complex, Jail Road, New Delhi.

Counselling and Guidance Bureau

A landmark service was commenced in the year 1960 to provide counselling and guidance to the children who are:

1. Problematic
2. School dropouts
3. On the verge of becoming deviant/delinquent.

A boy or a girl under the age of 16 and 18 years respectively is eligible for enrolment in the Counselling and Guidance Bureau which is located at Central Market, Gulabi Bagh.[12]

Integrated Child Development Scheme (ICDS)

A pioneering and single largest programme of children welfare is ICDS. Centrally sponsored scheme of ICDS was initiated in 1975 after the adoption of National Policy on Children on 22nd Aug., 1974. It is marked by multi-sectoral approach to child development and covers both mother and children. Its objectives are:

(i) Improving nutritional status of children.

(ii) Laying foundation for proper psychological and social development.

(iii) Reducing the rate of mortality and morbidity.

(iv) Achieving effective co-ordination of policy and its implementation among various departments to promote holistic child development.

(v) Enhancing capability of mother to look after normal health and nutritional needs of child through proper health and nutritional education. The strategy adopted in the ICDS is delivery of integrated package of services namely, (a) supplementary nutrition (b) immunization (c) health check-up and referral services (d) non-formal pre-school education to children (3-6) and (e) nutrition and health education to women. The target group is children of the age group of 0 to 6 years and pregnant women and lactating mothers. In Delhi the ICDS has been taken up in selected blocks in rural areas, resettlement colonies and urban slums.[13]

Urban Social Service Complex

This unit has been set-up in 1992 where a package of services is provided under one umbrella for family life counselling, day care, recreation centre, immunization programme, Anganwari for children of Grade III and Grade IV category, and vocational/short term training courses, etc.[14]

Grant-in-Aid to MCD and NDMC for Mid-day Meal Programme

To assure nutritious meal to children the Department provides grants-in-aids to MCD and NDMC for implementation of the scheme of Midday meal in the primary/nursery schools. The administration in its endeavour for healthy child tries to meet nutrition deficiency of the child.

Scheme of Financial Assistance to the Incarcerated or Released Prisoners

Under this scheme, financial assistance/grant is given to the children of the incarcerated or released prisoners for pursuing education. Financial help is also given in maternity cases.

Welfare of Handicapped

Different kinds of schools/institutions are taking care of the needs of different handicapped persons belonging to different age groups and sexes. Their objective varies from imparting basic education to vocational training so that they can become not only self-dependent but also a valuable part of the society.

Scheme of Stipends

Besides variety of centres, the Delhi Administration also introduced a scheme of stipends to physically handicapped students in 1976. Hitherto, a monthly assistance was provided to the blind, the deaf and the orthopaedically handicapped students, who were studying in classes I to VIII in Government recognised schools in Delhi. The quantum of assistance has been enhanced from Rs. 30 p.m. to Rs. 50 p.m. for physically handicapped to pursuing education upto primary classes and from Rs. 40 p.m. to Rs. 70 p.m. upto middle level. In 1995-96, 141 physically handicapped children were given financial assistance.

In yet another scheme of scholarship the Directorate of Social Welfare provides monetary assistance to the disabled persons to seek such education academic/ technical or professional training which would enable them to earn their livelihood. In 1995-96, 628 handicapped persons were provided scholarship for pursuing these educational and vocational/technical training courses.

Scheme of Assistance

The scheme of assistance to physically handicapped for the purchase of aids was introduced by the Delhi Administration in 1975. The following conditions are ascertained before granting assistance:

1. The person has a physical disability which causes interference with the normal functioning of bones, muscles and joints.

2. The person should be a domicile of Delhi for more than five years.

Prevention and Early Detection of Handicapped

'Prevention is better than cure', following this adage, the scheme provides for generating social awareness for prevention of disabilities and referring the detected cases to appropriate agencies for prosthetic aids and appliances to the handicapped persons to improve their mobility. The scheme is being operated in collaboration with voluntary agencies working for the handicapped persons.

Under the scheme, training facility through workshops, camps and Audio Visual means is provided. Home management of disabled is also proposed to be undertaken.[15]

Welfare and Development of Scheduled Castes, Scheduled Tribes and Other Backward Classes

The Directorate of Welfare of Scheduled Castes and Scheduled Tribes and other backward classes is responsible for implementation of various schemes for the children of socio-economic weak classes with the aim of their development. The notable schemes[16] are:

(1) Grant of vocational and technical scholarship to Scheduled Castes.

(2) Hostel for Scheduled Caste boys/girls.

(3) Meritorious scholarship to SC students.

(4) Free supply of books and stationery.

(5) Marriage assistance scheme for the girls of SC/ST has been introduced by the first BJP Government in Delhi State.

Welfare and Development Programme for Women

Women Bureau in the Directorate of Social Welfare is the nodal agency in the National Capital Territory of Delhi State. Established in 1980, the Bureau provides advice and assistance to the various departments for formulating plans for women welfare. It also co-ordinates the activities of the departments and voluntary organisations engaged in the field. Since independence the departments has launched a multi-pronged programme which is being expanded and strengthened further with the single aim of integrated development of women.[17] Some of the important on-going interventions are detailed below:

Women Welfare

Women welfare programme was launched in 1958 with the establishment of After Care Home for Women now in Nirmal Chhaya Complex (NCC). Having the strength of 100 it provides after-care services like education, training to those female inmates of custodial and non-custodial Homes/Institutions who after the completion of their stay in these Homes/Institutions are found to be in need of after care services. Free boarding, clothing, bedding and medical care facilities are also provided. Efforts are made to secure their placements in Private Sector and Government Institutions and arrange their marriage.[18]

In the year 1970 Widow Home, another wing now within the NCC came into existence to provide shelter, free boarding, lodging, educational and vocational training facilities to the deserving widows for their socio-economic rehabilitation. Deserving widows are characterised as women who are homeless or without any means of subsistence or in moral danger. They should be bonafide residents of Delhi and should not suffer from any incurable infection or any other communicable disease or physical disability or mental retardation. Eligibility age group is 18 to 45 years.[19]

In 1979 Nirmal Chhaya (Protective Home and Corrective Institution) within the NCC itself was also set-up. The girls and women are admitted in this Home under the order of the Courts.

It provides free boarding, lodging, medical care maintenance, protection, education and vocational training to the following categories:[20]

1. Women rescued from brothels.

2. Women in moral danger.
3. Connected with cases under Sections-363, 366 and 376 of Indian Penal Code etc.
4. Unmarried mothers.

The strength of the Institutions is 100 only.

In the year 1981 a Short Stay Home (SSH) was established in the NCC in which girls/women who are victims of socio-economic, physical and emotional circumstances or victims of dowry but not suffering from any incurable disease are admitted. It provides short term/temporary shelter, care, training and counselling services to the needy women/girls who are in distress pending their restoration/re-adjustment in their families or admission in a suitable institution.

Services

The Delhi Government with the aim of economic upliftment of women of the weaker sections launched its service programme by establishing Work Centres for Women (WCW) in 1976. Till date besides its main office in Jam Nagar House the Department is running 25 centres. Each centre with the capacity of 50 members caters to the poor and needy women/girls of J.J./resettlement colonies and villages and backward families.

In these centres main emphasis is on the vocational training of the person, so that they could supplement the income of their family. Out of 25, only 5 centres provide diploma in cutting and tailoring at par with I.T.I.

Scheme of Financial Assistance to Widows

Introduced in 1987, under this scheme, a financial assistance of Rs. 1500 in lump-sum is provided to the helpless and needy widow once in life for starting income generating profession/vocation. A solatium of Rs. 300 is paid to a widow to meet the contingency arising out of death of her husband, provided she applies within three months.

The eligibility conditions are as follows:

(1) They should be domiciled in Delhi for more than 5 years.

(2) They should have no regular means of subsistence.

(3) Their income from all sources including their dependents should not exceed Rs. 750 per month.

Educational stipend is also provided to children of widows for continuing their education through school. The rate of stipend has been revised upto primary level from Rs. 108 p.a. to Rs. 250 p.a., from VIth to middle level from Rs. 108 p.a. to Rs. 300 p.a., from IX to Higher Secondary level from Rs. 108 p.a. to Rs 400 p.a.

Anti-Dowry Scheme

An Anti-dowry Cell was established in 1978 under the Department of Social Welfare. Its activities include:

(1) To expose the evils of dowry system, carry out propaganda against this system through posters, pamphlets, articles in Newspapers and magazines, cinema slides, T.V. and radio.

(2) Counselling and reconciliation services are also provided to the affected married women/couples.

With the growing number of 'dowry deaths' in the State an Anti-dowry Cell was created in 1983 on a proposal dated 10.5.1982 made by Delhi Government to the Ministry of Home Affairs. The Cell was kept under the supervision of the DCP. VI Branch in the Delhi Police, with a skeleton staff of one inspector and one sub-inspector. The strength of the Cell was raised from time to time and on 13-9-85 on the recommendation of the Srivastava Commission and approval of Ministry of Home Affairs it was restructured to deal with crime against women in the Crime Branch of the Delhi Police. Renamed as the Crime (Women) Cell of Delhi Police was provided 44 additional posts and seven motor vehicles.

The Crime (Women) Cell 'the first of its kind in the country' enables police to intervene on behalf of women and open an avenue for the women where they could be warded. The Cell receives complaints directly from women. It acts as a counselling centre advising the women who come to the centre with their problems. It also oversees that the police stations deal with the complaints of women in a proper manner and take effective action thereon.[21]

Social Defence

Social Defence programme is a general programme encompassing both female and male persons and children and adults. Under this, by implementing Bombay Prevention of Begging Act 1959 the administration is committed to check the practice of begging in society. A Home for Able and Disabled female Beggars (for female under-trial beggars) was opened up in the year 1968 now in NCC. The female beggars who are found soliciting or receiving alms in a public place including railway compartment or wandering about having no means of subsistence are admitted to this institution by the court after arrest by any police officer or any other person authorised for this purpose. They are produced before the court within 24 hours of the arrest. The convicted females are also kept in this Home.

They are provided with free boarding, lodging, medical care and vocational training facilities.

Work Centres Scheme for Women Prisoner in Jail

Initiated in 1982 it provides vocational training in tailoring, cutting, embroidery and knitting to the women under trial/convicts with a view to equip them for supplementing their family income after release from prison.

Short Term and Condensed Courses

It aims to impart vocational training to children and women to equip them for self-employment. The training is marked by innovative and market oriented vocational training. The courses are arranged in collaboration with Shramik Vidya Peeth. The courses being offered are typing and shorthand, cutting and tailoring, scooter repair, dress designing, food craft and beauty culture, etc.

Hostels for Working Women

Thirteen women hostels are functioning for working women who come to Delhi from different parts of India. These hostels are being run by the Non-Governmental Organisation for which Government of India gives grants.[22]

Scheme of Financial Assistance for the Socially and Physically Handicapped Persons

Since 1968 Directorate of Social Welfare is providing financial assistance to the T.B. patients and their families, aged and infirm persons, sick and maternity cases and also stipend to the needy and deserving children of widows. The beneficiaries should be resident of Delhi and not in receipt of any assistance from Lt. Governor and other government agencies. Income conditions have also been levied.[23]

As the assistance of Rs 30 pm being provided to the T.B. patients was very meagre, same has been enhanced to Rs.100 pm, for meeting the cost of treatment and nutrition.

Scheme of Grant to Voluntary Organisations

A co-operative administration stands for both governmental and non-governmental efforts for the social cause. However, the former owing larger share of liability has to see that non-governmental efforts are obtained in maximum and in sustained form. The Delhi Government provides financial assistance to voluntary organisations for both 'recurring and non-recurring expenditure, with a view to give them certain measure of stability and to make them gradually self-sufficient in their finances. The recipient organisation should be engaged in social welfare activities of the handicapped, women, children, belonging to weaker/backward classes and scheduled castes/tribes.

Scheme of Medical Care Units

To provide care to the inmates of the institutions round the clock, four medical care units have been set-up. These are[24]:

(1) Medical Care Unit, Alipur

(2) Medical Care Unit, NCC

(3) Medical Care Unit, GLNS

(4) Medical Care Unit Ash Kiran Complex

Home for Aged and Infirm

Established in 1971 this Home provides free boarding, lodging, clothing, medical care and recreational facilities to the destitute, old and infirm persons who have none to support. Residents of Delhi of 60 years and above, who are not suffering from any infectious/communicable diseases are admitted to the Home.

Social Security

Old women are being assured social security under the scheme of Old Age Assistance. Under this scheme aged persons of 60 years. or above are given Rs. 200 since April 1994. In the year 1975, when the scheme was introduced the amount was Rs. 50 only which was increased to Rs. 60 in 1982, to Rs. 100 in 1987, and to Rs. 200 in April 1994. Under this scheme till 1995-96, 44947 persons have been sanctioned old age pension out of which a large number are women.[25]

Welfare Centre for Denotified Tribes

The scheme was launched in the year 1962. Until now six centres have been set-up in areas with sizeable population of denotified tribes. The aims of the scheme are:

(1) To provide pre-primary education children of 3-5 years are admitted.

(2) To provide craft training in sewing and embroidery to women and girls belonging to these tribes. The women and girls possessing aptitude for training are admitted.[26]

Employment-cum-Income Generating Production Units for Women

The NORAD (Norwegian Agency for International Development) assisted scheme started functioning from

1982-83 with the assistance of NOK (Norwegian Kroner).[27] The government of India, through Ministry of Human Resource Development, Department of Women and Child Development is implementing the scheme assistance projects sponsored by Public undertakings, corporations, women development centres of universities, autonomous organisations, VOs for setting-up of employment-cum-production units for women. The criteria of grant-in-aid is as follows:

(i) The project must require a substantial financial input.

(ii) Implementation of the project must be the responsibility of the recipient government or NGO acceptable to the government.

(iii) The project must have poor and needy women in urban slum and rural women as a major target group.

(iv) Emphasis of the project must be on income generating activities with the aim of achieving self-reliance on sustained basis.

(v) The project must be sustainable on a long-term basis. The Directorate of Social Welfare, Delhi has been receiving applications from VOs for onward recommendation to the Government of India.

Training and Orientation Cost of Staff

The various ongoing Social Welfare projects and new endeavours of Administration in the area of development require well-trained staff. Under the training and orientation cost of staff scheme the Department organises training, orientation and refresher courses for equipping the staff members of various institutions/services to carry out the welfare functions with optimum efficiency and achievement.

Promotion of Mahila Mandals in Villages

Under this scheme which was launched in late seventies, each registered Mahila Mandal is given an assistance of Rs.1285. The broad objectives of the scheme are as follows:

(1) Imparting technical know-how about improved farming and home practices.

(2) Promotion of leadership programme like Mahila Mandals and Youvati Mandals.

(3) Associating women with techniques of group work.

(4) Preparing women for effective extension work.

(5) Creating, awareness in matters like family planning improved nutrition, vegetable cultivation, backyard poultry, small savings etc.[28]

Incentive Awards to Mahila Mandals

This scheme came in operation in 1975-76. The awards were, however, given first time only in 1976-77. The awards are given for the best performance in the year.

Commission for Women

Another landmark in the history of women's development in the territory is the constitution of Delhi Women Commission, entrusted with powers of Civil Courts on 11.7.1995. The Commission will look into deprivation of women's rights and non-implementation of laws enacted to protect women and achieve the objectives of equality and development. It would check discrimination and atrocities against women and also undertake promotional and educational research. It would also advise on the planning process for socio-economic development of women and examine all laws relating to women to find out if they are sufficient and suggest new laws.

Women and Children Development Progress Report of Delhi Administration

The ongoing efforts of the Administration marked with gradual improvement and innovations have resulted in remarkable progress in the field of women and children development.

The decennial growth of population reveals that the increase of female population in comparison to their male counterpart had been quite low and thereby reducing the sex ratio low as 785 (rural 847; urban 737) per thousand males in 1961. The explanation for this low sex ratio is found in the migration of high number of males to Delhi from various parts of the country for want of jobs. However, sized with the problem the Government succeeded to raise the number of women to 830 (rural 820, urban 831) per 1000 males by various family welfare measures. But it is found less than the national sex ratio of 929 and far less than the highest sex ratio of Kerala, i.e., 1040.

It is heartening to note that due to various family welfare programmes adopted by Delhi Government, the mortality rate has gone down to 32.34 in 1991 from 70.8 per thousand in 1961. The corresponding number for 1991 census in Orissa, Madhya Pradesh and UP are 110, 106, 93 respectively. This achievement is the result of massive programme of immunization launched for expectant women and children during the last decade. I.C.Ds projects of Delhi played a significant role in Pulse Polio Programme. It was for the first time in the history of State that Polio drops were rendered to each and every child of the territory on 16.12.1995 after declaring that day as official holiday.

The literacy among women has also shown upward trends as against 42.5% of total literate women in 1961 the literacy among women went up to 66.99% in 1991.[29] Though in comparison to their male counter-parts, with 60.75 in 1961 and 82.01 in 1991 literacy rate among women is still quite low. The reason for this is revealed in the enrolment of less number of girl students at different levels of education and high level of dropouts among them.[30]

It is hoped that the literacy rate particularly among women will improve with the passing of Girl Child Bill 1994 and campaign for universal literacy launched by the Government in June, 1996.

As the participation of women in the economic

activities is considered as most effective indicator to rate the level of women development, the statistics also reveal the gradual progress in this context.

Prospective Programme for Children and Women Development

(1) The matter for setting-up separate Women and Child Development Department is under active consideration of the Administration. The decision will be taken in due course of time when the matter is finalised.

(2) Through the integrated Child Development Services work relating to gender sensitisation programme will be vigorously pursued.

(3) The Girl Child (Compulsory Education, Upbringing and Welfare) Bill, 1994, when passed will ensure compulsory and free education to girl child upto senior secondary level with all accessories, e.g., school uniform, shoes, free transport etc. The commendable feature of the Bill is its provision making head of the family duty-bound to send the girl child to school. Any case of contravention will be considered as a punishable offence.

(4) The plan of action has been approved by the Government of India for the girl child decade.

(5) The Department has got the scheme approved by the Planning Commission for the upgradation of protective home Nari Niketan being run under the Immoral Traffic (Prevention) Act, for providing better facilities of counselling services and vocational training during the Eighth Five Year Plan (1992-97). The vocational training courses are being conducted successfully by the Department through Shramik Vidhyapeeth.

The up-graded Nari Niketan is being managed by the government. of NCT, Delhi after it was taken over from voluntary sector due to mismanagement in 1979.

(6) The Planning Commission has approved construction and expansion of working women's hostel building for working women with day care centres.

The Directorate of Social Welfare has recommended the case of a voluntary organisation namely Indian Council of Social Welfare to the government of India for release of grant to construct a hostel in R.K. Puram.

(7) Model rules under Dowry Prohibition Act have not yet been framed by the government of India. These should be framed in consultation with other concerned departments.

Dowry Prohibition Officer(s) appointed by the Directorate of Social Welfare should be given powers of trial of cases relating to dowry. They should also be delegated with some semi-judicial powers as are delegated to the Police department Therefore, under the provisions of Section 8(b) (i) of the Dowry Prohibition Amendment Act, 1986 regarding appointment of Ex-officio Dowry Prohibition Officer they should be given powers of Civil Courts for investigation of Dowry cases.

To conclude, though the administrative endeavour has achieved some advancement there is still scope to achieve more. This process of development of children and women is an ongoing process. Started with humble origin, it became multi-dimensional and multi-faceted in Delhi to meet the social needs of the needy and the progress had earlier been good. Its pace of achievement became slow as the programmes, though implemented, could not be pursued vigorously as there was lack of manpower and owing to abolition of posts (due to economic restructuring) which has affected the implementation of the schemes in proportion to the rate of development of the Department. Thus the quality of services is marked by various deficiencies. The achievements in the department have also been affected due to financial constraints as funds have not been made available due to economic policies and financial cuts in various plans. Now prospective planning, while identifying its new horizons, should also envisage to improve upon the pace and quality of existing programmes, because for sustained development quality rather than quantity matters. And for that adequate financial support is needed.

It is also suggested that with the emphasis on universal literacy the reasons for the large number of drop outs at the school level should be detected and measures to tackle the problems be devised accordingly. More emphasis be laid on professional training and education on need based education particularly among girl students. Above all, there is need to take rigorous measures to check growing population by controlling birth rate and migration from outside. Otherwise the growing unwieldly numbers will nullify all the resources and sincere efforts on the part of the government The health awareness programme be taken up on war footing and the number of Family Welfare Centres both in rural and slum areas increased and quality services ensured.

REFERENCES

1. *Gazetteer of Rural Delhi*, Delhi Administration, Delhi, 1987, pp. 384.
2. *Ibid.*

2a. *Annual Administration Report (AAR). 1990-91*, Delhi Administration (DA) p. 46.

3. *Ibid*, 1994, p.
4. *Annual Administration Report* (AAR) 1993-94.
5. *Ibid.*
6. Schemes and Services (S&S), 1995 D/O Social Welfare Government of National Capital Territory of Delhi, pp.10-11.
7. *Ibid.* pp.12-13.
8. *Ibid.* pp.9-10.
9. *Ibid.* p.40.
10. *Ibid.* p.13.

11. *Ibid.* p.14.
12. *Ibid.* p.15.
13. *Ibid.* 1994, p.16.
14. *Ibid*, p.42.
15. *Ibid.*
16. Gazetteer *of Rural Delhi*, p.385
17. *National Perspective plan for Women's Report 1988-2000 A.D.* D/o HRD, Ch. III, p.18.
18. S.S., p.26
19. *Ibid.* p.25
20. Report of the Committee to go into the Functionary of the CRIME (WOMEN) CELL, Delhi Police 1991, Delhi Administration, Delhi Home Deptt., pp.1-4.
21. *Mahila Uthan Aur Vikas Ek Vihangam Drashti*, Records of D/SW.
22. S&S, p.37.
23. AAR, 1993-94.
24. Official Records, DISW.
25. S&S, p.39.
26. India, 1992, p.289.
27. Records of Ad. D/SW.
28. Gazetteer of Rural Delhi op. Lit., p.387.
29. Delhi Statistical Hand Book 1991, Bureau of Economics and Statistics, D.Ad., Delhi, p.284.
30. Statistic on Children in India, NIPCCD, 1995. At the primary level as against 19.25 per cent of boys 28.83 per cent of girls dropped out and for middle classes the corresponding figures for boys and girls are 19.89 and 31.24.

7 ORGANISATION AND FUNCTIONS OF DELHI DEVELOPMENT AUTHORITY

S.C. VAJPEYI AND RAKESH BIHARI

Delhi which served as the Capital of many kingdoms, came to be the capital city once again after a long interval when the British government shifted its capital from Calcutta to Delhi in 1912 and established a new city, known as New Delhi. The city of New Delhi was planned as a garden city, around a central vista— with the Secretariat complex at its Western end and the National Stadium at its Eastern end. A city centre known as the Connaught Place Complex was also established.

In 1936, the Government of India appointed AP Hume, ICS to study the housing problem in Delhi. His report indicated a two-fold congestion— congestion of people in houses and of houses on land. There are many slum areas, abounding in insanitary conditions constituting a menace to public health of the whole of urban Delhi. In order to ameliorate living conditions of the residents of Delhi and to shift the excess population, Mr. Hume suggested several schemes of urban development to be executed on the existing government and acquired lands. In order to execute the above schemes, the Delhi Improvement Trust was set-up in 1937 to execute these schemes and lands belonging to Government, known as nazul lands, were also placed at the disposal of the Trust under an agreement.

As the Delhi Improvement Trust did not succeed in bringing about the desired improvement, especially in the wake of influx of refugees into the Capital pursuant to the partition of the country, the government appointed a Committee, known as the Delhi Improvement Enquiry Committee, in 1950. This committee identified several shortcomings in the working of the Delhi Improvement Trust, main of which are listed below:

(1) Several agencies in Delhi were entrusted with the development of the city and there was neither co-ordination of effort nor overall supervision and planning of the activities of these agencies.

(ii) The work of the Trust has been handicapped to some extent on account of the agency for execution of its works being CPWD, an authority independent of the Trust.

(iii) The Trust has not been able to produce either a Civil Survey or a Master Plan with the result that the growth of Delhi has been proceeding in a haphazard way, with little foresight and imagination and without any coordination.

(iv) There has been no proper zoning, and all the essential requirements of a community have not been provided for in the layouts of the Trust.

(v) The policy followed by the Trust in selling land to the highest bidder or tenderer regardless of the considerations whether the buyer was a genuine builder or only a speculator in land, has prevented even a partial solution of the housing problem in Delhi.

The Committee, therefore, concluded that conducting a survey and preparation of a Master Plan would be a pre-requisite for proper development of the city. In the circumstances, the Committee suggested setting-up of a single Planning and Controlling Authority for the development of the whole of the urban area of Delhi and devolution of adequate financial resources by earmarking certain incomes to the Authority.

These recommendations of the Committee seem to have received the attention of the Government of India in as much as a Town Planning Office was set-up sometime in 1955 to prepare a detailed plan for the development of urban Delhi. With the assistance of the Ford Foundation Consultants, the organisation prepared an Interim General Plan. Simultaneously, the Government set-up a Provisional Development Authority in October, 1955 by promulgating the Delhi (Control of Building Operations) Ordinance, 1955. Under this legislation, the Provisional Authority was charged with the responsibility of preventing "bad lay-out of land, haphazard execution of buildings or growth of sub-standard colonies" and ensuring "development and expansion of Delhi according to proper planning". For this purpose, the legislation empowered the Provisional Authority to declare, by notification in the Official Gazette, any area falling within Delhi as a "Controlled Area". The legislation remained in force from 22nd October, 1955, up to 30th December, 1957. In September, 1957, the Government came forward with the Delhi Development Bill to replace the Delhi (Control of Building Operations) Act, 1955. The Delhi Development Act, 1957— establishing the Delhi Development Authority, thus came to be passed and was brought into force with effect from 30th December, 1957.

Objectives of DDA

The Delhi Development Act, 1957, hereinafter referred to as the Act, defines the objects of the Authority as "To promote and secure the development of Delhi according to plan", and for the purpose, the Authority shall have the power to acquire, hold manage and dispose of land and other property, to carry out building, engineering, mining and other operations, to execute works in connection with supply of water and electricity, disposal of sewage and other services and amenities, and generally to do anything necessary or expedient for purpose of such development and for purposes incidental thereto.

In order to ensure an integrated and planned development, the Masterplan of Delhi that came into force on 1.9.1962, provided the necessary framcwork for planned development of Delhi. Since its inception, the Authority has endeavoured to ensure planned development by creating community facilities near the employment centres so as to reduce burden on public utilities, providing functionally utilitarian, economically viable and aesthetically satisfying shelters to all the sections of society as per their family requirements and paying capacity, relocating dilapidated and unauthorised structures to conforming areas, providing re-creational/sports-centres in all parts of the city, preserving the cultural heritage of Delhi and its historical landmarks, while developing Delhi as a modern city which can withstand pressures of urbanisation in the years to come.

Functions of DDA

Far from being merely a central planning authority, DDA has played a role in each and every activity connected directly or indirectly with the development of Delhi as a metropolitan city. While it is difficult to compartmentalise functions of DDA, these can be broadly grouped into acquisition and assembly of land of residential, industrial, commercial, institutional and recreational purposes, construction of houses, re-settlement of squatters, construction of recreational centres, sports complexes, developing infrastructure facilities for smooth functioning of the city, e.g. bus terminus, flyovers etc. constructing Commercial District Centres, Local and Convenient Shopping Centres etc., relocation of industries from non-conforming areas to conforming areas and development of Industrial Estates, provision of basic services and amenities for so developed areas, developing and preserving green-areas and historical monuments. Thus, in brief, DDA has combined in itself the functions of a Central Planning Organisation, a Housing Board, a Slum Board, an Agency for execution of public works and commercial functions of a private developer.

Administrative Organisation

The main executive body of DDA, known as the "Authority", has 13 members and its Constitution is as follows:

1. Lt. Governor of Delhi (Chairman).
2. Two representatives of the Municipal Corporation of Delhi.
3. Three representatives of the Legislative Assembly of NCT of Delhi.
4. Commissioner of the Municipal Corporation of Delhi.
5. Three persons nominated by the Central Government— one of them having experience of town planning and architecture.
6. Vice-Chairman, Finance Member and Engineer Member of DDA.

The Central Government appoints the Vice-Chairman, Finance Member, Engineer Member, Secretary and Chief Accounts Officer of DDA. The Authority, subject to such checks and balances as may be provided under various rules, may appoint such other officers and employees as are necessary for efficient working of the organisation.

The functions of DDA have been organised into the following main departments:

(i) Planning and Architecture

It deals with:

(a) Perspective planning urban transportation, urban extension and National Capital Region, Walled city, Trans-Yamuna and other areas.

(b) Development controls, land-use planning, Master Plan and Zonal plans, Buildings Bye-laws.

(c) Development Projects, e.g., Rohini, Dwarka, Narela, Jasola, etc.

(ii) Engineering—

Engineering wings is headed by the Engineer Member. DDA has been divided into six construction zones and each zone is under charge of a Chief Engineer. Functions of the Engineering wing, are multifarious, e.g., development and assembly of land, construction of various structures over developed land, providing infrastructure like roads, storm-water drains, sewerage, water supply and other facilities. Horticulture wing deals with development and maintenance of green areas.

(iii) Lands

The Lands department is headed by two Commissioners— Commissioner (Land Management) and Commissioner (Land Disposal) who are assisted by five Directors for management and disposal of lands under the Revenue Estates entrusted by the Government of India to the erstwhile Delhi Improvement Trust under the Nazul Agreement 1937, and the lands placed at the disposal of DDA since 1961 under the Scheme of Large Scale Acquisition, Development and Disposal of Land in Delhi. In addition, this department also manages the lands transferred by the Ministry of Rehabilitation. Management functions include preparation and maintenance of land records, land protection and disposal of land (i) through allotment for residential purpose to co-operative societies, for institutional purpose to government departments, public institutions and charitable organisations, for industrial purpose to non-conforming industrial units for shifting to conforming areas, and (ii) through auction for all other purpose. Other important function of Lands department include disposal of commercial estate in Commercial Centres developed by DDA, enforcement of land use as per Master Plan provisions, eviction of land realisation of damage charges from unauthorised occupants of DDA lands and administration of lease-deeds in respect of lease-hold lands and commercial estate.

(iv) Housing

Allotment and lease-administration of houses

constructed by the engineering wing of DDA is done by the Housing Department initially, a part of Lands department, Housing was established as a full-fledged department during mid-seventees when it was decided, owing to paucity of land, to discontinue the practice of disposal of residential plots and consequent increase in the number of flats constructed by DDA. The department is headed by a Commissioner.

(v) Finance

The Finance and Accounts wing of the Authority is headed by the Finance Member. The Accounts of the Authority are maintained in the following four divisions:

1. Nazul Account I,
2. Nazul Account II,
3. Nazul Account III, and
4. General Development Account.

(vi) Personnel

The Personnel Department is headed by the Commissioner (Personnel). It plays an important role in manpower planning, training, placement and career-management of DDA employees.

(vii) Law

The Law Department has been assigned the job of looking after the entire litigation work of the Authority. It also renders advice on all important legal matters which are referred to it by various departments of Authority. The Department is headed by the Chief Legal Adviser.

(viii) Vigilance

The Vigilance Department is responsible for implementation of anti-corruption measures as per instructions issued from time to time by the Department of Personnel and Administrative Reforms, Ministry of Home Affairs and the Central Vigilance Commission.

(ix) Welfare

It looks after welfare of all categories of employees of

DDA. It also helps in creating a healthy employer-employee relationship by organising cultural programmes, social get-togethers and other allied activities.

(x) Secretariat

It is headed by Secretary DDA whose main function is to deal with records and all matters connected with the meetings of the Authority. A Parliament and Co-ordination Cell also functions in the department that deals with co-ordination meetings held periodically under Vice-Chairman to review progress of various schemes and disposal of time-bound references pertaining to public-grievances and Parliamentary matters.

(xi) Slum Wing

Slum Wing has the main responsibility for improving quality of life of the slum areas and jhuggi dwellers. The Slum Areas (Improvement and Clearance) Act, 1956, remained a source of guidance for various activities of the slum wing, with main stress on clearance of slums until the end of the Sixth Five Year Plan, 1980-85. Due to some functional problems, e.g. resistance from slum-communities against relocation, physical and financial constraints to provide alternative housing stock to all the affected families, non-availabilities of vacant land adjoining the slum areas for relocation and political opposition to the slum clearance, there was shift from the clearance to slum improvement and upgradation of existing slums. The Seventh Five Year Plan(1985-90) saw the beginning of definite efforts to restructure/revamp the activities of Slum Wing, by incorporating innovative and Imaginative approaches to solve the problems of the slum areas. One such major endeavour was to facilitate/promote house building by economically weaker sections and jhuggi dwellers themselves through formation of co-operative group housing societies by providing access to land, finance and technology, NGOs are also used for motivational efforts.

Achievements of DDA—An Overview

Main achievements of DDA are given below:

(i) The number of dwelling units constructed by DDA has crossed the 201, 617 mark thus exceeding those constructed by any other development agency in India. Many big housing colonies like Janakpuri, Vasant Kunj and Rohini— comprising both residential flats and plots have been developed by DDA and many more such housing colonies in Dwarka, Jasola, Narela, etc. are in progress. Special emphasis has been laid on providing houses at reasonable and affordable price to economically weaker sections.

(ii) DDA has been acquiring and developing lands for residential, industrial, institutional, commoercial and recreational purposes to functionally balance future growth of Delhi. It has also been developing spaces and vast green areas to provide adequate lung space to contain pollution and to satisfy aesthetic needs of the city.

(iii) One of the guidelines provided for development of Delhi under the Master Plan is to decentralise commercial activities so as to reduce burden on public utilities. DDA has developed office-complexes at five places viz. Nehru Place, Laxmi Nagar, Bhikaji Kama Place, Rajendra Place and Janakpuri. As many as 25 Community Centres, 64 Local Shopping Complexes and 346 Convenient Shopping Centres have also been developed. Special consideration is accorded in allotment of shops to members of Scheduled Castes and Scheduled Tribes, physically handicapped, ex-servicemen, freedom-fighters and those whose land has been acquired.

(iv) Due concern has been shown for preserving the historical millieu of the city by preserving and maintaining its monuments, river fronts, ridge-forests and natural greens.

(v) DDA has made significant contribution towards providing sports facilities at the 8 Sports Complexes constructed by it in Delhi. At all these sports-centres, facilities are provided for playing cricket, football, hockey, squash, badminton, table-tennis and volley ball. These sports centres are expected to go a long way in promoting love of sports and games among the citizens of Delhi.

(vi) The Slum Wing, DDA which is responsible for providing basic amenities to the inhabitants of notified slums, sub-standard areas and squatter settlements has done a commendable job over the years in the parts of the city.

The foregoing achievements will have to be weighed against the criticism voiced about the functions of the DDA. The main role of the DDA envisaged at the time of its creation was to undertake perspective planning, determine land use and develop land required for future development of Delhi. This role according to many has receded to the background. It was not envisaged that the DDA would engage in commercial activities such as construction of Shopping Centres, auctioning of lands and so on. It has also been represented that this has contributed substantially to escalation in prices and to scarcity of land and housing, as also growth of authorised colonies. Another charge is that DDA has failed to prevent encroachments on acquired lands. It has not been able to finalise most of the Zonal development plans, detailed development and layout plans for rural villages. It has also been alleged that there has been a mis-match between the pace of acquisition of land by the Delhi Administration and that of utilization of lands by DDA for development. Although, there is a Master Plan for land-use, there is none for essential services. There is no time frame laid down for providing social and physical infrastructure like schools, hospitals, etc. There are also charges of corruption, inefficiency etc. in the organisation.

The Estimates Committee of the Lok Sabha in its 8th Report on the then Ministry of Works and Housing had, after examining the working of the DDA, made the following observations:

> "Delhi Development Authority has been burdened with a variety of functions, so much so that it has lost its direction and sense of priorities, it has also become unwieldy-housing problems of management and administration".

The DDA had entrusted the study of its organisational structure to M/s Tata Consultancy Services in 1986. Their report submitted in September, 1986 contains the following pertinent observations:

> "The DDA has drifted away from its main objectives of planning and development of Delhi. The basic role of planning and ensuring planned development of Delhi was increasingly being relegated, having been over whelmed by the enormity of engineering operations and allied activities. This resulted in a lack of focus purpose and significant retardation of the development process. Such has been the growth in the volume and nature of DDA's activities that the organisation's structure has become unwieldy and a work overload situation has arisen. There is no focus on the mission goal and the basic purpose of the organisation itself seems to has been diffused".

The Balakrishnan (Sarkaria) Committee on Administrative set-up for Delhi pointed out several deficiencies in the functioning of the DDA. Some of these are:

The DDA being the first urban development organisation to regulate the growth of Delhi in a planned way, did not have any precedent or model to follow. Being one of India's first experiments in this regards DDA was modelled on concepts taken from UK and USA Its statutory objectives as well as the additional functions taken over by it from time to time, cast a multitude of responsibilities upon the DDA. The DDA came to be utilized to perform a variety of extraneous functions, not contemplated in its Charter, especially in times of emergency and crises, such as during epidemics, floods or during international events like Asiad, 1982. This has not only seriously impaired its operational efficiency but caused financial strains upon it too.

Co-ordination with the Local Bodies and other agencies in regard to development plans and housing projects has been presenting difficulties for DDA. Problems have arisen in regard to expeditions acquisition of land required by DDA for development because procedural delays resulting in progress of acquisition and delivery of land. The desired level of co-ordination between DDA and the service agencies such as those connected with water supply, sewage disposal, electricity etc. has not been achieved in regard to the development of land. Further all large projects are required to be cleared by the Delhi Urban Arts Commission and this also involves delays and difficulties in submitting modified plants in conformity with the requirements of the Commission.

Management structure in the DDA is not such as to ensure efficiency. There is considerable overstaffing in the DDA leading to inefficiency and diffusion of responsibilities. That the supervision over the staff has not been adequate is clear from the allegations of large scale corruption, various forms of malpractices and harassment to citizens. A very common complaint is regarding the poor quality of construction of houses. The implementation and enforcement of the terms of leases in leasehold lands is another area of DDA's activities in regard to which serious complaints have been made.

The DDA is solely responsible for implementation of Master and Zonal plans. It has, therefore, a duty to ensure that its own building and other activities are carried out strictly in accordance to these plans so as to effectively monitor implementation of the Master Plan and the Zonal development plans by other agencies. The distorted growth of urban Delhi, according to some, is attributable to slackness on part of DDA to strictly enforce requirements of the Master Plan and the Zonal Development plans.

There has also been slackness in regard to development of land. The pace of such development has not been adequate or sufficient to have any impact on the availability of developed land at reasonable prices in Delhi. This number of dwelling units constructed by DDA has fallen far short of requirement—leading to the present problems like escalating prices and rents, growth of unauthorised colonies, etc.

The Balakrishnan Committee and Estimates Committee made various recommendations for effective functioning of DDA. These are briefly summarised below :

(i) The DDA should concentrate on, and effectively perform, its main functions of planning, monitoring and co-ordinating activities connected with implementation of the Master Plan approved by the Central Government. In the matter of development of land, it should act in accordance with the policies and guidelines issued from time to time by the Central Government. The DDA should be responsible for preparation and revision of the Master Plan and Zonal Development Plans etc. for approval by the Central Government. It should be responsible for monitoring land-use and carrying out horticulture development, especially the development and maintenance of important green areas in the Union Territory other than the work relating to laying out and maintenance of public parks/ gardens or recreation grounds in residential colonies, commercial complexes, institutional areas, etc., which have been developed or may hereafter be developed by other agencies.

(ii) As regards land made over to the DDA for various purposes like housing, commercial complexes etc. its development should be the responsibility of the DDA which should follow the general requirements of the Master Plan and specific directions, if any of the Central Government. The allotment of such land should be in accordance with the principles or guidelines in force from time to time.

(iii) There should be a Housing Board set-up under a separate law of Parliament to undertake construction of houses and such other work incidental thereto as is allocated to it. Land should be made available to the Housing Board either by the DDA or by the Government for the purpose of such construction. The Housing Board should be an autonomous body with respect to its day to day functioning. The general powers to give directions should be vested in and exercised by the Central Government.

(iv) The functions now being performed by DDA relating to administration of Lotteries and Inter-State Bus Terminal should be the concern of the Delhi Administration which may assign them to such agencies as it considers proper.

(v) In particular, that part of the work of administering lease deeds relating to land vested in the Central Government which is now being looked after by DDA and the Land and Development office of the Ministry of Urban Development should be made the concern of Delhi Administration in the interest of better co-ordination to the extent functions in this regard are entrusted to the Lt. Governor. Since the subject of land is responsibility of the Central Government, the Administration of these lease deeds would, of course, be subject to the overall direction and control of the Centre.

(vi) The Slum Wing should be taken out of the purview of DDA and transferred to Local Bodies.

(vii) Consequent on transfer of functions from DDA as detailed above, the staff in DDA, now dealing with the functions transferred such as "Housing Slums" lease deeds, lotteries and ISBT, should be assigned to the respective organisations concerned.

(viii) To ensure that development conforms to the Master Plan and Zonal Development Plans, and generally to facilitate enforcement, the Act provides for powers, including power to demolish unauthorised constructions. The DDA has not been able to enforce these provisions effectively. While the general responsibility regarding the formulation, implementation and monitoring of the Master and Zonal plans should, as required by the Act, be the responsibility of the DDA, the government of Delhi should be directly and effectively involved in the enforcement of the penal provisions and taking measures to prevent encroachments or other contraventions of law. As land in Delhi is a subject under jurisdictions of the Union, this arrangement may have to be secured either by amending the Delhi Development Act, 1957 or by taking resource to Article 259 of the Constitution.

In brief, DDA should concentrate on its main functions of planning and co-ordinating all activities bearing on implementation of the Master Plan approved by the Central Government. While the Slum Wing has been transferred to Municipal Corporation of Delhi, and the Lotteries and ISBT to Delhi Administration, most of the other recommendations of the Balakrishnan (Sarkaria Committee) are yet to be implemented.

As already mentioned, DDA—being one of India's first experiments in Urban Planning, was modelled by and large, on concepts taken from UK and USA The modern system of planning law was initiated by the Town and Country Planning Act, 1947 in UK The outstanding features of the Act of 1947 were that each local planning authority was required to prepare a detailed development plan for its area; that all development required permission and was exposed at once to enforcement proceedings. If permission was not obtained or not an overall plan for the area had been brought into effect; that no compensation was payable for refusal of permission; that on the grant of permission a 'development charge' was payable equal to the excess of the value of the land with such permission over its 'existing use value'. As a corollary, compensation on the compulsory acquisition of land was limited to existing use value. The local planning authorities, established under the Act of 1947, were the county councils, and the countory borough councils. Today, however, in non-metropolitan counties both the county council and district councils are local planning authorities—with special provision being made for the division of planning functions between them. In the metropolitan counties the district councils, and in Greater London, the borough councils, are the local planning authorities. Each local planning authority designated by the Act of 1947 was required to prepare its unitary development plan that would incorporate a structure plan consisting of a written statement of the general policies of development and land-use, and a local-plan consisting of detailed maps and designating the areas selected for comprehensive development, re-development or improvement. The local planning authority is required to comply with regulations regarding public participation in drawing up local plans that are subject to quinquennial review.

The Secretary of State has a wide range of statutory powers in UK that enables him to intervene in many aspects of the planning process either by calling plans for his approval or issuing directions for preparation of plans in a particular way or himself granting planning permission in several ways. Owing to the excessively slow and cumbersome process of preparation of local plans and demands for more public consultation, the Town and Country Planning Act was enacted in 1968 to delegate much of the detailed work from the Whitehall to local authorities subject, of course, to the planning guidance—regional and strategic, given by the Secretary of State, including the national planning policies. The Secretary of State must be sent a copy of unitary development plan, and may call it in for approval. Thus, although virtually the whole procedure for adoption of structure, local and unitary development plans is subject to the federal control—by making regulations or through powers of Secretary of State to direct the making or alteration of a plan, the drawing up of these plans is intended to be and has come to be essentially a local process in UK.

In the case of DDA, however, the local Government viz., the Government of National Capital Territory of Delhi has little say in the planning and other functions of DDA notwithstanding the inordinate delay in preparation of Zonal and lay-out plans and existence of countless number of public grievances against DDA. Tight federal control over even the day-to-day activities of DDA has political overtones, and more often than not based on considerations other than merit. While statutorily, only the Vice-Chairman is to be appointed by the Central Government, Lt. Governor, Delhi (who is the Chairman of DDA) has been deprived of powers to appoint even lower functionaries, like the Commissioners, etc. Moreover, Section 42 of the DDA Act, contemplates issue of directions largely on policy matters, the experience during the past 3 years would show that these powers have been used in such day-to-day matters as change of land-use of particular pieces of land or reinstatement of a Stenographer dismissed for corruption.

Redressal of public grievances leaves much to be desired. During the past 3 years, the High Court and the Supreme Court have not only passed severe strictures against the top management of the DDA but have enforced the concept of "public accountability", treating DDA as a trustee to carry out public functions and holding concerned officers personally responsible for their failure to discharge statutory functions or for abusing their jurisdiction. A celebrated example of enforcement of much needed accountability of officers is the case relating to *DDA* vs. *Skipper* (1966) SCC 2732 in which the conduct of top officers of DDA has been adversely commented upon, and in respect of some disciplinary proceedings have been initiated. A system of Lok Adalats for redressal of public grievances associating responsible citizens needs to be introduced. This would also reduce the enormous unproductive litigation in which the DDA and citizens of Delhi are embroiled.

There is a need to incorporate greater transparency into the working of DDA. Rules and procedures need be codified and these be given appropriate publicity amongst their clients by bringing out brochures incorporating all the relevant information reducing their dependence on the officials who, due to their immobility, tend to develop vested interests. The top management in DDA—presently drawn on All India basis, due to their transient character, is largely dependent upon the middle and lower rungs of DDA officials who often develop common interests with unscrupulous property dealers and pairvikars who claim to fix up public hearings even with top managers of DDA for a consideration. Obviously, there is need of greater localisation of the top management and rotation of the lower rungs of officials of DDA.

At the official level, three issues need to be addressed. First, the Chairman/Lt. Governor should not be in a position to where he is held responsible without exercising real authority. Second, even though land is reserve subject under the NCT Act, the local government must have adequate opportunity to interact with the DDA. Third the top officers posted in the DDA should necessarily be conversant with the local conditions of metropolis and should have a sense of accountability to the citizens of Delhi. Obviously, deputationists from other States posted for a three years' stint in DDA have neither the necessary knowledge nor adequate stake and incentive for tackling the complex problems of the metropolis for which separate cadres of both. All India and State Civil Services exist.

8 SETTING UP OF TRAINING INSTITUTIONS TO PROFESSIONALIZE CIVIL SERVICE

M.K. GAUR AND KUL BHUSHAN RAI VASHISHT

INTRODUCTION

In the present-day context of fast-changing realities, the role of training in equipping the civil service to handle newer challenges can hardly be overemphasised. All developmental efforts through governmental channel are planned, programmed and implemented through the instrumentality of civil service. The scenario of total dependence on civil service in this regard prevailed till 1990 though emphasis have tended to shift slightly with the advent of New Economic Policy and its attendant reforms since 1991. But that, in fact, has reinforced the emphasis on training, instead of diluting it, as the civil servants have to be oriented and equipped through familiarisation drills in training situations so that the administration does not get out of step with the changes inspired by technological change, and liberalisation, marketisation and globalisation thrusts which have to be assimilated quickly in administrative processes, procedures and behavioural patterns of civil servants. As such, this compulsion itself has made emphasis on training more pronounced.

The aim of civil service training is broadly to contribute to a continuing improvement in administrative processes and procedures and thereby enabling civil servants to fulfil developmental aspirations of the people at an accelerated pace.

National Training Policy

Government has to play a crucial role in the development process and promotion of appropriate conditions which would lend dynamism to the national effort in personnel development.[1] With the changing policy of the Government with regard to economic liberalisation, decentralisation, and technological advancement, the civil servant needs to adapt himself to face the new challenges. Training is one of the effective tools to improve the quality of performance. Realising this necessity, the Government of India has come up, though rather belatedly, with a "National Training Policy, 1996" which seeks to achieve the following major objectives:

—Keeping up-to-date and enhancing professional knowledge and competence needed for better performance.

—Promoting better understanding of professional requirements as well as sensitization to professional, socio-economic and political environment in which work is done.

—Up-dating and enhancing professional skills for improving actual performance of individuals and organisations.

—Bringing about right attitudinal orientation.[2]

The objectives of National Training Policy envisages training to be imparted to all rungs of the civil service from the lowest and cutting edge to the highest in policy-making. It proposes that each department should set apart 1.5 per cent of its salary budget to be used solely for training purposes.

A systematic development of the attitudes, knowledge, skills, and behavioural pattern required to perform adequately a given task or job would help in speeding up the process of development to full capacity, increased output, improved quality, lessening of wastage, better utilisation of men and machines, etc.

Civil Service Training in NCT of Delhi

Let us now take a look at the prevailing arrangement of training for the benefit of civil servants in the NCT of Delhi. It is proposed to cover in our discussion the training effort under two broad categories, i.e., training for civil servants and training for police personnel in Delhi for the obvious reason of basic difference in the nature of the roles of the two categories.

Training Infrastructure—Directorate of Training (UTCS)

The Directorate is the agency for discharging training function mainly for Union Territory Civil Service manning different echelons of Government of Delhi. It was set up in 1962 under the Union Government (Ministry of Home Affairs). Its administrative control was transferred to the Government of Delhi only in April, 1974. It imparts both induction and in-service training now, though it was primarily established to impart Foundation Training to directly recruited probationers of Union Territory Civil Service (UTCS) officers. Its functions have now been enlarged as it has been entrusted with imparting orientation/refresher courses to other officials of the Government of Delhi, its local and autonomous bodies and undertakings. In the case of officers/officials other than Delhi, Andaman Nicobar and Lakshadweep Civil Service (DANILCS), it is imparting only skeletal in-service training. It has a target of covering two percent of the total employees per annum for some training or the other.

Organisational Set Up of the Directorate

The Directorate is headed by a whole-time Director, usually an IAS officer. He is assisted by one Joint Director, two Deputy Directors, four Assistant Directors and other Group C & D officials. The officers assist in organisation of various training courses/programmes; arranging for guest faculty; providing facilities to the faculty and the trainees; administrative work; maintenance and upkeep of hostel, etc.

Training Campus

The Directorate is located in the Institutional area, Vishwas Nagar (about 8 kms away from ISBT, off ITO) on the eastern bank of river Yamuna. It has got a complex of buildings built at a cost of about Rs. 2.5 crores with well ventilated classrooms, conference halls and an auditorium. It also has good hostel facilities to accommodate about 60 participants at a time. Hostel accommodation is provided at a nominal rate of Rs. 10- per day for single room and Rs. 20- per day for double room. Some of the officials working in the complex are also provided residential accommodation on the campus.

The huge infrastructure is presently underutilised for want of gearing up of training activity. Though it has a vehicle (van) to provide mobility to trainees and staff, yet its location, being not easily accessible through public transport, is another cause of low rate of participation. The Directorate many a times organises courses at the door-steps of the concerned organisation for which the courses are specially designed.

Library

The Directorate has a spacious library which is equipped with some of the latest books, periodicals, etc. on public administration and related inter-disciplinary areas. It has a collection of over 10,000 titles. The library facilities are provided to the trainces which includes borrowing of books. The Directorate proposes to expand and modernise the library facilities to enhance its utilisation.

Faculty

What is most surprising is that the Directorate has no regular faculty of its own. As such, it is wholly dependent on borrowed faculty from institutions like IIPA,

ISTM, University Colleges, etc. Owing to pre-occupation of guest faculty, finding faculty for its training programmes is a major handicap and the Directorate is forced to depend more on non-academic staff, like serving officers and Superintendents of the Government of Delhi or its retired officers. Most of these are neither professional trainers nor accustomed to teaching. Therefore, they are unable to do justice to the avowed task of training. Comparing the situations regarding faculty with Union Government's Institute of Secretarial Training and Management, which is also located in Delhi and discharging similar training function without regular faculty of its own, the big difference between the two is that the ISTM follows the practice of taking such officers on deputation basis who have a flare for training and teaching. The ISTM also offers them financial incentive by way of 15 per cent deputation allowance. Though this itself is not an ideal practice, yet it could be followed by UTCS with advantage. The UTCS seems to be alive to this major basic problem as it has proposed to appoint some academicians as regular faculty of its own during the Ninth Five Year Plan. By and large, a feeling prevails in the Directorate that disgruntled staff is posted here who have no interest whatsoever in maintaining, let alone improving, and expansion of training functions of the Directorate. This is also evident from the fact that five of the officers posted in the Directorate have taken voluntary retirement which does not signify a healthy or a positive trend.

Audio-visual Aids

The Directorate has audio-visual aids and equipments necessary for imparting training. But there have not been used to the optimum level in the absence of trained faculty. Even the auditorium is also sparingly used for similar reasons.

Computer Training

The Directorate has made a modest beginning in imparting Computer Training to its officers and staff. It has set-up a separate computer cell and equipped it with

PCs. Presently, it is running two courses of two weeks each but these are likely to be geared up when regular faculty joins.

Funding

The Directorate draws financial sustenance through a regular budget of its own. Its activities are not funded through any fee-based courses. However, Union Ministry of Home Affairs compensates the Directorate for the expenditure incurred on DANILCS training. The annual budget of the Directorate is presently Rs. 65 lakhs approximately. The expenditure involves maintenance of infrastructure, salaries of employees, payment of honorarium to faculty and other training related expenditure.

Training Programmes

Classification

At present, 21 training programmes[3] are being conducted by it. These could be broadly categorised in terms of their duration as: *(i)* Long-term courses, *(ii)* Medium-term courses, and *(iii)* Short-term courses.

In the long-term category falls the Foundation Training Course for DANILCS. The tenure of this course is one year.

The medium-term course comprises the Foundation Course for Pondicherry Civil Service probationers. Duration of this course is four months.

Short-term courses include the Urban Training Module for IAS officers, which is of 4-week duration. It is meant for AGMUT Probationers. The remaining courses (eighteen) in this category are only of one-to-two weeks, duration. Nine of these courses are meant for gazetted officers and another nine for non-gazetted officers.

Course Content

The content of course for DANIL is prescribed by Union Ministry of Home Affairs. It includes both indoor and outdoor training. The participants are familiarised with basic economic principles, Indian Economy, Principles of Management, Political Science, provisions in Indian Constitution, District Administration, provisions in Criminal and Civil Procedure Codes, etc. In outdoor training, through swimming, shooting, musketeering, horse-riding, etc., the physical fitness aspect of the participants is emphasised on.

The contents of courses of shorter duration are related to specific topics pertaining to demands of specific job situations at various levels. These courses, for example, focus on office management, conduct rules, leave rules, retirement benefits, maintenance of ACRs, punctuality, noting and drafting, records management, provisions under Sales Tax Act, accounting procedures, etc.

Since the Directorate has been following religiously a set pattern, which itself was adopted from somewhere long ago, the contents of the courses have not been examined from the angle of relevance in the changed scenario of public administration. Therefore, the need for a thorough review of the course contents by an expert committee is long overdue. This is the minimum that can be done periodically in a systematic manner to save training from becoming a ritualistic exercise.

Quantum of Training Effort

Let us now take a look at the number of training programmes organised by the Directorate during 1992-96 and the number of participants attending these programmes. Details of these are as follows:

Year	*Number of Programmes*	*No. of Participants*
1992-93	45	1414
1993-94	25	689
1994-95	61	1335
1995-96	85	3904

As we see from the above table, training activity of the Directorate was at the lowest ebb during the four-year period under review in 1993-94. It more than doubled in 1994-95 and more than trebled during 1995-96. This certainly is a healthy trend as it indicates not only greater emphasis on training but also higher productivity of the Directorate, as for as quantum of training programmes go, towards meeting mounting challenges of training.

Methodology

By and large, the traditional method of lectures in classroom situation is adopted for training purposes in most of the Directorate's courses. Use of modern techniques, like distribution of case material, questionnaire, response sheets, group discussions, *viva-voce*, field study, etc., are not common and rarely used. However, probationers are exposed to some of these techniques by the expert guest faculty in a limited way as demanded by the training situation. The participants are also taken out for field visits to familiarise them with ground realities of administration.

Evaluation of Training Programmes

The participants are systematically asked towards the end of each training programmes to give their assessment about the training exposure to them during the programme, its course contents, duration, methodology etc. They are also expected to give their views on performance of individual faculty members. Likewise, the faculty's views are also sought on the need to improve upon the courses.

Future Plans of the Directorate

The Directorate proposes to cover following activities during the Ninth Five Year Plan:

—Strengthening its faculty and administrative set-up,

—Extension of training facilities to local bodies and people's representatives, like MLAs and members of different Houses of legislature, Committees, etc.,

—Visit of staff and trainees to sister training institutions,

—Upgradation of hostel and library facilities, and

—Purchase of training equipment and setting-up of a sports complex.

An educational institution does not grow suddenly. It has to establish a tradition to raise itself from the ground slowly. But despite a lapse of 22 years, the Directorate is still at an infancy stage and a lot more needs to be done to build its image as an apex training institution for administrative personnel of NCT of Delhi.

The aims and objectives adopted by National Training Policy needs to be suitably adapted to impart both induction training and in-service training to personnel working on different echelons in the Government of NCT in a phased manner. For this, the Directorate itself would have to be revamped.

Now let us take a brief look at the existing arrangement of training police personnel in the NCT of Delhi.

Police Training School

Delhi Police had no training school for its force till the end of 1967. On the recommendation made in Khosla Committee report[4], i.e., the Delhi Police Commission, an independent Police Training School (PTS) has come up at Jharoda Kalan, a West Delhi village. Prior to this, the training of Head Constables, Assistant Sub-Inspectors (ASIs) and Sub-Inspectors (SIs) was conducted at Phillaur in Punjab. The present school is serving the dual purpose as a Police Training School for Constables and Head Constables and also as a Police Training College for upper level subordinate officers, *i.e.* ASIs, SIs, and Inspectors.

The school conducts both induction and in-service training. It also imparts capsule courses on specialised subjects. The overall sanctioned strength of Delhi Police has got a specified number of police personnel to serve as trainee-reserves and contingency proportion of which is normally 6.5 per cent. Thus, training is a regular activity for which staff has to be deputed by rotation.

Organisational Set-up

The PTS is headed by an Additional Commissioner of Police, who is assisted by one Deputy Commissioner of Police (DCP) and four Assistant Commissioners of Police (ACPs), 27 Inspectors, 21 Sub-Inspectors, 14 Assistant Sub-Inspectors, and 492 other functionaries. However, demand has been made to strengthen further by adding about 300 more posts for PTS.

There is also a proposal to set-up a Police Training College, with a staff strength of 660 posts, separately for imparting training to officers of the rank of Assistant Sub-Inspector and above.

The Additional Commissioner of Police is the overall chief to supervise the activities of PTS and the DCP is the head of the Institute. The ACPs supervise the indoor and outdoor training activities. Training is imparted by Inspectors/Sub-Inspectors and ASIs, some of whom are designated as Instructors. They serve as their regular training faculty. However, specialists are also invited for important training courses from time to time as and when needed. The training facilities are provided at the following locations:

— PTS, Jharoda Kalan, Delhi;

— Provision and Lines Unit, Civil Lines, Delhi; and

— Wazirabad.

Besides, most of the Districts/Units/Battalions also provide in-service and on-the-job training of short duration to their own staff according to prescribed syllabus therefor.

Courses

The following types of entrance, promotional and specialised courses for in-service police officers are being organised, durations of which range from one month to two years.[5]

Basic/Initial Courses	**Duration**
1. Probationary Sub-Inspectors and Women Assistant Sub-Inspectors	24 months

2.	Head Constables (Ministerial) and Assistant Sub-Inspectors (Steno)	3 months
3.	Recruits Training Courses	9 months

Promotional Courses

1.	Upper School Course	4 months
2.	Intermediate School Course	4 months
3.	Lower School Course	3 1/2 months

Specialised Courses

1.	Drill Instructor's Course	9 Months
2.	Motorcycle Rider Training Course	15 days
3.	Training of Technical Hands	2 months
4.	Training of Inspectors of Central Excise and Customs	3 weeks
5.	UAC Course	3 months
6.	Training of Class IV employees	1 month

During a period of five years from 1990, the PTS has conducted 168 initial/promotional/specialised training courses, covering a staff strength of about 20,000 police personnel.

The PTS chalks out a calendar of training programmes for each year and circulates it to all Units for follow up action and sponsoring of names.

Syllabus

The PTS is, by and large, following the curriculum prescribed by the Khosla Committee Report and the Report of the Committee on Police Training, popularly known as Gore Committee. It includes both indoor and outdoor training. The syllabus is prescribed for all long-term courses which is strictly followed.

The basic objective of training of Police Officers is to inculcate in them knowledge and professional skills as also development of attitudes appropriate to their work and the people they come into contact with. It provides for positive bias for relevant advancements in the fields of science and technology as also the latest relevant techniques. While the training provides for development of professional leadership, positive attitude and technical and analytical skills, it also encourages ability to anticipate situations and builds capacity to innovate for achieving organisational goals.

It imparts training to keep the force abreast of the latest techniques in crowd control, detection and control of crime, traffic management, security of VVIPs, protection, promotion of cultural values, etc.

Topics connected with investigation, maintenance of records, communication, tension handling during agitation and communal frenzy are also covered. It provides knowledge about the provisions made in latest laws and rules *vis-a-vis* judicial pronouncements. The other aspects covered by such training are: technical interaction, counselling techniques, departmental enquiry proceedings, horse riding, motor-cycle riding; behavioural science, human rights, provisions in Custom and Central Excise rules, handling of arms and ammunition, video coverage, protection of under-trials, etc.

Infrastructure

The school is located in tented accommodation, and classes are also held in tents. There is no built-up accommodation even for the faculty. They have to face rough weather. At least barracks need to be constructed to accommodate the school, which is the basic minimum requirement.

Boarding and Lodging

The trainees are housed in the school during training period and they have to undergo drill, physical training (PT), marchpast, and participation in games period as per curriculum in a strict manner. Mess facilities are provided to all trainees during the course.

Support facilities, like services of cobbler, tailor, carpenter, barber, gardener, washerman, plumber, bookbinder, electrician, radio mechanic, tubewell operator, etc., are made available to the trainees in the school.

Library

The existing library facilities are nominal in nature and need to be geared up. The school has already sent a proposal for augmentation of library facilities.

The existing functioning of the school is appreciable inspite of various constraints. But much needs to be done. The Gore Committee on Police Training of 1973 was, however, critical of the existing training practice and dubbed it as a 'ritual'. The existing training facilities have not been found satisfactory qualitatively as well as quantitatively. It has been found that there is lack of genuine conviction about the value of training. Numerous committees have recommended modernisation of training techniques and provision of latest facilities.

The Tenth Finance Commission has also stressed for special allotment of funds for upgrading training facilities of police personnel. In view of these recommendations, further improvements need to be introduced without further delay.

REFERENCES

1. India, *"Trainers' Development: The Key to Human Resource Development"*, Training Division, Ministry of Personnel, Public Grievances and Pensions, 1996.

2. National Training Policy, Training Division, Ministry of Personnel, Public Grievances and Pensions, 1996.

3. Delhi Training Calendar 1995-96, Directorate of Training, Government of NCT of Delhi, 1996.

4. *Khosla Committee Report*, Ministry of Home Affairs, New Delhi.

5. *Delhi, Calendar of Training Programmes*, 1995, Delhi Police.

6. India, *Gore Committee Report on Police Training*, Ministry of Home Affairs, 1973.

9 LANDMARKS IN DELHI LEGISLATIONS

M.K. GAUR AND KULBHUSHAN RAI VASHISHT

Federal Constitution of India establishes a dual polity with the Union at the Centre and the States at the periphery, each endowed with sovereign powers to be exercised in the field assigned to them by the Constitution.

Constitutional Position

Both the Union and the States derive their respective authority to legislate from the Constitution. But still one is not subordinate to the other in its own field. The authority of one is to coordinate with that of the other, according to Dr. Ambedkar.[1]

The Constitution does not make any fundamental changes in the pattern of distribution of legislative powers as was done under the Government of India Act, 1935. The distribution of legislative powers has been done in such a manner as would make India a single economic unit for the purpose of economic development of the country and its cultural growth. The Constitution, while conferring exclusive jurisdiction on the State Legislature through prescribing a State List, also provides for certain contingencies as safeguards when Union Parliament can legislate on the State List, e.g. when it is in the national interest, when a proclamation of emergency is in operation or when two or more states, by consent, require the Parliament to do so. Besides the States, the Indian Federation has also got a number of Union Territories, which are administered by Ministry of Home Affairs and their legislative business is transacted by Parliament.

Dr. Ambedkar realised that the Federation being a dual polity, based on divided authority with separate legislative, executive and judiciary powers for exercise of the two polities is bound to produce diversities in laws, in administration and in judicial protection.[2] As such, it was realised that Delhi, being the capital city of India, will have a unique position. Due to certain historical reasons, the administrative set-up of Delhi has seen many changes, which changed its legislative role, from time to time.

Historical Background of Delhi's Legislature

Although presently called the Government of National Capital Territory of Delhi, Delhi has not much in common with the other State Governments of Union Territories. Historically it may be recalled that in 1857 when the British reoccupied Delhi, it was made a District of the then province of Punjab. On December 12, 1911 on the occasion of the Coronation Durbar, Delhi was proclaimed as the Capital of India.[3] On October 1, 1912, Delhi was separated from Punjab and organised into a separate territorial entity headed by Chief Commissioner, Administration. In 1915, some territory across the river Jamuna, comprising 65 villages, was detached from the Meerut District and added to Delhi. During the next over four decades, i.e. up to 1950, Delhi was run as a separate local administration under a Chief Commissioner, under the provision of Government of India Acts of 1919 and 1935. On July 30, 1947, the Constituent Assembly of India appointed a Committee to recommend constitutional changes in respect of the five Centrally administered areas, including Delhi, which suggested that Delhi will be administered by the President through a Chief Commissioner.

Delhi's First Legislature

After independence, with the enforcement of the Constitution of India on January 26, 1950, Delhi became a Part 'C' State. By a further enactment, i.e., Government of Part 'C' States Act, 1951, Delhi came to be administered by a regularly constituted Ministry, responsible to the legislature, consisting of 48 members with a Council of Ministers to aid and advice the Chief Commissioner in the exercise of his functions in relation to matters in respect of which the State Assembly was given powers to make laws. The legislative powers of the Delhi Assembly were, however, subject to certain special limitations.

But this arrangement too was short-lived, as in pursuance of the recommendations of the States Reorganisation Commission, Part 'C' States were abolished in 1956.

Union Territory Without Legislature

Delhi now became a Union Territory without any legislative body. As a consequence, the administration of Delhi became the direct responsibility of the Government of India through an Administrator. However, a Municipal Corporation for Delhi was constituted in April, 1958, under the provisions of Delhi Municipal Corporation Act, 1957 to look after municipal functions.

Creation of Metropolitan Council and its Limited Legislative Role

The rearrangement caused great discontentment amongst Delhi citizens which kept growing and in order to meet their persistent demand for a popular Government for Delhi the Delhi Administration Act, 1966 was enacted by the Government of India, which provided for setting-up of a Metropolitan Council and an Executive Council in Delhi. This Metropolitan Council on the legislative side could only discuss and make recommendations on the following legislative matters:

1. Proposals for undertaking with respect to any of the subjects enumerated in the State List or the Concurrent List in the VII Schedule;

2. Proposals for extension to Delhi of any enactment in force in any other State related to any matter enumerated in the State List or Concurrent List;

3. Proposals for legislative references made to it by

the Administrator with respect to any matter enumerated in State List or Concurrent List.[4]

The recommendations made by the Metropolitan Council in these matters were considered by the Executive Council, and, wherever found necessary, forwarded by the Lieutenant Governor to the Central Government with the views, if any, expressed therein by the Executive Council, barring reserved subjects, such as law and order, services, land and building, which were under the executive domain of the Lt. Governor and the Central Government. Thus, the Metropolitan Council was recommended as a debating forum and as a recommendatory body which could not yield the desired results.

It resulted in multiplicity of authorities and other administrative problems in Delhi. As such, in June, 1988 the Metropolitan Council house passed a unanimous resolution demanding a 'Legislative Assembly' for the Union Territory of Delhi.[5]

Committee For Reorganisation of Delhi Set-up

In the meantime, the Government of India appointed a committee on Re-organisation of Delhi Set-up in 1987. On the basis of its recommendations, the Government of National Capital Territory of Delhi Act, 1991, was passed and it has been provided with an Assembly and a Council of Ministers.[6] This Act empowers the Assembly to legislate on most of the subjects enumerated in the State and Central List barring reserved subjects, like law and order, police, land, etc. It is subject to the provisions of Transaction of Business of the NCT of Delhi Rules, 1993 issued by the Ministry of Home Affairs which calls for clearance of the Administration or the Government of India in some matters, prior to introduction of the Bills. Specially those where government funds are involved.[7]

LEGISLATIVE LANDMARKS

The historical background given in preceding paras shows that barring a short spell of five years, from 1951 to 1956, Government in Delhi had no legislative powers of their own and they were solely dependent on the national

Parliament for all legislative matters, through Central Ministeries. The legislative landmarks of Delhi can, therefore, be broadly categorised as:

(a) Legislative Enactments by Delhi Assembly; and

(b) Legislative Enactments by the national Parliament for Delhi.

Enactments by Delhi Assembly

The Delhi Assembly, in a short spell of five years in early 50s made the following main enactments alongwith their rules:[8]

1. The Delhi Panchayat Raj Act, 1954,
2. The Delhi Bhoodan Yagna Act, 1955,
3. The Delhi Shops and Establishments Act, 1954,
4. The Delhi Homoeopathic Act, 1956,
5. The Tibbia College Act, 1952,
6. The Delhi Nursing Homes Registration Act, 1953,
7. The Delhi Anatomy Act, 1953,
8. The Delhi Land Reforms Act, 1954,
9. The Delhi Land Revenue Act, 1954,
10. The Delhi Public Gambling Act, 1955, and
11. The Delhi (Places of Public Entertainment) Prohibition of Smoking Act, 1953.

Taking a view that the above mentioned enactments were made-when the democratic set-up in Delhi was in its infancy, each of the above pieces of legislation appears to be a landmark in its own perspective. The subjects of legislation chosen in that era continue to be very meaningful as welfare measures even in the wake of the present focus on democratic decentralisation, modernisation, socio-economic and environmental requirements.

The Delhi Panchayat Raj Act, 1954

Panchayat is a heritage of Indian life and culture.

The main emphasis of Panchayati Raj is on creation of community spirit among the people of local level so that they may prepare plan for their development and executing their programme with self-help and active help of voluntary organisations and government departments. Mahatma Gandhi was of the view that "true democracy could not be worked by 20 men sitting at the Centre. It had to be worked from below by the people of every village".

As such, Delhi was one of the fore-runners to introduce the Panchayati Raj system in Delhi, way back in 1954. It provides for setting-up of *Gaon Panchayat* through the democratic process of fair elections, with a *Pradhan* and *Upa-Pradhan*. The term of Panchayat has been kept as five years. The Act and the rules framed thereunder provide for elaborate procedure for holding elections; convening meetings of *Gaon Sabha* and passing resolutions. The duties of *Pradhan*, *Gaon Sabha* and *Gaon Panchayat* have been well defined. The system provides for setting up of committees and holding of *Panchayat Adalats*, governing disputes, enquiring into allegations and deciding the petitions and their execution procedures.

It empowers the *Gaon Panchayat* to acquire and hold land, maintain *Gaon Sabha* property and its records. The Panchayat may establish and maintain their libraries, organise and maintain a village volunteer force to perform watch-and-ward duties; promote goodwill and harmony; to assist in relief operations, calamities, shramdan, melas, markets, etc.

The Delhi Bhoodan Yagna Act, 1955[9]

In order to facilitate the activities in connection with the Bhoodan Yagna, initiated by Acharya Vinobha Bhave and to provide for the Bhoodan Yagna Board, the donation of land to the said Board, the distribution of land received in donation to landless persons and to provide for matters ancilliary thereto, the Delhi Bhoodan Yagna Act, 1955 was enacted. The Act and rules made thereunder lay down procedure for donation of land, gifts, and its leasing out to the landless persons. The land so vested in the board was made non-attachable and, free from Stamp Duty fee. The lessee was entitled to hold the land as long as it continued to be vested in the Board and then could be passed on to his heirs. But he cannot transfer his interest in the land to others nor can he sub-let the land without previous sanction of the Board. The lessee acquires the right in the land after expiry of ten years of continuous holding it as a lessee. The Act and rules lay down procedures for regulating the working of the Board and other allied matters.

The Delhi Shops and Establishments Act, 1954[10]

This is a social welfare measure enacted to amend and consolidate the law relating to regulation of hours of work, payment of wages, leave, holidays, terms of service and other conditions of work of persons employed in shops, commercial establishments for public entertainment or amusement and other establishments. It prohibits child employment and regulates working of young women during day hours. It requires the establishment to maintain cleanliness, ensure proper ventilation and precautions against fire hazards and empowers the Government to take both remedial measures and punitive action against defaulters and protects the interests of the employees through regulatory measures.

The Tibbia College Act, 1952[11] *and the Delhi Homoeopathic Act, 1956*[12]

In order to preserve and promote the ancient Ayurvedic and Unani Systems of Medicine and also the Homoeopathic system founded by Hienemann, these enactments were made so that these medical systems can play a vital role in modern times also. The Tibbia College Act provides for transfer of the management of the Ayurvedic and Unani Tibbia College of Delhi, founded by late Hakim Ajmal Khan, from its then trustees to a Board constituted under the Act. It empowers the Board to maintain the college and impart higher education and promote and conduct research in these systems and improve the Hindustani Dawa Khana and Rasayanshala. The Homoeopathic Act also provides for setting up of a separate Board for systematic growth of the Homoeopathic system of medicine. It provides for regulatory measures to conduct examination, impart training, grant diplomas and degrees, and to maintain adequate standards and proficiency in the practice of homoeopathic system. The Board is empowered to control, admissions, prescribes syllabus, recognises institutions and registers the practitioners.

Delhi Nursing Homes Registration Act, 1953[13]

In order to regulate the working of the Private Nursing Homes opened in Delhi, the Act makes it mandatory that these should be registered with the State Government's Medical Department. The licences issued are periodically renewable. The keepers of the nursing homes are required to keep proper records of health of every patient admitted by them. They are also required to keep proper record of maternity cases, child births, miscarriages, abortions and still-births. They are required to intimate to the authorities about deaths occurring in the nursing homes within 24 hours. However, the Act is not comprehensive enough to check mushroom growth of private nursing homes, the quality of treatment and medical care being provided, and to regulate the essential safety and hygienic measures and other allied matters, including the fee to be charged.

The Delhi Anatomy Act, 1953[14]

It is an act to provide for supply of unclaimed bodies of deceased persons to teaching medical institutions for anatomical examination and dissection. It also provides for procedure for the disposal of unclaimed bodies in hospitals, prisons and public places, who had died under suspicious circumstances.

Delhi Land Reforms Act, 1954[15] *and Delhi Land Revenue Act, 1954*[16]

At the time of independence, Delhi territory primarily comprised agricultural land with 358 villages and most of its population was rural oriented. In order to regulate the land revenues and consolidate land reforms laws, two new enactments—The Delhi Land Reforms Act, 1954 and Delhi

Land Revenue Act, 1954—were made. Prior to enactment of these laws, the land revenue was regulated under the provisions of Land of Punjab/Revenue Act, 1887 and United Provinces. Land Revenue Act, 1901 in the constituent areas which originally belonged to the State of Punjab and United Provinces.

The new Act recognises only two categories of tenure holdings, viz., *Bhumidar* and *Asamis*, thus, doing away with the several intermediary interests between the Government and the actual tillers of land.

The Delhi Land Reforms Act provides for acquisition of certain rights of properties and vest them in *Gaon Sabha* after repayment of compensation. It regulates the holdings by various types of persons, such as proprietor, tenants, sub-tenants, to be declared as Bhumidars and Asamis under the various provisions of the Act, and land revenue payable by them and its realisation. It lays down the procedure for implementation of the provisions, general consequences of the termination of intermediaries' rights, use of land and improvements, transfers, partition, surrender, abandonment, extinction, acquisition and ejectment. It also takes care of the land revenue, its procedure for determination, collection, payment, refunds, etc., and maintenance of proper records thereof and provides for penal provisions, such as arrest, detention, attachment, lease or transfer of land.

The Act also takes care of setting-up of a *Gaon Sabha* and *Panchayat* and prescribes their duties, functions, roles and responsibility. It also encourages cooperative farming and consolidation of land.

The Land Revenue Act and Rules prescribe the role, responsibility, qualification and service provisions of various revenue functionaries, such as Patwaries, Girdawar, Kanoongo, Sadar Kanoongo, Naib Tehsildar, Tehsildar, Revenue Assistant, etc., and their channel of control and appeals. It clearly defines and demarcates their respective duties and obligation for maintenance of land revenue records, preparation of maps, Khasra Girdawari, Khatuani and other records and their procedures for inspection, issue of copies, disposal of mutation cases and other allied matters.

The Delhi Public Gambling Act, 1955[17]

This social legislation was enacted to control the evil of gambling, which came into force in February, 1956. It provides for penal action against those indulging and abetting gambling. The responsibility for its implementation rests with Delhi Police, as per provision made in Delhi Police Act, 1978.

The Delhi (Places of Public Entertainment) Prohibition of Smoking Act, 1953[18]

Prohibition of intoxicating drinks and drugs is a national goal and its implementation is an obligation of the respective State Governments and Union Territories. In the interest of health and welfare of the society, the Act was enacted and certain places of public entertainment declared as prohibited areas for smoking and all hours of the days and night have been specified as prohibited for all classes of entertainments. But the legislation, being incomprehensive, the evil of smoking has dug its root, resulting in polluted atmosphere and large number of deaths every year due to cancer caused by consumption of tobacco. The present Government has, therefore, enacted another legislation on the subject to widen its scope and take care of this evil in a more effective manner.

Enactment By Parliament for Delhi

After abolition of Delhi as 'C' Class State, it became a Union Territory administered by the Ministry of Home Affairs through the Lt. Governor. In the absence of duly elected Government, following major enactments were made by the Parliament between 1956 to 1966 during which it was granted a Metropolitan Council:

1. Delhi Tenants (Temporary Protection) Act, 1956,
2. Delhi Municipal Corporation Act, 1957,
3. Delhi Development Act, 1957,

4. Delhi Rent Control Act, 1958,
5. Delhi Primary Education Act, 1960,
6. Delhi Land Holding Ceiling Act, 1960,
7. Delhi High Court Act, 1966,
8. Delhi Administration Act, 1966.

All these Acts were enacted by the Central Government without taking into consideration the aspirations of the local political leaders and their parties. As such these cause certain socio-political problems. The passing of the recent Delhi Rent Control Bill, 1995 by Parliament is a glaring example which has created resentment amongst all classes of society and has placed the Government of India in an embarrassing position. Local political parties have raised their voice against it. With the setting up of Metropolitan Council in 1967, the legislative work got some momentum and it passed 85 bills during its tenure extending over two-and-a-half decades.[19] Eighty-three Bills were, however, referred to the Government of India by the Executive Council for enactment through Parliament. But only 37 of these Bills could be enacted into laws, 20 Bills were rejected/dropped, one was substituted by another Bill, while 25 Bills remained pending with the Government of India. The process of legislation during this period was quite time-consuming and cumbersome. Statistics show that the pace of disposal of these Bills was quite slow. Out of 37 Bills enacted, only 20 were cleared within one year, six in one to two years, three in two to three years and remaining eight after three years.

The following important legislations enacted by Parliament deserve to be mentioned:

1. Delhi Sikh Gurudwara Act, 1971,
2. Delhi Cooperative Societies Act, 1972,
3. Delhi Lands Restriction on Transfer Act, 1972,
4. Delhi School Education Act, 1973,
5. Delhi Sales Tax Act, 1975,

6. Delhi Agricultural Produce Markets (Regulation) Act, 1976,
7. Delhi Police Act, 1978,
8. Delhi Fire Preservation and Fire Safety Act, 1986,
9. Delhi Apartment Ownership Act, 1986, and
10. The National Capital Territory of Delhi Act, 1991.

Though Delhi was represented by MPs and some of them even enjoyed the rank of Cabinet Ministers, yet much could not be achieved due to Parliament's own limitation, and pre-occupation in national and international matters, with the result that Delhi had to be regiven its legitimate right of legislation by providing a Legislative Assembly in December 1993 with some checks and controls.

PRESENT LEGISLATIVE ASSEMBLY AND ITS ENACTMENT

As per the recommendation of The Balakrishnan Committee on Reorganisation of Delhi set-up, Delhi has been granted the status of National Capital Territory of Delhi (hereinafter NCT of Delhi, through an enactment of 1991.[20] It has been provided with a Legislative Assembly consisting of 70 elected members. The political executive comprises a Council of Ministers headed by a Chief Minister, who can be appointed by the President of India, instead of the Lt. Governor. The enactment still provides a pivotal role for Central Government in administering the NCT. The Transaction of Business of Government of NCT of Delhi Rules, 1993 stipulate certain conditions, which could cause administrative delay in legislative business. Yet, despite such delays, the newly constituted Assembly of 1993 has been able to carry out the following four important legislations which have now become Acts.

The Delhi Lokayukta and Upalokayukta Act, 1995[21]

It provides for setting-up of Lokayukta system in Delhi to attend to allegations against public functionaries, including the Chief Minister, Ministers, MLAs, Chairman, Vice-Chairman or Managing Director or a Member of Board of Directors of an Apex Cooperative Society, Government

Company, Local Authority, Corporation, Commission or a body set up by the Government of Delhi, and a Member of Municipal Corporation of Delhi. The Lokayukta will be assisted by one or more Upalokayukta, who are to be appointed by the Lt. Governor with the prior approval of the President of India. The Lokayukta can be appointed after consultation with the Chief Justice of High Court of Delhi and the Leader of the Opposition in the Legislative Assembly. The Upalokayukta can be appointed in consultation with the Lokayukta.

The Lokayukta or Upalokayukta on receiving complaint or other information can *suo motu* proceed to inquire into all allegations made against a public functionary. Their respective jurisdictions have been defined in the Act. They are, however, debarred from inquiring into any matter which has been referred for inquiry under the Commission of Inquiry Act, 1952. They have been given powers for summoning and enforcing attendance, requiring the discovery and production of documents, receiving evidence on affidavit, requisitioning of public record, issuing commission for examination of witnesses, etc. They can utilise the services or any officer of investigating agency of Government for investigation purposes. The Lokayukta and Upalokayukta are to report their findings in writing and make recommendations which are normally required to be implemented within three months of the date of receipt of the report. The departments are to submit action taken reports to the Lokayukta. The Act is likely to serve as a deterrent to indulgence in malpractices at the levels stated above.

The Delhi Commission for Women Act, 1994[22]

It provides for constitution of a Delhi Commission for Women consisting of woman Chairperson, committed to the cause of women and five other members to be nominated by the Government. It is to look into complaints, investigate and examine all matters relating to safeguards provided for women under the Constitution and other laws. It can also make recommendations for effective implementation of these safeguards for improving the condition of women in the capital. It may review the existing provisions of the Constitution and other laws affecting women and recommend amendments thereto to suggest remedial measures to meet any lacunae, inadequacies or shortcomings in such legislation. It can take up isolation of provisions of the Constitution and other laws. It can also undertake *suo motu* studies and investigation work and evaluate the progress of development of women in the capital. The legislation is meant for upliftment of women's social status.

The Delhi Agricultural Cattle Preservation Act, 1994[23]

It provides for the preservation of animals suitable for milch, drought, breeding or agricultural purposes. It prohibits slaughter of cattles, like cows, calves of cows, bulls, and bullocks. It also imposes certain restrictions on export of such cattle to avoid slaughter to other States/ UTs. It contains provisions for prohibition of possession of flesh of agricultural cattle and also empowers certain officers to enter, search and seize. Its penal provisions provide for imprisonment for a term which may extend to five years and fine which may extend to Rs. 10,000 for violation of rules, This legislation is expected to help in protection of cows, calves, bulls, etc.

The Delhi Preservation of Trees Act, 1994[24]

It provides for preservation of trees in NCT of Delhi and contains provisions for establishment of Tree Authority, consisting of Secretary (Forest) as its Chairman, and five members, viz., Deputy Commissioner, Delhi; two MLAs and two representatives of local bodies nominated by the Government. The Deputy Conservator of Forests is its Member-Secretary. Its main duties are preservation of all trees within Delhi, carrying on census of the existing trees, development and maintenance of nurseries, supply of seeds, saplings and trees, planting and trans-planting of trees, organisation of demonstrations and extension services, undertaking studies and projects in allied areas.

It imposes restrictions on felling and removal of trees, and provides for regulatory measures to obtain prior permission to fell, cut, remove or dispose of trees, if required. It also provides for adoption of trees for their maintenance and preservation. Penal provisions for violation have also been made which may extend to one year's imprisonment or with fine up to Rs. 1000 or both. It is a welcome step for preservation of environment of Delhi.

The other two landmark enactments by the Delhi Legislative Assembly so far pertain to banning smoking in Delhi and adoption of family planning measures. A brief description of these is as under:

The Local Government in Delhi (Disqualification for Membership) (Small Family) Act, 1996[25]

It provides for disqualification of an incumbent for election as a member to an office of a local government, such as Panchayat, Municipality, Improvement Trust, District Board, Mining Settlement Authority and any other Local authority in the Capital Territory of Delhi, if he or she has more than two children.

The Delhi Prohibition of Smoking and Non-Smokers Health Protection Act, 1996[26]

It provides for prohibiting smoking in places of public work or in public service vehicles in the Capital Territory of Delhi. The place of public include auditoria, hospital buildings, health institutions, amusement centres, restaurants, public offices, court buildings, educational institutions, libraries and the like which are visited by general public, but does not include any open place. It also provides for a ban on smoking in a public service vehicle. The Act also envisages a ban on sale of cigarettes, beedies, etc., to a person below the age of 18 years. It imposes restrictions on advertisement of cigarettes in any public place and any public service vehicle as also its sale within 100 metres of area around any college, school or other educational institutions. The offender can be fined up to Rs. 100 for the first offence and Rs. 200 and Rs. 500 for second and subsequent offences. It also contains penal provision for imprisonment in certain cases.

Thus, during a short span of about three years, the Delhi's Legislature has been able to pass six important bills of which four have been enacted for the well-being of citizens of Delhi.

CONCLUSION

The discussion in the preceding paras presents a picture of chequered carrier of legislative work in the Union Territory which is now rechristened as NCT of Delhi.

Legislative Assembly carried out its legitimate legislative functions only for a short spell of about five years from 1950-56 with due participation of people's elected representatives. We have covered in our discussion a selection of such enactments which could be considered as landmarks. Then followed the phase of total Central Government control on Delhi's legislative activities. This long phase lasted nearly a spell of about 26 years wherein Metropolitan Council, though entrusted technically with legislative function, was at best functioning as an advisory/ recommending body of the Central Government.

Delhi's legislative activity is now in its present new *Avtar*. As was expected, it has started off well despite inherent restrictions imposed by the Central Government, particularly relating to Bills on fiscal matters. As is evident from the nature of enactments (both completed as well as in process), the present phase seems to be geared to discharging a more fuller and satisfying role expected from a representative legislature.

REFERENCES

1. Sharma, S.K., *Union Territory Administration in India*, Chand Publishers, Chandigarh, 1968.
2. *Op. cit.*
3. *Delhi Gazetteer*, Delhi Administration, Government of India Printing Press, New Delhi.
4. *Delhi Administration Act*, 1966.
5. *Status Paper on Delhi*, Delhi Administration, A.R. Department, Delhi, 1968.

6. NCT of Delhi Act, 1991.
7. The compilation of statutory rules and orders, issued under the Acts enacted by Delhi Legislative Assembly and included in Delhi Code, Vol. II, Delhi Administration, 1968.
8. The Delhi Panchayat Raj Act, 1954.
9. The Delhi Bhoodan Yagna Act, 1955.
10. The Delhi Shops and Establishments Act, 1954.
11. The Tibbia College Act, 1952.
12. The Delhi Homoeopathic Act, 1956.
13. The Delhi Nursing Homes Registration Act, 1953.
14. The Delhi Anatomy Act, 1953.
15. The Delhi Land Reforms Act, 1954.
16. The Delhi Land Revenue Act, 1954.
17. The Delhi Public Gambling Act, 1955.
18. The Delhi (Places of Public Entertainment) Prohibition of Smoking Act, 1953.
19. *Status Paper on Delhi*, Delhi Administration, 1988.
20. The Constitution (Sixty-ninth) Amendment Act, 1991.
21. The Delhi Lokayukta and Upalokayukta Act, 1995.
22. The Delhi Commission for Women Act, 1993.
23. The Delhi Agricultural Cattle Preservation Act, 1994.
24. The Delhi Preservation of Trees Act, 1994.
25. The Local Government in Delhi (Disqualification of Membership (Small Family) Act, 1996.
26. The Delhi Prohibition of Smoking and Non-Smokers Health Protection Act, 1996.

10 AN UNIFIED METROPOLITAN TRANSPORT AUTHORITY FOR DELHI

ASHOK KUMAR

Commuting in Delhi indeed will not be feasible without the Mass Rapid Transit System for it would require at least 10,000 buses by 2001 in order to serve its commuters. In this context consider that the length of roads in Delhi in 1992-93 was only 24,402 km. Therefore, it would be extremely difficult to create required road length for 10,000 buses by 2001. This scenario clearly predicts doom whereby the transport arteries of Delhi would clog leading to the sudden death of the city.

At this point it is appropriate to note that alternatives to shift complete reliance from the bus service to the Mass Rapid Transit System have been considered since 1969 but nothing significant has been achieved. How did we come to such a pass? Is it the lack of an organisational framework at metropolitan level that has led to a situation of complete helplessness. Therefore, this author looks at the transport problems and issues of Delhi from the organisational standpoint. It is argued that appropriate public transport systems could be adopted only after an unified metropolitan transport authority is established.

This research study begins by providing an analysis of the traffic and transport problems and issues that face Delhi today. In the third section, the sudden demise of the

Delhi Transport Corporation (DTC) and the accidental introduction of private bus service is discussed. The vacuum in respect of policies on the privatisation of bus service, according to author of this study, points to the accidental introduction of the private bus service. An analytical guide to policies and proposals forms the fourth section. In the backdrop of this analytical guide, Unified Metropolitan Planning Authority is proposed in the last section of this work.

Traffic and Transport Issues and Problems of Delhi

Travel demand in cities has increased, firstly because more people are required to be moved as a result of sharp rise in population. Secondly, mobility as expressed in terms of Per Capita Trip Rate (PCTR) has increased because of change in the socio-economic characteristies of the trip makers and more number of opportunitics offered by the cities (Sahoo, 1995: 407). For instance Delhi offered work to more than 2.2 million in 1991. A large number of informal commercial establishments (33,094 in 1982) further encourage people to travel longer distances to their places of work. Jacobs *et al* add that "with the increase in city size and area, trip lengths will increase and the burden of commuter travel will increasingly fall upon the public transport sector as longer trips will discourage walking and cycling as convenient alternatives" (Jacobs *et al*, 1986: 1).

The Average Trip Length (ATL) has also increased as a consequence of continuous physical expansion of the cities and distribution of the activities over a wide spatial frame (Sahoo, 1995: 402). For instance the total land area of the Union Territory of Delhi in 1991 was 1483 sq. kms. (51.90 × 48.48 kms.). In addition to this, people travel from as far flung places as Aligarh, Agra, etc., for employment purposes. As a result the Per Capita Trip Rate or the PCTR (vehicular trips only) in Delhi has increased from 0.49 in 1970 to 0.72 in 1981. It is expected to rise to 1.1 by 2001 (Sahoo, 1995: 405).

Road Length, Human Population and Vehicle Population

Length of Roads in Delhi

Length of roads in Delhi was 8,231 kms., in 1970-71. This figure increased sharply to 18,065 by 1986-87. However, since then road length has only increased to 24,402 km., by 1992-93 (see Table 1). Whereas the number of vehicles on the roads have crossed the 2.5 million mark in 1993 from a mere 0.2 million in 1971.

Table 1. Length of Roads in Delhi between 1970-71 to 1992-93

Year	*Length in km*
1970-71	8,231
1986-87	18,065
1990-91	21,564
1991-92	22,487
1992-93	24,402

Source: Government of the National Capital Territory of Delhi, 1995.

Number of Vehicles

Number of vehicles, particularly, motorized vehicles has increased from just 204,078 in 1971 to 1,923,787 in 1991 and 2,198,908 in 1993 (Government of the National Capital Territory of Delhi, 1995: 181). Between 1985 to 1993, the number of non-motorized vehicles has also increased from 6,305 to 24,637 (See Table 2).

Table 2. Number of Motorized and Non-Motorized Vehicles in Delhi

(Motorized Vehicles)

Type of Vehicles	*Year*			
	1971	*1991*	*1992*	*1993*
Goods Vehicles	15,262	106,052	110,465	114,294
Cars and Jeeps	61,521	427,743	468,809	510,242
Motorcycles and Scooters	109,112	1,294,066	1,381,582	1,467,182
Autorickshaws	10,812	65,829	69,974	71,568
Taxis	4,105	10,426	11,212	11,679
Buses	3,266	19,671	22,640	23,943
Total (A)	204,078	1,923,787	2,064,682	2,198,908

(Non-motorized vehicles)

Type of Vehicles	Year			
	1985	1991	1992	1993
Rickshaws	1,411	12,411	1,3847	15,579
Tongas	1,354	974	954	927
Rehras	346	269	203	190
Handcarts	6,517	4,886	5,075	4,998
Bullock Carts	775	521	473	442
Cycle Rickshaws Trollies	6,305	11,476	18,198	24,637
Total (B)	16,708	30,537	38,750	46,773
Total (A)+(B)	220,786	1,954,324	2,103,432	2,245,681

Source : Government of the National Capital Territory of Delhi (1995 : 181).

It is estimated that at present the number of all types of vehicles is more than 25 lacks (Ranganathan, 1995) which is more than the total number of vehicles in Mumbai, Calcutta and Chennai put together.

There were 46,773 men and animal driven vehicles, most of them in the Municipal Corporation of Delhi area in 1992-93 (Government of the National Capital Territory of Delhi, 1995 : 187). The plan envisaged that all manned and animal driven vehicles are to be phased out but no specific phasing out time schedule is mentioned. Neither an authority is identified which will implement this phasing out scheme, although the Municipal Corporation of Delhi is the organisation which should take up this responsibility.

Now consider that the human population in two decades has doubled but the number of vehicles increased ten-fold. As a result the number of vehicles per lakh of population increased from 4,433 in 1971 to 19,246 in 1991. On the other hand development of road network has been marginal but number of vehicles grew enormously resulting in more vehicles per 100 km of road length. In

1971 vehicles per 100 km of road length were 2,463. This increased to 8,918 in 1991. Consequently one experiences more congestion on roads (see Table 3).

Table 3. Population, Road Network and Numbers of Vehicles

Year	*Population in lakhs*	*Road network (km)*	*Numbers of Vehicles*	*Vehicles (in lakh)*	*Vehicles/ 100 km of road length*
1971	40.7	7,327	180,434	4,433	2,463
1981	62.2	13,904	536,011	8,618	3,855
1991	94.2	1,812,967	1,812,967	19,246	8,918
2001(E)	218.0	564,09	18,216,352	83,561	32,293

Source: Sahoo (1995: 408).

Note: E stands for 'estimate'.

Traffic Composition and Traffic Volume

Traffic composition has also changed since 1971. Percentage of motorcycles and scooters to total motorized vehicles has increased from approximately 50 per cent in 1971 to 66.72 per cent in 1993. The number of auto rickshaws have increased 7 times between 1971 and 1993. "The volume of traffic in Delhi has increased with the level of urbanization, with 9.27 million person trips per day in 1993, up by 138 per cent over a period of 12 years, while the population increased by only 46.1 per cent during 1981-91. The development in the public transport system, however, has not matched this development, with only one additional public vehicle being inducted in the transport system per 2,600 people in 1993 as against one every 1250 people in 1985" (National Steering Committee: India, 1996: 48). This has resulted in a shift to personalized modes. The ownership of personalized modes has gone up at an annual rate of 10.2 per cent between 1985-1993 causing a significant change in the modal split.

Modal Split

Modal split of work trips for Delhi demonstrates that

more than 50 per cent of total work trips are made by buses alone. Unlike Mumbai, Calcutta, Chennai, Delhi completely depends on buses. But it is significant to note that 33 per cent work trips were made by personalized vehicles including cars, two wheelers and cycles (see Table 4). "However, from population point of view it would be desirable to encourage a modal split that would restrict the use of personalized vehicles, particularly in the inner cities" (National Steering Committee: India, 1996: 47). Modal split also affects average travel time per kilometre.

Table 4. Percentage to Total Work Trips

City	*Car*	*Train*	*Bus*	*Two-wheeler*	*Cycle*	*Walk*	*Others*
Delhi	6.00	0.50	52.20	17.00	8.00	14.00	2.30
Mumbai	3.98	60.27	19.15	2.23	3.40	6.30	4.67
Chennai	1.50	4.10	37.90	7.00	14.20	29.50	5.80

Source: National Steering Committee: India (1996: 46).

Note: Others include Auto Rickshaws, Tempos, Cycle-rickshaws and Tongas.

Consequently Delhi has the highest automobile ownership among the Indian metropolitan cities, according to a study conducted by the Society for Development Studies for India Habitat II Report (see Table 5). Delhi has 205 vehicles per 1,000 driving license age group population whereas it is only 51 vehicles for Mumbai. That is why Delhi has 23 per cent personalized motorized vehicles.

Table 5. Automobile Ownership, 1993

City	*Vehicles per 1000 driving license age group population*
Delhi	205.41
Mumbai	50.91
Chennai	101.82
Bangalore	130.23

National Steering Committee: India, (1996: 47).

Average Travel Length and Time

The Average Trip Length in Delhi has also increased. It has increased in Delhi from 5.4 km. in 1970 to more than 8 km. (see Table 6). On DTC buses it has increased from 6.2 km. in 1971-72 to 14 km. in 1988-89. This is happening because people are increasingly commuting from the National Capital Region to Delhi (Sahoo, 1995: 407).

Table 6. Average Travel Time, 1993

City	*Average time in minutes for a work trip*		
	Trip length (km)	*Travel time (min.)*	*Travel speed (min./km.)*
Delhi	8.50	44.34	5.10
Mumbai	12.40	33.37	2.70
Chennai	7.30	21.62	3.00
Bangalore	6.70	17.60	3.30

National Steering Committee: India (1996: 48).

Average trip length is the highest in Bombay i.e. 12.4 km. For Bombay this may have to do with the linear form of the city. But for Delhi it is because of its spatial spread. At the same time bus route length of "over 70 per cent routes have lengths between 10 km to 25 km. Average route length is around 20 km." (Sarna *et al*, 1994: 428).

Due to its most sophisticated modal split, Mumbai has the lowest average travel speed per kilometre i.e., 2.7 minutes per kilometre whereas average travel speed is the highest for Delhi i.e. 5.1 minutes per kilometre. Average travel speed is also highest in Delhi as compared to other metropolitan cities.

Average travel time in Delhi is 44.34 minutes in 1993. It was 30 minutes in 1985. One of the factors responsible for this increase is because journey speeds have come down as one approaches from particular areas to inner city areas (refer Table 7).

Table 7. Journey Speeds in Delhi, 1985

Area	*Travel speed in km per hour*
Periphery Areas	37
Outer Areas	30
Central Business District	21 to 24

National Steering Committee: India, (1996: 49).

The mobility rate i.e. average trips per person is also consistently increasing in Delhi (see Table 8).

Table 8. Daily Trip Rates per Person per Day in Delhi

Purpose	*Year*			
	1969	*1981 Observed*	*1981 Modified*	*2001 Projected*
Work	0.29	0.300	0.352	0.450
Education	0.80	0.088	0.102	0.150
Others	0.12	0.012	0.196	0.400
Non-home Based	*	0.040	0.070	0.100
All Purpose				

Source: Ranganathan (1995: 87).

*included in other trips.

Cost of a Similar Trip Length

The ratio between the cost of a similar trip length by public bus and the private bus is 1 : 2. However, the same ratio between the public bus and the personalized two-wheeler is approximately 1 : 3 (also see Table 9).

Table 9. Cost of a Similar Trip Length (10-11 km)

Mode	*Cost in Rs.*
Public Bus	2.75
Private Bus	4.11
Personalized Two-wheeler	5.50

National Steering Committee: India, (1996: 49).

It will take at least 20 years and Rs. 8,000 crores (at 1992 prices) to complete both phases of the Mass Rapid Transit Service. By that time i.e. by 2014 number of vehicles will be around 2 crores (Sahoo, 1995: 409).

As the data demonstrates, expenditure has been steadily increasing. But expenditure on roads has been clubbed together with items such as conservancy, drainage, sewage and public lighting. In all Municipal Corporation of Delhi spent Rs. 5,486.53 lakh in 1994-95. However, the New Delhi Municipal Council in the same year spent Rs. 1,181.30 lakh which is much more considering that it has only four per cent of the total area of the National Capital Territory (See Table 10).

Table 10. The MCD Expenditure on Roads and Lighting

(Rupees in Lakhs)

Period	*MCD*	*NDMC*
1990-91	3307.45	1041.42
1991-92	4468.63	1074.76
1992-93	4914.32	1178.81
1993-94	5221.84	1175.83
1994-95	5486.53	1181.30

Source: Government of the National Capital Territory of Delhi (1995 : 126-127 and 130-131).

The NDMC separately makes allocations for water, electricity and roads (see Table 11).

Table 11. Fleet and Passenger Characteristics in Delhi

Period	*Total Buses in Fleet*	*Buses on Road (daily average)*	*Passengers (in lakhs)*	*Daily average passengers (in lakhs)*
1970-71	1238	870	2688	7.36
1987-88	4353	3443	13975	38.18
1990-91	4392	3722	16001	43.84

Table Contd. on next page

Table Contd.

Period	Total Buses in Fleet	Buses on Road (daily average)	Passengers (in lakhs)	Daily average passengers (in lakhs)
1991-92	4375	3750	15630	42.70
1992-93	3840	3665	13685	37.49
1993-94	3502	3247	8901	24.39

Period	Kilometres operated (in lakhs)	Kilometres operated daily average (in lakhs)	Break down (000)	Accidents by DTC Buses (Total)	Major Accidents
1970-71	529.72	1.45	88	1002	63
1987-88	2640.01	7.21	78	3519	345
1990-91	2977.82	8.16	24	3065	283
1991-92	2916.50	7.97	19	2769	344
1992-93	2834.83	7.77	16	2406	304
1993-94	2558.20	7.01	16	1790	258

Source : Government of the National Capital Territory of Delhi (1995: 182-185).

Organisational Maze

Delhi does not has a unified organisation at metropolitan level to look into transportation problems and issues. While the Plan goes on to make proposals for the Mass Rapid Transit System (MRTS) for faster intra-city movement, it fails to indicate any time schedule for its completion and no mention is made of the approximate costs involved in this project. If the transport networks are the components of the city's personality, the Plan must have given more details on the vital aspects of authority, time and cost. Even if the Plan's perspective year 2001 is taken into account for the completion of the MRTS, the ongoing haggling by the Ministry of Surface Transport, the Government of Delhi, and the private sector including national and international funding agencies leaves no scope for its even beginning let alone the completion of this project. While costs escalate, demands on the MRTS and needs of the people of the city and region will also change in the new perspective year. According to a RITES study, it is estimated that "as a result of the delay in taking up the work, the project cost is going up by Rs. 2 crore per day" (HSMI, 1996: 9).

The first phase of the MRTS measuring 55.3 km. (out of a total of 198.5 km) got the long awaited approval of the Union Cabinet on 18 September, 1996 to meet the deadline set by the Japanese Overseas Economic Cooperation Fund which is to provide loans equivalent to 60 per cent of the project cost. The fixed cost of the first phase would be Rs. 4,860 crore at April 1996 prices. It will cross Rs. 8,000 crore by the time the project is completed in 2005-06. After the completion of the first phase, the system is expected to carry 32,00,000 passengers daily. The first phase comprises three corridors: north-south, east-west and north-west.

The project will be implemented by the Delhi Metro Rail Corporation on a 50: 50 basis joint venture between the Union and Delhi Government formed in May 1995. Its Chairman is the Union Urban Affairs Secretary and Managing Director to be appointed by the Delhi Government.

The MRTS would save approximately Rs. 1,901 crore annually in terms of vehicular operating costs, road congestion, time saving, reduction in accident rates, and pollution. Additionally, savings will be made on account of additional road infrastructure. Fuel savings alone will amount to Rs. 465 crore per day.

Lack of Discipline on the Road and the Increasing Accidents

The first thing that comes to one's mind when one makes a mention of transport problems of Delhi is the unrestrained Red Line buses. Another aspect is that of a very little discipline maintained both by the drivers as well as the passengers. To top it all Delhi Traffic Police seems unable to implement traffic rules and regulation in spite of issuing about 40,000 challans in 1995. In six months Red Line prosecutions exceeded 19,000 (*Indian Express*, 1993: 4). This clearly established that punishment alone cannot help to enforce the rule of the road.

According to the Delhi Police on an average 2,800 accidents occur every year. More than 17,900 drivers jump red light and some 1,773 drivers are caught for overspeeding in addition to 2,220 are punished for reckless driving. More than 1,600 drivers are found to be driving without driving licenses. A lesser number of drivers that is 353 are punished for drunken driving. More than 2,900 drivers use pressure horns and 1,337 are caught for triple driving. A large number of 8,235 drivers violate the provision of wearing the helmets while driving (*Indian Express*, 1993: 4).

Privatisation of Bus Service in Delhi

It was in 1935 that a public limited company called the Gwalior Northern India Transport Company Limited was established for giving licences to operate buses in Delhi (see Table 13). After independence the bus services, as everything else, was nationalized under the direct control of the Delhi Transport Service of the Union Ministry of Surface Transport. As things settled after independence, the Delhi Roads Authority was created in 1950 which replaced the Delhi Transport Service. However, the control remained with the Union Ministry of Surface Transport. The Delhi Transport Corporation was born in 1971 by replacing the Delhi Road Transport Authority. The Delhi Transport Corporation continues to survive, but just, till today. But the bus service was largely privatised in 1992 in Delhi.

Table 12. Historical Perspective of a Transport Authority in Delhi

Year	*Event*
1935	The Gwalior Northern India Transport Company Limited was given license to operate city buses in Delhi.

1948	Bus service was nationalized and the Delhi Transport Service (DTS) was established under the Ministry of Transport, Government of India.
1950	The Delhi Road Transport Authority (DRTA) was constituted by an Act of Parliament and it replaced the Delhi Transport Service.
1971	The Delhi Transport Authority was converted into the Delhi Transport Corporation (DTC).
1992	Red Line private bus service was introduced on Delhi roads under the control of the State Transport Authority which issues permits.

Source: History up to 1971 is adapted from Singh (1991: 11).

At present Delhi has developed a range of privatised bus service to supplement (read replace) the government owned fleet of the Delhi Transport Corporation. Based on a combination of fare structured and stoppages between specific points the Delhi transport scene has acquired many hues. The privatised services comprise Red Line, White Line, and Blue Line buses. At present, however, most of Red Line buses have been painted blue and white.

Demise of the Delhi Transport Corporation

Privatisation of bus services cannot be considered to be the precursor to the demise of the Delhi Transport Corporation and its shrinking fleet. To begin with it has been consistently experiencing financial losses. Financial mismanagement has been the hallmark of the Delhi Transport Corporation since its inception in 1971. Furthermore, it has been over staffed up to the hilt. In a bid to reduce staff, the Delhi Transport Corporation dismissed 3,000 employees which it had to take back as per proviso of the RTC's Act. In order to provide them with gainful employment, the Delhi Transport Corporation requires another 2,000 buses in addition to the existing 1,500 buses. In 1991 the Delhi Transport Corporation had 2,500 buses which has come down to 1,500 in 1995. It is expected that Delhi Transport Corporation fleet will be reduced to 1,000 by the end of 1996. The Voluntary Retirement Scheme really did not work out.

The Delhi Transport Corporation had perpetually

made losses till 1992 when private bus service was introduced. The Delhi Transport Corporation continues to make losses. Secondly, new buses were required to be introduced, firstly as replacement to the aging Delhi Transport Corporation's fleet, then increasing demand due to increase in the number of commuters. Government did not have that kind of investment particularly for an organisation which piled upon itself huge financial losses. Then came Prime Minister Narsimha Rao's liberalization and privatisation policies. According to Dhingra (1996: 3) "4000 private bus operators were running the city services by 1994".

Privatisation, however, has given birth to its own unique problems. For example, routes of 900 buses were changed to more remunerative routes without any reference to operating costs. This had adversely affected other routes and the needs of the commuters.

Further, the State Transport Authority did not look into the parking needs of the private bus operators. No provision was made for terminal requirements other than that they may offer terminal space for Rs. 250 per month for each bus. This has led to parking of the Red Line buses all over the residential areas of the city.

Every regulatory body like the State Transport Authority requires staff to enforce its rules and regulations. The State Transport Authority at least should have employed timekeepers and route inspectors for monitoring and enforcement. No additional timekeepers have been provided for the Red Line bus service.

Financial Mis-management of the Delhi Transport Corporation

The Delhi Transport Corporation funds its operations through Government loans including social costs such as money waived to students as free bus passes. It has to pay interest rates as high as 21.25 per cent on some loans. The Delhi Transport Corporation has accumulated a debt of Rs. 122 crore which it has to pay to oil companies, spare parts suppliers and other enterprises. But more alarming is the fact that its "latest balance sheet shows an amount of Rs. 834 crores as interest due to the Centre" (Raina, 1996: 12). This interest consists both accumulated and penal interest on refundable loans. This financial crisis has deepened due to the Delhi Transport Corporation buses plying on unrenumerative routes, lower utilization of assets, higher operating costs and stagnant pricing framework (see Table 13).

Table 13. Public Transport System: Key Indicators in Mega and Metro Cities, 1993

City	*Fleet Utilisation (%)*	*No. of passengers per day (lakh)*	*Average passenger lead (km)*	*No. of passengers (km per day lakhs)*	*Buses per lakh population*
Delhi	86	43.67	13.50	589.55	75
Bombay	86	38.45	7.75	298.18	24
Calcutta	59	7.06	9.20	65.12	18
Madras	89	28.95	7.75	224.56	42
Ahmedabad	75	6.34	5.34	33.85	21
Pune	80	5.45	6.52	65.12	11

Source : Planning Commission, Compendium of Transport Statistics, 1993.

Operating efficiency is affected because the Delhi Transport Corporation has to serve resettlement colonies located far and wide in the metropolis.

Capital Structure

The Delhi Transport Corporation has no equity capital base:

(a) The Delhi Transport Corporation has been financing its operations through the interest bearing repayable Capital Loans and the Ways and Means Loan.

(b) Fifty per cent of the Capital Loans are refundable at 17 per cent interest rate and the remaining 50 per cent carry concessional rate of interest of 6.25 per cent.

(c) The Ways and Means Loan are extended to the Delhi Transport Corporation at 18.5 per cent interest rate.

(d) Non-payment of interest on Government loans attracts penal rate of interest of 2.75 per cent.

(e) The total Capital Loan outstanding on 31 March. 1995 was Rs. 79.65 crore of which Rs. 10.06 crore was non-refundable and Rs. 69.59 crore was refundable.

(f) In addition the outstanding Ways and Means Loan on 31 March, 1995 stood at Rs. 481.26 crore.

(g) It may be pertinent to mention here that this scenario existed in spite of the partial capital restructuring implemented from 1986-87 when Rs. 277.27 crore of outstanding Ways and Means Loans were written off and Rs. 164.61 crore Refundable Loan was converted into Non-Refundable Capital Loan.

(h) Central Government had also approved the conversion of Non-refundable Capital Loan amounting to Rs. 126.10 crore together with Rs. 119.26 crore interest into equity for a period ending March 1992.

Losses of the Delhi Transport Corporation

(a) In the absence of an economic fare structure similar to the increase in prices of various consumable items as also in the absence of a proper debt equity ratio, the Delhi Transport Corporation has been incurring losses on a year to year basis since its inception.

(b) At the time of its formation on 3 November, 1971, the Delhi Transport Corporation inherited an accumulated loss of Rs. 15.22 crore. In view of the in-built flawed financial structure, the accumulated losses had snow-balled to

Rs. 1683.48 crore on 31 March, 1995. For example, the net losses sustained by the Corporation during the year 1994-95 were Rs. 309.29 crores of which Rs. 225.11 crore (72.78 per cent) was the interest burden alone. Expressed in terms of total expenditure, the interest burden was as high as 47 per cent.

(c) The extent of depreciation was Rs. 14.76 crore in terms of fleet and Rs. 1.15 crore on other assets.

(d) The residual working cash losses during the year 1994-95 were of the order of Rs. 68.26 crore i.e. Rs. 18.70 lakh per day.

(e) It may be pertinent to mention here that the Delhi Transport Corporation has the lowest fare per passenger per kilometre among city transport undertakings in India, the average fare being 11.5 paise for the Delhi Transport Corporation as compared to 22-23 paise of the BEST in Mumbai and 18 paise each for the PTC in Chennai and the CSTC in Calcutta.

(f) A large chunk of losses of the Delhi Transport Corporation are also attributed to various concessions being given to students, residents of re-settlement colonies etc. No such comparable concessions are being given in other metropolitan cities and whatever students' concession passes are being given in those cities are restrictive. In case of Chennai, the cost of student concession is actually recovered as a subsidy from the Tamil Nadu Government.

Some other reasons for the called losses to the Delhi Transport Corporation are as follows :

(a) *Low Fare Structure*

Delhi has 11.4 paise per passenger kilometre as compared to 24 paise in Mumbai, 20 paise in Chennai and 18 paise in Calcutta.

(b) *Concessional Passes*

To students, press, police and residents of re-settlement colonies, general all route passes.

(c) *Free Passes*

Disabled, freedom fighters, sportsmen, national award winners, war widows and their dependents enjoy free passes.

(d) *Operation of Uneconomic Services on Social Considerations*

Routes not covering even the working expenditure are being run by the Delhi Transport Corporation. The special services for officegoers and the University Specials add to existing financial burden.

(e) *Surplus Manpower*

If one has to adopt manpower norm of 8 men per bus, the ideal manpower should be 28,000 for a fleet of 3,500 of the Delhi Transport Corporation. Excess manpower in the region of 3,000 is another addition to the Delhi Transport Corporation's losses.

Table Net Losses of the Delhi Transport Corporation

(Rs. in Crores)

Year	*Low Fare*	*Concessions*	*Interest*	*Depre-ciation*	*Net Loss*
1986-87	18.61	20.00	11.94	11.71	62.26
1987-88	25.85	20.00	20.96	12.07	78.88
1988-89	32.07	20.00	32.99	13.93	98.99
1989-90	35.85	21.00	49.05	13.95	119.85
1990-91	92.22*	21.00	69.95	14.31	197.48*
1991-92	60.86	23.00	106.74	13.22	203.82
1992-93	30.94	23.00	176.24	15.10	245.28
1993-94	55.48	16.00	195.87	14.49	281.84
1994-95	51.10	15.00	225.12	15.91	307.04
1995-96	70.24	21.00	281.98	18.83	392.05

Source : Chopra (1996: 21).

* It includes payment of arrears of 'Fourth Pay Commission' as well as 50 per cent wages paid to the dismissed employees (March 1988 strike) taken back in service.

Analytical Guide to Policies and Proposals Formation

According to a study by Murthy (1995: 683-684) a passenger looks for punctuality, safety, reliability, regularity and customer service in choosing and operator. But free for all market cannot provide all of this. "The market cannot be relied upon to safeguard the interests of either the customers, the staff or innocent third parties. It would be intolerable to leave it to private market choices to weed out the unsafe operators, and in any case the mechanical complexities of transport are such that as to prevent the layman from forming any opinion in advance about the safety of the vehicles that he is about to board" (Hibbs, 1984: 32). Diandas concludes that "competition is not a useful strategy to obtain efficient, effective and high quality public transport. Rather, Government monopoly operation is more likely to innovate and to achieve these objectives" (Diandas, 1996: 155). Further, it could be argued that "continued use of quantity and quality control measures are essential to ensure vehicle and passenger safety, operator viability and the avoidance of wasteful service duplication" (Maunder and Mbara, 1996: 153). It is in this backdrop that a framework of regulations is discussed below :

Economic Regulations

(a) Fare Regulation

Fare regulations entail a system of fares that must be developed and enforced. Many classifications can be offered to categorise fare systems. Reddy (1996: 216) classifies fare systems into five categories viz., flat fares, distance fares of stage fares, zonal fares, schedule fares, multi-mode fares and discounted fares.

(b) Entry Regulation

Entry regulation pertains to the issue of which company is most qualified to enter transport industry. This issue is vital because less responsible companies may create havoc on the roads which can result in more number of accidents. The Red Line bus service on the roads of Delhi is one such example.

(c) Quality of Service Regulation

This regulation includes regulation of licenses and regulations to improve the service and safety of passengers.

(d) Tax Regulation

Tax regulations entail a tax structure to foster development transportation.

Physical and Infrastructure Regulations

The 'rules of the road' are meant to ensure operational discipline. These include quality of roads, adhering to minimum standards and fitness of vehicles to prevent accidents. Further, pneumatic doors in city buses can also prevent accidents as power steering and automatic gears can relieve the drivers of fatigue.

Social Policy Regulations

A balanced regional and urban development in the form of even spread of transport could help to disperse population. Environment and consumer protection are further important issues. Equity i.e. poor spend more on transportation than rich as percentage of their income must be maintained.

The Policy Framework of the Master Plan 2001 for Delhi

The Master Plan for Delhi 2001 encourages self-containment at zonal level. It proposes to develop an hierarchical system of road network. However, a major emphasis has been placed on arterial roads and lower levels of road systems have been ignored resulting in reduced levels of service. The Delhi Development Authority conceives that the Delhi Urban Area's transportation problems should be handled both at regional and city level. In respect of traffic and transportation major goals of the Master Plan for Delhi 2001 are:

(a) To establish a reliable, efficient and attractive multimodal public transport system;

(b) To create conditions for safe usage of bicycles;

(c) To establish a reasonable freedom to automobile traffic;

(d) To establish safe pedestrian movement; and

(e) To encourage innovative management techniques to resolve the problems of critical areas.

One of the critical areas, the Plan identifies, is the Old City for which the Plan has two pronged strategy. First, transport generating non-conforming commercial and industrial uses will be shifted to designated areas such as integrated freight complexes. As a consequence, it is expected that the associated traffic will cease to exist. Secondly, vehicles of all kinds will be allowed only on certain roads, during particular hours and some areas will be declared as traffic free areas for pedestrians. The multi-modal transport system, it is proposed, would include the electrified ring rail, bus transport, and light rail transit on selected corridors.

On the other hand, the number of vehicles in private ownership as a percentage of the total number of vehicles has increased many fold. According to the Transport Department of the Government of the National Capital Territory of Delhi, there were 21,98,908 vehicles out of which 19,77,424 were (Government of the National Capital Territory of Delhi, 1995: 181). To improve the safe use of bicycles, the Plan proposes fully segregated tracks, partially segregated cycle tracks, and the traffic management measures in the five identified areas (Government of India, 1990: 132-35). However, no progress has been made as far as the safer use of bicycles is concerned. But the Delhi Police has already started implementing traffic management plans particularly in the areas in and around Connaught Place. For the Walled City a medium capacity mass transit system like Tramway is proposed. It will cover and area of 10 km. between Chandni Chowk, Esplanade Road, Chawri Bazaar and Asaf Ali Road. Private modes of transportation will be discouraged but where used will be provided with adequate parking facilities at interchange points. The Plan also proposes an unified single transport authority as proposed by the National Transport Policy Committee at metropolitan level in order to run the multi-modal metropolitan transportation system. Then the Plan goes on to enlist the hierarchy of roads along with details such as the right of way etc. It also identifies intersections where Grade Separators need to be provided.

In order to serve the transport needs of the ever growing number of commuters at the metropolitan level, the Plan proposes four metropolitan passenger terminals one each in Trans-Yamuna area, Okhla, Bharthal, and North Delhi other than the existing three—Delhi Junction, New Delhi and Nizammudin. Within the metropolitan railway terminals, four new inter-state bus terminals are also proposed to cater to the inter-state bus movement. Each one will have an area of 10 hectares. Additionally, a bus terminal is proposed either at Dhaula Kuan or Nizammudin. A total of 2,260 hectares of land is earmarked for the International Airport Authority for its extension needs. Further, more than one-third of the gross annual freight movement to and from Delhi is carried out by road whereas, nationally this freight movement is only slightly more than 17 per cent and the rest is by the railways. This phenomenon puts the roads of Delhi under greater stress.

In order to redirect through goods and passenger traffic movement from Delhi, the Plan proposes a new railway line joining the existing Delhi Mathura Railway Line with the Delhi Punjab Railway Line in the National Capital Region. The Intergrated Freight Complexes are proposed in order to provide integration of goods movement by road and rail at Madan Pur Khadar (NH-2), Patparganj (NH-24), G.T. Road (NH-1), and Bharthal (NH-8). These are the locations where maximum regional goods traffic may be intercepted. The Integrated Freight Complexes would consist of wholesale market, warehousing facilities, road and rail transport terminals.

Major commercial centres such as Karol Bagh, Chandni Chowk and Connaught Place will be developed as vehicles free pedestrian precincts. The sub-centre business district and district centres should be provided with pedestrian piazzas. Residential areas may be so designed so that the bus stop, shopping area and nursery school can be accessed without confronting the vehicular traffic. The Plan proposes that the bus transport system will act as the feeder service by connecting residential areas and the ring rail.

The Study Group on Alternative Systems of Urban Transport

The Study Group on Alternative Systems of Urban Transport recommended in 1987 that the Unified Metropolitan Transport Authority should be established at city level in order to perform the functions of planning, funding and coordination. We will take up these issues for discussion one by one:

Planning Function

The planning function includes the following major areas of concern:

(a) Participation in the integrated land use transport planning and development of a city;

(b) Evolving a transportation system on a metropolitan level;

(c) Ensuring the operation of various modes in an integrated manner so that each mode is not only complementary to the others but also designed to reduce transportation costs including the energy costs;

(d) Interfacing of various modes in an integrated manner so that transfers from one system to another are quick and without undue delay;

(e) Envisaging the needs and potentials of different sub-systems like roads, rail, bus transport, etc. projects, in order to take care of them while planning the total transport system;

(f) Undertaking or commissioning continual studies on all systems;

(g) Evolving transport operations to cover regional aims and objectives;

(h) Ensuring the proper modal splits of public and personalized transport;

(i) Evolving rational fare policies for all modes in an integrated manner; and

(j) Controlling air, noise and other environmental pollution arising out of such transport systems.

Operational Supervision

The Unified Metropolitan Transport Authority must oversee the functioning of the transport organisations under its umbrella. It would therefore:

(a) Monitor and budget the activities of the Transport Organisations under its umbrella;

(b) Ensure operational efficiency by monitoring such factors as cost per kilometre, vehicle utilization, maintenance etc.;

(c) Monitor modal splits;

(d) Monitor fuel consumption in the city, accidents, pollution, trip lengths, traffic flows, occupancies etc.;

(e) Act as the 'client' on behalf of the city in all matters and projects concerning transportation; and

(f) Organise and implement traffic measures in consultation with the police.

Financial Function

The Unified Metropolitan Transport Authority functions could be:

(a) Assume financial responsibility on behalf of the city for all matters regarding urban transportation;

(b) Evolve annual budgets encompassing the

finances of the transport organisations and the level of support required;

(c) Justify the budget to the city, state and Central Government.

(d) Ensure that municipal finances, land use (real estate) operations and transport dovetail, and each provides part of the required finances;

(e) Monitor farebox recovery, and adjust fares as required after due consultations;

(f) Organise and implement any other measures required e.g. dual pricing, parking charging etc.; and

(g) Work with city, state and Central Government to raise and disburse financial support to the transport organisations.

Status of the Unified Metropolitan Transport Authority

The Unified Metropolitan Transport Authority should be a part of the City Authority (similar to the Development Authority), but as a separate division, needing as it does, specialist multidisciplinary expertise.

It is emphasized that the acronym "Unified Metropolian Transport Authority" is used in generic terms and that the word 'Metropolitan' should not be misconstrued. The organisation defined need not necessarily carry this name if it causes misunderstanding over its role which includes planning, supervision and financial responsibility.

The Unified Metropolitan Transport Authority should be created when a city has reached a level of one million population. It will start small and expand with city size.

Authority of the Unified Metropolitan Transport Authority

Given all its responsibilities and functions the Unified Metropolitan Transport Authority must be given the necessary statutory authority to perform effectively and efficiently.

At the metropolitan city level, a three-tier structure is proposed as under:

(a) An Apex Metropolitan Planning Authority;

(b) An Unified Metropolitan Transport Authority;

(c) The transport operating agencies/authorities like Bus Corporation, Metro Rail, Parking Authority, Terminal Authority, Para Transit Authority, Traffic Management Authority, etc.

The Metropolitan Planning Authority is envisaged to be the apex authority at the city level and it will be responsible for planning. It shall comprise the chiefs of the functional and sectoral authorities of which the Unified Metropolitan Transport Authority is one. Only such an apex authority will be able to formulate overall policies, prepare integrated city development plans, ensure inter-sectoral coordination and monitor the plan implementation. In case of Delhi, the present efforts at trifurcation of the Delhi Development Authority provides an opportunity to structure and established the apex Delhi Planning Authority with proper structure and authority.

The Unified Metropolitan Transport Authority in its composition will comprise the chiefs of the sub-system agencies and authorities like the bus, rail, parking, terminal, para transit, traffic management, etc. Such a composition will enable translation of city level policies to transport sector policies and also ensure intra-sectoral coordination. The Unified Metropolitan Transport Authority shall be coordinating agency.

At the third level, the operating agencies will be responsible for day to day operations of the sub-systems like bus, rail, etc. within the framework of policies and guidelines laid down by the Unified Metropolitan Transport Authority under its overall supervision and guidance.

Why Delhi Needs an Unified Metropolitan Transport Planning Authority

There is no going back to pre 1992 situation. Even the kilometre scheme whereby the Delhi Transport

Corporation hired private buses could not be contemplated at this stage because it did encourage back door monopoly and discouraged competition. Furthermore, the private operators may not be keen to accept rates offered by the Delhi Transport Corporation. Then the Delhi Transport Corporation could not be trusted for it always had made losses.

There are many reasons why the Unified Metropolitan Transport Authority should be established for the National Capital Territory of Delhi:

Implementation of the Vital Proposals

The Rail India Technical and Economic Services or the RITES in its recent study of May 1995 for the Union Urban Affairs has recommended that:

1. The cost of the first phase of 55 km. of the Mass Rapid Transit System is Rs. 5,000 crores.
2. As a result of the delay in taking up the work, the project cost is going up by Rs. 2 crores per day.
3. The government should enact an Urban Transport Act.
4. It should create an independent authority for each city including Delhi handling all aspects of transport (HSMI, 1996: 9).

Cost and Efficiency Considerations of the Options

One rail-car can replace over 155 automobiles. But the proposal of the Mass Rapid Transit System has been delayed beyond imagination. The Mass Rapid Transit System proposal was first mooted in 1969. While more than 70 cities of the world have already acquired mass transport system with London starting its Tube Rail in 1863, the Mass Rapid Transit System for Delhi linger on.

In order to fulfill the growing transport demand broadly four options could be considered. Firstly, authorities could strengthen the road transport system. However, this is a short-term (5-10 years) measure.

Secondly, High Speed Tram (HST) may be introduced. Thirdly, one could go for the construction of heavy Mass Rapid Transit System (MRTS). Fourthly, authorities could adopt a combination of the above options.

We are only left with the alternative of HST consisting of elevated tracks supported by one metre thick single new pillars erected in the central verge of the road and spaced at about 25 to 30 metres apart. The clear height below the track may be 4.5 metre to allow the free movement of double decker buses. There are many benefits if Delhi adopts the High Speed Tram:

(a) Very little land acquisition is necessary for High Speed Tram Tracks can be constructed over the right of way of roads.

(b) This system is Capacity Flexible Mode and can carry between 10 to 15 lakh commuters at a 1 to 4 km. stretch.

(c) Project completion period is shorter than the Mass Rapid Transit System. The High Speed Tram projects can be completed between 10 to 15 years.

(d) The High Speed Tram System is less capital intensive. It can be erected at the cost of around Rs. 3200 crores at 1992 prices.

(e) It is commercially viable for external rate of return is 12 per cent.

Coordination at Regional and Sub-Regional Level

Keeping in line with the 73 and 74 Amendments to the Constitution of India, the Transport Committee of the ward members and the MLAs could oversee the Unified Metropolitan Transport Authority. This committee could provide a strategic direction with the help of proposed technical departments.

Conductive to Act as a Leverage for Private Investment

Provision of an efficient transport system at a metropolitan level is in line with the profit-making strategies of the national as well as international private companies. It surely enhances the wealth creation and accumulation processes of the free market. Therefore, the private sector is willing to make huge invests in this sector. The recent evidence to this effect has been provided by the Japanese private companies which have committed large amounts of funds for the MRTS in Delhi. With further liberalization and political commitment of the Union Government as reflected in the formation of the Infrastructure Finance and Development Corporation of India, it is expected that more funds are likely to flow to this sector.

Prospoed Organisational Structure of the Unified Metropolitan Transport Authority

But before that what Delhi needs is an organisation at metropolitan level which should be able to perform as an enabling organisation for the private sector. At present public monopoly of the Delhi Transport Corporation, which has been transferred to the Government of the National Capital Territory of Delhi, has been replaced by private monopolies of individuals. Public interest has been completely ignored. Unlike the proviso of Section 71 of the Central Motor Vehicles Act, the Unified Metropolitan Transport Authority should require individual owners of buses to organise in the form of competitive private companies which should be able to operate, maintain and introduce new buses as and when required. Private limited companies should be issued time-bound franchises to maintain competition. Fatal accidents by buses, particularly, Red Line buses could be reduced by these private companies because they can be compelled to comply with the standards on training of drivers and conductors and upkeep of the fleet.

The Central Motor Vehicles Act should be amended and a fresh legislation should be enacted to formulate the Unified Metropolitan Transport Authority. The Unified Metropolitan Transport Authority could include the following departments:

Policy and Planning Department

Policy and Planning Department of the Unified Metropolitan Transport Authority would perform major policy formulation tasks. It would be the Policy and Planning Department which will coordinate with the Delhi Development Authority and the National Capital Region Board, State governments and the Union government. This will be the most powerful Department of the Unified Metropolitan Transport Authority. It will act as the General Body.

Revenue Department

On the basis of the policies formulated by the Policy and Planning Department of the Unified Metropolitan Transport Authority, the Revenue Department will ensure enforcement and collection of taxes. It will prepare budget for the Unified Metropolitan Transport Authority indeed after prior consultations with the Policy and Planning Department. It may seek approval of the general body of the Unified Metropolitan Transport Authority if it wants to pursue any financial transactions with an external organisation.

Building and Operations Research Department

The Building and Operations Department will look into the operation of buses etc. It would also ensure the timely construction of roads as and when proposed by the Unified Metropolitan Transport Authority. It will be the spending Department.

Traffic Engineering and Management Department

The Traffic Engineering and Management Department will look into innovative techniques for the management of traffic of the metropolis.

Training and Orientation Department

Training is very significant aspect of transport industry. This Department would establish institutional framework for the training of drivers, conductors, inspectors and other staff. This will also impart orientation training to the Delhi Traffic Police which could have got its basic training from the Delhi Police. Over 80 per cent of the drivers and conductors have only informal training about their job. Average load factor on peak time is more than 100 per cent and staff ratio is 4.6 against a standard of 8 for STUs and 11.8 for the Delhi Transport Corporation (Dhingra, 1996: 4-5).

Enforcement Department

The Rules of the Road are of no significance until and unless they are enforced. The Enforcement Teams will enforce the traffic rules and regulations of the Unified Metropolitan Transport Authority.

Other Major Proposals the Unified Metropolitan Transport Authority

Following is a list of measures that are required along with the establishment of the Unified Metropolitan Transport Authority:

1. In order to enhance competition and reduce the likelihood of violation of allocated routes or frequent changes to more remunerative routes, private limited companies may be offered franchises for particular routes rather than a general permit to ply on the roads of Delhi. This condition would require that a company owns at least a fleet of 10 buses. This would also mean that the Enforcement Department may have to look after fewer companies rather than 4,000 individuals. This would help to maintain more road discipline and timetables. This will also discourage selling of permits on a power of attorney basis. Therefore, large private companies should be offered franchises with a mix of profitable and unprofitable routes.
2. The Delhi Traffic Police which requires entirely a different kind of training and orientation should become a part of the Unified Metropolitan Transport Authority which will be responsible for enforcement as far as transportation is

concerned. However, traffic police may secure their basic training with the Delhi Police.

3. The issue of driving licenses has assumed fatal dimensions. Fake licenses apart, there are organised motor driving institutions which covertly facilitate the issuing of driving licenses to half-trained drivers for all kinds of vehicles including cars, buses and two-wheelers. If the UMTA starts operating from its Zonal Offices under the general control of a Zonal Manager, this menace could be stopped. This will help in reducing speeds as well as accidents.

4. The Unified Metropolitan Transport Authority should open a training cell where all the drivers whether from public or private sector should be asked to take orientation courses once they offend on the road or violate traffic rules. Driving licences of drivers should be cancelled who offend three times.

5. The Unified Metropolitan Transport Authority should also perform as a coordinating authority with the Delhi Development Authority as well as the National Capital Region Board. Whereas, the Delhi Development Authority and the National Capital Region Board perform policy formulation functions at metropolitan and regional level respectively, it should be the Unified Metropolitan Transport Authority which should prepare zonal level transport plans for implementation.

6. Whereas, the Delhi Development Authority or whatever planning organisation replaces it, should prepare a development plan for Delhi, the Unified Metropolitan Transport Authority should become a statutory consultant to the planning authority on traffic and transport matters. Furthermore, it should advise planning authority on transport policies keeping in mind

efficiency and optimisation of the entire transport system.

7. The Unified Metropolitan Transport Authority should take those policies from the planning authority and implement them. Its area of operation for implementation should be the National Capital Territory of Delhi. This would mean that projects such as the MRTS should directly come under the general control of the Unified Metropolitan Transport Authority. The Unified Metropolitan Transport Authority should be a regulatory body for public as well as para-transit transport systems.

8. The Unified Metropolitan Transport Authority should fix minium wages for the drivers, conductors and other staff along with their age, qualifications and training.

9. The Unified Metropolitan Transport Authority should declare its transport planning zones after consultation with the Delhi Development Authority and Delhi Administration, and prepare and implement transport plans at that level. The Revenue Department, the Building and Operations Research Department, the Traffic Engineering and Management Department, the Training and Orientation Department, and the Enforcement Department will have zonal offices.

10. Unlike the Delhi Transport Corporation, the Unified Metropolitan Transport Authority should have capital grant for rolling stock and infrastructure development. It should only charge commuters to cover the operating costs. A part of the revenue expenditure should also be subsidised. The Unified Metropolitan Transport Authority should also formulate policies on road pricing, vehicle tax, road tax, etc.

REFERENCES

1. Chopra, T.S. (1996) *Bus Transit System in Delhi*, Delhi Transport Corporation Delhi, Delhi. (an unpublished document).

2. Diandas, J. (1996) Competitive Efficiency in Public Transport: Some Important Aspects in Policy Operation and Management, *India Journal of Transport Management*, Vol. 20, No. 3, pp. 155-168.

3. Dhingra, K. (1996) *Review of Policy Regarding Shape of Private Sector Role in Public Transportation*, the background paper for the Workshop on Delhi Transport System—Priorities and Action Plan, SPA, New Delhi.

4. Government of India (1990) *Master Plan for Delhi, the Gazette of India, Part II-Section 3-Sub-Section (ii)*, Union Ministry of Urban Affairs and Employment, New Delhi.

5. Government of the National Capital Territory of Delhi (1995) *Delhi Statistical Hand Book*, Directorate of Economics and Statistics, Government of the National Capital Territory of Delhi, Delhi.

6. HSMI (1996) RITES Suggests A Unified Urban Transport Act, *HSMI News*, Vol. 3, No. 1, p. 9.

7. Hibbs, J. (1984) Privatisation in the Transport Sector, The Economic Review, pp. 31-34.

8. *Indian Express* (1993) Traffic Police Drive Fails to Check Road Fatalities, 1 May, 1993, p. 4.

9. Jacobs, G.D., Maunder, D.A.C. and Fouracre, P.R. (1986) *Characteristics of Conventional Public Transport Services in Third World Cities*, Overseas Unit, Transport and Road Research Laboratory, Surry.

10. Maunder, D.A.C. and Mbara, T.C. (1996) Liberalization of Urban Public Transport Services : What are the Implications, *Indian Journal of Transport Management*, Vol. 20, No. 3, pp. 147-154.

11. Municipal Corporation of Delhi (1994) *The Delhi Municipal Corporation Act 1957 (Act No. 66 of 1957)*, Akalank Publications, New Delhi.

12. Murthy, C.P. (1995) Customer Service in Bus Passenger Transportation, *Indian Journal of Transport Management*, Vol. 19, No. 11 pp. 681-688.

13. National Institute of Urban Affairs (1991) *Basic Services and the Urban Poor*, NIUA Research Study Series No. 46, NIUA, New Delhi.

14. National Steering Committee: India (1996) *Second United Nations Conference on Human Settlements Habitat II India*, Draft Final National Report, Society for Development Studies, New Delhi.

15. Padam, S. (1995) Transport and Regulation, *Indian Journal of Transport Management*, Vol. 19, No. 5, pp. 341-347.

16. Raina, J. (1996) Will the DTC Join the Dodo ? *The Hindustan Times*, Vol. LXXII, No. 201, p. 12.

17. Ranganathan, N. (1995) National Urban Transport Policy, *Indian Journal of Transport Management*, Vol. 19, No. 2, pp. 85-98.

18. Reddy, T.S., Chand, K. and Parida, P. (1996) Pricing Policy for Urban Bus Transport Systems, *Indian Journal of Transport Management*, Vol. 20, No. 3, pp. 213-220.

19. Sahoo, M.S. (1995) High Speed Tram: An Appropriate Public Transport System for Metropolitan Cities—A Case Study of Delhi, *Indian Journal of Transport Management*, Vol. 19, No. 6, pp. 401-413.

20. Sarna, A.C., Marwah, B.R. and Sachdeva, Y.P. (1994) Planning of an Urban Bus System—A Case Study of Delhi, *Indian Roads Congress Journal*, Vol. 55, No. 3, pp. 409-444.

21. Singh, T. (1991) Bus Transit System in Delhi, *Journal of Transport Management*, Vol. 15, No. 10, pp. 11-14.

11 MANAGEMENT OF THE ELECTRICITY SUPPLY IN DELHI

ASHOK KUMAR

Electricity supply in Delhi existed even prior to its being declared capital of India in 1911. The John Flaming Company was granted license by the Government in 1905 under the Indian Electricity Act 1903 to engage in the business of electricity supply in Delhi by establishing a small diesel generating station near Lahori Gate. This Undertaking was purchased in 1908 by a British company called "the Delhi Tramway and Lighting Company" which later changed its name to the Delhi Electric Supply and Traction Company Limited.

To meet the capital's requirement of electricity, Government of India installed steam generating station at Kingsway Camp which was operated and maintained by Central Public Works Station. Consequent to the shifting of Government of India's headquarters from Civil Lines to New Delhi, the power station was shifted to Rajghat and named as Central Power House.

The Delhi Municipal Committee took over the Power House from the CPWD in 1932. Later, Government of India appointed the Pit Ketly Committee to look into the question of electric supply in Delhi and on the recommendations of this committee, the Government established the Delhi Central Electric Power Authority Limited to whom the Rajghat Power House was transferred, followed by transfer to Distribution Undertaking of the Company in 1947.

The Delhi State Electricity Board was established in March 1951 when the Electric Supply Undertaking of the Delhi Central Electric Power Authority Limited was transferred to it. At the beginning of the First Five Year Plan, the Delhi State Electricity Board, the New Delhi Municipal Committee and the Upper Yamuna Valley Electricity Supply Company were the three organisations distributing and supplying electricity in Delhi, New Delhi and Shahdara area respectively.

With the formation of the Municipal Corporation on 7 April, 1958, the Delhi State Electricity Board stood dissolved and its functions were taken over by Municipal Corporation of Delhi who has since been performing these functions through Delhi Electric Supply Undertaking. The function of the Yamuna Valley Electric Supply Undertaking were also taken over by Delhi Electric Supply Undertaking.

The Delhi Electric Supply Undertaking also supplies bulk power to New Delhi Municipal Committee, the distribution licensee for the area is under its jurisdiction. Till sometimes back Delhi Cantonment was managed by MES. Now even this area has come under the jurisdiction of Delhi Electric Supply Undertaking.

This study is divided into three sections. After this brief introduction, major issues related to power demand and supply are discussed. Most of this discussion reveals the complete helplessness of the people of Delhi in respect of power supply. It is in the last section of this study that has been discussed for partial privatisation of electricity in Delhi. A partial privatisation is argued because of strategic significance of this service and impact on the quality of life of citizens.

PROVISION OF ELECTRICITY IN DELHI

Generation and Distribution

The electricity demand, at present, is around 1,700 to 1,800 MW per day and during peak days it exceeds even 1,800 MW. The Delhi Electric Supply Undertaking produces only 400 MW. The National Thermal Power Corporation contributes 500 MW from Badarpur Thermal

Power Station. This plant is currently suffering from coal shortages. Due to non-payment or partial payment of dues by the State Electricity Boards including the Delhi Electric Supply Undertaking the National Thermal Power Corporation left with no option but to resort to low generation.

However, the Delhi Electric Supply Undertaking heavily relies on the Northern Grid's Dadri Plant from where it gets about 900 MW. This still leaves another 250 MW demand unmet due to low generation in the Northern Grid. The Northern Grid comprises Delhi, Jammu and Kashmir, Himachal Pradesh, Rajasthan, Uttar Pradesh, Haryana and Punjab (see Tables 1 and 2).

Table 1. Generation and Distribution of Electricity

(in M.U.)

Item	*1970-71*	*1980-81*	*1990-91*	*1991-92*	*1992-93*
Locally generated	1027	1313	2351	2415	2433
Purchased from other states	362	1613	6378	6973	8115

Source: Government of the National Capital Territory of Delhi (1995: 104-107).

Table 2. Consumption Patterns of Power

Consumed for domestic purpose	233	701	2316	3110	3741
Commercial purpose	210	453	1093	1002	1024
Industrial purpose	208	590	1952	1843	2067
Public Water and Street Lighting	107	175	347	363	378
Licenses (NDMC & MES)	272	453	707	781	786
Total	1036	2372	6415	7099	7996

Source : Government of the National Capital Territory of Delhi (1995: 104-107).

The peak demand has been steadily rising on average at a rate of 100 MW annually. In winter peak demand has been more than during summer (see Table-3).

Table 3. Peak Demand in MW

Period	*Winter*	*Summer*
1992-93	1,583	1,514
1993-94	1,631	1,616
1994-95	1,898	1,820
1995-96	1,984	1,976

Source : Srivastava (1996 : 3).

Bijli cards for slum dwellers entitles households to use electricity at a flat rate. This experiment is operating in 30 settlements. Notable among them are Indira Camp in Naraina, Jawahar Camp in Kirti Nagar and G.P. 6 in Pitampura.

Consumer of Electricity Power

Number of domestic consumers of power was less than half a million in 1970-71. This figure even declined to 0.31 million in 1980-81. But after that the number of domestic consumers sharply rose to 1.42 million in 1990-91 and 1.53 million in 1991-92 (see Table 4). This trend is expected to continue at least for foreseeable future. Consequently, the ratio between industrial consumers and domestic consumers began declining in spite of the fact that number of industrial consumers has also risen. The ratio between industrial and commercial consumers was 1 : 4 in 1970-71, remained the same for the year 1980-81. But later on this ratio started declining and it was 1 : 3 in 1990-91 which further declined to 1 : 2.5 in 1991-92 and 1992-93.

Table 4. Number of Consumers of Electricity in Delhi

Category	*1970-71*	*1980-81*	*1990-91*	*1991-92*	*1992-93*
Domestic	417173	306812	1420214	1483227	1533935
Commercial	62501	162241	201725	206402	210483
Industrial	16766	41370	79385	83281	85915
Public Water Works & Street Lighting	725	1073	1898	1960	2027
Licenses (NDMC & MES)	2	2	2	2	2
Total	517167	1011498	1703224	1774881	1832362

Transmission and Distribution System

The distribution system of electricity is inadequate and not maintained according to laid down standards. Augmentation of distribution network has not kept pace with growing demand. The distribution network is capable of transporting only 1,600 MW of power. At present the system is stretched beyond its maximum limit. Majority of Power and Distribution Transformers are overloaded and 220 KV lines are saturated. The present system lacks the capability to fall back on alternative feeds in the event of its one section becoming faulty. A slight disturbance in the system is bound to lead to unannounced load shedding which the Delhi Electric Supply Undertaking covers up by attributing it to local breakdowns.

The 400 KV ring around Delhi with five steps down sub-stations is the lifeline for power distribution in the capital. Initiated long time ago, it is still far from complete. Many important 200 KV lines have also been delayed. In case the Northern Grid is able to spare more power for Delhi, the Delhi Electric Supply Undertaking system is neither capable of receiving nor distributing power to the consumers. This is demonstrated by the fact that for every unit of electricity sold by the Delhi Electric Supply Undertaking, another unit is lost during transmission or stolen by the unregistered consumers (refer Table 5).

Table 5. Power Theft Cases in Delhi between January 1995 to June 1996

Police Dist.	*Number of cases*	*Number of persons arrested*	*Number of cases pending investigation*	*Number of cases pending trial*	*Number of cases sent as untraced*	*Number of conviction*
South	242	182	166	67	9	0
South-West	15	22	10	5	—	—
North-East	60	104	27	32	1	—
Central	7	36	—	7	—	—
North	11	9	6	5	—	—
East	26	106	15	11	—	—
North-West	212	408	74	134	2	2
West	31	120	10	21	—	—
New Delhi	—	—	—	—	—	—
Total	604	987	308	282	12	2

Source: Delhi Electric Supply Undertaking (1996)

Note: —Not Applicable

Transmission losses shot to an unprecedented 50.2 per cent in January 1996 as the Delhi Electric Supply Undertaking sent out bills only for 48.2 per cent of the total number of units it distributed. This far exceeds the 7 per cent maximum transmission loss permitted by the Central Electricity Authority for intra-city distribution, technically for a network of grids with capacities of 11 KV and below (Raj, 1996: 1). Although all the circles make huge losses, the maximum loss of 68 per cent is experienced by the North-West Circle. This is closely followed by the East Circle. (see Table 6).

Table 6. Transmission and Distribution Losses of the Delhi Electric Supply Undertaking

DESU Zones	*Per cent Losses*
North-West Circle	68
East Circle	66
West Circle	61
South Circle	40
Central Circle	32
North Circle	27

Source : Raj (1996: 1).

Installed Capacity

The installed capacity in 1971-72 was just 296,200 kilowatt. This capacity declined to 275,800 in 1981-82. But the installed capacity sharply rose to 551,600 kilowatt in 1991-92 (see Table 7).

Table 7. The Installed Capacity of Electricity in Delhi

(in Kilowatt)

Period	*Installed Capacity**	*Derated Capacity**
1971-72	296,200	282,600
1981-82	275,800	258,000
1991-92	551,600	544,000

Source : Government of the National Capital Territory of Delhi (1995: 103).

Note: *Excluding the share of the HSEB at I.P. Station.

The Delhi Electric Supply Undertaking's Inability to Spend Plan Funds

The Delhi Electric Supply Undertaking is unable to spend its plan funds. The Delhi Electric Supply Undertaking was allocated Rs. 85 crore in 1993-94 and Rs. 150 crore in 1994-95 for strengthening the transmission and distribution system which it could not spend fully. The Delhi Electric Supply Undertaking's Additional Manager (Transmission and Distribution) himself admitted that it could not spend Rs. 3.5 crore meant for the installation of shunt capacitors-devices used to control voltage fluctuations. Then out of a total of 22 cable fault locating vans, only two are in a working condition.

Power Tariffs

Power tariffs were last revised in October 1993. At present every unit costs DESU Rs.1.80. Now 50 per cent increase is expected in industrial tariffs from October 1996 from the present Rs. 100 per kilo volt ampere to Rs.1.50. Fuel adjustment charges, i.e., hike in tariff due to hike in the price of raw material used in the production of electricity is allowed only on industrial users and the Delhi Electric Supply Undertaking looses Rs. 30 crore every month due to FAC which cannot be levied on agricultural and domestic users (see Table 8).

Table 8. Power Tariffs Before and After 1993

Power Tariff before 1993	*After 1993*
0.40 paise for the first 100 units	0.60 paise
0.50 paise for the next 100 units	Re. 1.00
Rs. 1.50 for the next 100 units	Rs. 1.80
Rs. 2.00 for over 300 units	Rs. 2.40

At present the Delhi Electric Supply Undertaking's inability to collect revenue for the energy used by the consumer is probably one of the major causes of its inability to pay for the power purchased, and consequently leading to reduced availability of power. Average price of power purchased by the Delhi Electric Supply Undertaking's gas turbines is Rs. 1.60 per unit and by thermal plants it is Rs. 1.35 per unit.

Average price of the Delhi Electric Supply Undertaking's own generation is around Rs. 1.45 per unit. In turn the Delhi Electric Supply Undertaking sell it to the consumers at an average price of Rs. 1.80 per unit inclusive of penal charge.

The Debt Trap of the Delhi Electric Supply Undertaking

The vicious circle of debt trap not only affects the operational efficiency of the Delhi Electric Supply Undertaking but also the concerned organisations (refer Table 9). For example, the Badarpur Thermal Power Station has very little coal to produce electricity because the Delhi Electric Supply Undertaking has not paid the Power Station for the power purchased by it. Consequently, the Badarpur Thermal Power Station owes Rs. 700 crore to the Indian Railways and Rs. 358 crore to the Coal India Limited. Whereas the NTPC supplies power worth Rs. 75 crore per month, the Delhi Electric Supply Undertaking pays only Rs. 55 crore. Similarly the Delhi Electric Supply Undertaking draws power worth about Rs. 46 crore per month from the Badarpur Station and pays only Rs. 10 crore plus Rs. 22.5 crore from the Central Appropriation to Delhi. The Delhi Electric Supply Undertaking's debt is nearly one and a half times of Delhi's annual budget. Based on current estimates, it is possible to construct a brand new power plant of 1,000 MW with the amount owed to Badarpur Thermal Power Station. In 1989, Government wrote off Rs. 1,109 crore leaving the debt at Rs. 380 crore only.

Table 9. The Debt Trap of the Delhi Electric Supply Undertaking

Thermal	*Rs. in crores*		
Badarpur Thermal Power Station	Power	4,800	since 1989
National Thermal Power Corporation	Power	600	
Indian Railways	Coal	100	
Coal India Limited	Coal	32	
Total		5,600	

Source : Pandey (1996: 1).

Safety from Electricity

The Delhi Electric Supply Undertaking has provided standards for the removal of those buildings/parts of buildings as per stipulations of the Indian Electricity Rules 1956, which have become accessible to the electric mains and may cause accident due to that accessibility (refer Table 10).

Table 10. Standards for the Minimum Clearances from the Buildings

Voltage Level	*Horizontal (mts.)*	*Vertical (mts.)*
Upto 650 Volts	1.2	2.5
Above 650 Volts and upto 11 KV	1.2	3.7
Above 11 KV and upto 33 KV	2.0	3.7
Above 33 KV and upto 66 KV	2.3	4.0
Above 66 KV and upto 220 KV	3.8	5.5

When the Delhi Electric Supply Undertaking lays lines it secures permission in the form of right of way from the competent authority. But people while making illegal and unauthorised constructions and alterations encroach upon the right of way of the Delhi Electric Supply Undertaking's electric lines. This causes a grave danger to both human life and property. Moreover, the Delhi Electric Supply Undertaking experiences frequent interruptions in the distribution of power supply. Therefore, the Delhi Electric Supply Undertaking has devised a set of norms whereby minimum voltage levels in respect of horizontal and vertical distances from buildings are expressed (see Table 8). The Delhi Electric Supply Undertaking has also provided that people who have encoached upon its right-of-way can be helped whereby the Delhi Electric Supply Undertaking will remove and/or shift lines provided a payment to that effect is made. One such accident occurred in Delhi where more than 19 people died in Khari Baoli area due to the fire caused by an electric short circuit.

Load-Shedding

The Delhi Electric Supply Undertaking contends that they are shedding load because the frequency is dipping below the normal 50 Hertz. Basically load-shedding is generally used for the maintenance of the grid system. But the Delhi Electric Supply Undertaking uses it for emergency purposes as a load management tool.

The frequency of power supply from the Northern Grid hovered dangerously around 48 Hertz or Hz. Additionally, the voltage generally hovers around 170 volts. The ideal frequency that the Delhi Electric Supply Undertaking gets from the Northern Grid is 50 Hertz. If the frequency level goes down to 47.6 Hertz, the Northern Grid will collapse. To maintain the frequency well about 47.6 Hertz the Delhi Electric Supply Undertaking had installed 'under frequency relay system' to avoid complete collapse of the Northern Grid. However, other states follow no such discipline. Another operational difficulty is that of shortage of coal supplies to power plants in Indraprastha Estate, Rajghat and Northern Grid power plants. Quality of coal is also very poor. Consequently boilers get spoiled and pollution levels increase. In a recent move the Delhi Electric Supply Undertaking has also removed its 'under frequency relay system' until after other states install theirs. But this has led to a lot of uncertainty.

Work Culture in the Delhi Electric Supply Undertaking

The Delhi Electric Supply Undertaking's losses due to theft of power are as high as 50 per cent of the total transmission and distribution. Further the Delhi Electric Supply Undertaking officials are extremely inaccessible. Consequently the complaints of the public are not attended to and the complaint centres do not function. To make things worse there are large number of cases of overbilling by the Delhi Electric Supply Undertaking. The Delhi Electric Supply Undertaking employs 25,000 strong workforce.

POLICY PROPOSALS FOR EFFECTIVE MANAGEMENT OF POWER

Minor Policy Changes Resolve Nothing

Minor policy changes have been taking place throughout the 1990s. But minor policy changes have not been able to resolve any of the problems and issues. At the most the major issues of power have been postponed hoping for the better. For example, attempts to curb power thefts have led to some policy changes. The Delhi Government has made the following policy changes:

(a) The circle-heads have been given the responsibility of billing and recovery.

(b) Commercial establishments in residential areas have been allowed sanctioned load of two kilowatt instead of one kilowatt allowed earlier.

(c) Khurana Government also introduced a scheme of voluntary declaration and regularisation. According to this scheme, commercial and industrial consumers can declare the actual load they are drawing and get that load regularized after a small payment. This is applicable to unregistered residential consumers.

(d) Government would also allow one point and two-point regular electricity connections to the residents of slums for a flat monthly fee.

(e) It is expected that the Delhi Electric Supply Undertaking may be transferred to the Delhi Government from Union Government. It is also expected that its losses may not be transferred to the Delhi Government. This means that the Delhi Electric Supply Undertaking will have another chance to renovate itself under the administrative control of Delhi Government.

Take another example for illustration. The Delhi Electric Supply Undertaking has enforced regulatory measures in July, 1996 to improve power shortage situation in the capital under the proviso of the Delhi Electric Control Order 1959 :

(a) All industries in Delhi will observe 5 days week.

(b) Air-Conditioning load is not allowed to any consumer during peak period.

(c) Neon signs, decorative lights, advertising lights etc. are banned even with DG sets.

(d) Temporary connections are prohibited even for marriages. The consumers may, however, use DG sets.

(e) Industries shall continue to strictly observe peak load restrictions as already in vogue.

But little attention has been paid to devising appropriate enforcement mechanisms. To begin with a great deal of policy change is required in respect of operationalisation of enforcement teams including their training.

Privatisation is the Master Strategy

Government of Delhi has been in favour of privatisation of electricity since long. Speaking in 1995 Delhi's then Lt. Governor PK Dave noted "A private operator will not allow thefts, slowing of meters and illegal connections, Calcutta which faced almost similar power crisis as Delhi sometime back, is now finding its power position very satisfactory, the power being supplied by a private company of RP Goenka Group" (Mohapatra, 1995: 3). Consequently, the Delhi Government was engaged in finding out a solution to power crisis through privatisation. At present the top bureaucrats of Delhi Administration are busy in completing a study about the fate of the Delhi Electric Supply Undertaking when it is handed over to it by Central Government. The study group has indicated that they will recommend that the Delhi Electric Supply Undertaking should be completely privatised and Delhi Administration should completely withdraw from the loss making power sector. Major proposals are:

(a) To hand over government managed power generation plants to private companies.

(b) The Delhi Electric Supply Undertaking employees should be rehabilitated in a phased manner.

(c) Two organisations will be created. The Power Generation Corporation of Delhi will handle power generation, and the Grid Corporation of Delhi will work for power transmission and system operations, and distribution. However, initially only one company will look after generation and distribution.

(d) The Grid Corporation of Delhi will create its distribution divisions and sub-let "the divisions" rights to other small companies through competitive bidding.

(e) There will be the Delhi Electricity Regulatory Board which will oversee but have no involvement in operations. It will only regulate the private companies handling power distribution, generation and transmission.

(f) The Delhi Electricity Regulatory Board will be a policy making body and license issuing authority.

The Delhi Model of electricity privatisation is based on the Orissa Model of power reforms. It is expected that the tariffs may rise both for the bulk supply as well as for the retail supply. But reforms will introduce the practice of private sector management of power plants which is presumed to be more efficient than the public management. It is further expected that this process will result in the decentralization of power generation.

The Power reforms introduced in Orissa have remained a 'non-starter'. Although on the face of it, the concept may look to be a rational step, it would create a lot of confusion and paralyse the pattern of coordinated working and dilute accountability. It may also lead to the introduction of different tariffs for different licensee areas in the same state.

Therefore, it could be safely argued that private sector's involvement in the power sector will also not work if the following factors are not taken into consideration. First, negotiations and the MoU route should not be adopted to replace competitive bidding method for the selection of power suppliers. Second, the consumers of power should be involved in decisions about privatisation at all levels. Lack of transparency in deals between the private sector and the Delhi Government would eventually fail the strategy of privatisation. Further, poor financial viability of the State Electricity Undertaking may not inspire the confidence of the private sector. Therefore, the Delhi Electric Supply Undertaking has to take steps to augment its paying capacity for the power purchased from the private sector.

Experiences with Privatisation

In June 1996 the Trans Yamuna area was chosen for partial privatisation of electricity on experimental basis. By the end of 1996, billing, meter reading and distribution of power will be privatised in the Trans Yamuna area. Delhi Government argues that this area has been chosen for there exist two clearly identifiable grids which supply power to this area. This clear demarcation of area will help to carry out this experiment.

In August 1996, the Delhi Electric Supply Undertaking floated tenders to invite participation of the private sector in the distribution of bills and disconnection notices. Many reputed courier companies will be engaged in the distribution of almost 5.5 lakh electricity bills every month. The Delhi Electric Supply Undertaking expects that private sector's involvement would help in breaking the nexus of corruption among various departments of the Undertaking. This will also improve revenue collection. Note that the Delhi Electric Supply Undertaking is loosing Rs. 400 crore every year from inadequate revenue collection methods alone.

It is not that the Delhi Electric Supply Undertaking is not making efforts to set its house in order and to shore up its plunging revenues. The Delhi Electric Supply Undertaking is going to create a new internal audit cell. This proposal has been sent to the Delhi Electric Supply Committee for approval.

(a) It has not been able to check leakages and prevent other losses.

(b) The Delhi Electric Supply Undertaking has not been able to respond adequately to the external audit observations, reviews/drafts and reports received from Municipal Chief Auditor and/or the Accountant General Delhi.

(c) Responding to the objections of these audits is a task entrusted to the same staff who makes the Delhi Electric Supply Undertaking's monthly/ annual accounts and thus the compilation of these accounts suffers from chronic delays.

Strategic Planning by the National Capital Region Board

The National Capital Region Board is working to prepare a strategy to reduce the demand of power on the Delhi Electric Supply Undertaking. It has proposed gas based captive power plants for 12 districts including Ghaziabad, Bulandshahar, Hapur, Meerut and Khurja in Uttar Pradesh; Faridabad, Gurgaon, Rewari, Rohtak and Panipat in Haryana; and Bhiwadi and Alwar in Rajasthan. This project will cost Rs. 3,600 crore at current prices. However, it will be able to produce power with tarrif rates lower than the Delhi Electric Supply Undertaking. Among other things cheaper power will be an added attraction for polluting industrial units which are beginning to relocate in the National Capital Region excluding the Delhi Metropolitan Area. This will bring down not only the pollution levels but also the demand for electricity distributed by the Delhi Electric Supply Undertaking. It is pertinent to note that 25 per cent demand for power in Delhi is by the industrial sector which comprises of more than 90,000 units. But this plan may be realized only by the end of the Ninth Five Year Plan.

Application of the Law and Other Experiences

Power consumers of the metropolis have learnt to live with the darkness. Small interruptions and power breakdowns no more evoke reactions. Poor quality of supply does not bother the consumers who are happy as long as lamps light up and fans hover over their heads, especially in a situation where the top administrative and technical managers in the Delhi Electric Supply Undertaking continue in their present attitude of justifying the Delhi Electric Supply Undertaking and proceed on the basis that consumer is generally wrong. This is a radical contrast to the consumer orientation of the BEST, also an undertaking of the Municipal Corporation Mumbai along with the BSES, a private sector company in Mumbai. Further example is that of the Ahmedabad Electricity Company which serves Ahmedabad city as well as Gujarat's state capital Gandhinagar.

Political will and unstinted administration support is a prerequisite for any meaningful change in the prevailing sordid affairs of the Delhi Electric Supply Undertaking. So far it has been lacking any bold policy steps and half hearted efforts have not made any dent.

To commence with, a public utility like the Delhi Electric Supply Undertaking should be subject to all the proviso of the Indian Electricity Act 1910 and its Rules as may be applicable to any private licensee. This will help to ensure that relevant aspect of the operations of the utility are transparent to the public and the consumer to the same extent, as in the case of a private licensee. The fact that the Municipal Corporation controls the Delhi Electric Supply Undertaking cannot be taken to be an adequate condition for the transparency of its operations or for protecting the entitlements of consumers, as experience has shown in more than ample measure.

At present, the Delhi Electric Supply Undertaking by virtue of Section 277 of the Municipal Corporation Act 1957 has been exempted from the proviso of Sections 3 to 11 of the Indian Electricity Act 1910 as well as from the

Clauses I to IX of the Schedule of the Indian Electricity Act which include stipulations regarding preparation of Annual Accounts as a licensee and submission of the same to the State Government within a specified time limit. Further, the Delhi Electric Supply Undertaking being a wing of the local authority has also been exempted from the provision of the Sixth Schedule of the Electricity (Supply) Act 1948, which regulates licensee's charges to its consumers. It may be mentioned here that private licensees such as the BSES of Mumbai and the Ahmedabad Electricity Company do not have the privilege of enjoying above mentioned exemptions and are, therefore, answerable to the Government in respect of maintenance of an economic supply system as well as reasonableness of charges levied on the consumers.

The spread between the cost of the utility per unit bought and the sale price per unit was 27.28 paise in 1990-91, 26.53 in 1991-92 and 41.88 paise in 1992-93 in the BEST of Mumbai and minus 34 paise in 1990-91 in the Delhi Electric Supply Undertaking. Since the Delhi Electric Supply Undertaking is running in loss, it is essential to urgently explore a predetermined schedule of rates and also reduce the surplus staff which is almost twice that of the justifiable number as compared to Mumbai utilities. Similarly there is a need to reduce the transmission and distribution losses to around 13 per cent.

The present policy of revising tariffs as per stipulations contained in paragraph one of the Sixth Schedule to the Electricity Supply Act 1948 which is to permit the licensee to so adjust his charges for the sale of electricity, whether by enhancing or reducing them that his clear profit in any year of account shall not, as far as possible, exceed the amount of reasonable return. This does not leave any scope for covering the operational and other inefficiencies of the utility.

REFERENCES

1. Government of the National Capital Territory of Delhi (1995) *Delhi Statistical Handbook*, Directorate of Economics and Statistics, Government of the National Capital Territory of Delhi, Delhi.

2. Mohapatra, S. (1995) I am not Enthused by Trams : Dave, *The Hindustan Times*, p. 3.

3. Pandey, V. (1996) The DESU puts a load of Rs. 5,600 crores on creditors, *The Times of India*, Vol. CLIX. No. 179, p. 1.

4. Radhika, V. (1996) DESU Likely to Make Way for Private Companies, *The Pioneer*, Vol. 6, No. 207, p. 1.

5. Raj, Y. (1996) Power Theft Bludgeons DESU Reforms, *The Times of India*, Vol. CLIX. No. 128, p. 1.

6. Srivastava, A. (1996) Power Cuts are More Due to Thefts than Demand, *The Times of India*, Vol. CLIX, No. 113, p. 3.

7. Tewari, V. (1996) New Plan may Help Provide Better Power Supply for Delhi, *The Times of India*, Vol. CLIX, No. 150, p. 3.

12 AN AVOIDABLE CRISIS OF THE SAFE DRINKING WATER IN DELHI

ASHOK KUMAR

The decade of 1981-91 was decleared the International Drinking Water Supply and Sanitation Decade. The Government of India, in response, prepared a National Master Plan for Water Supply and Sanitation Sector in 1983. The Government also committed itself "to provide safe drinking water on a sustainable basis to the entire population in the rural areas and to a larger population in the urban areas with local participation" (Eighth Five Year Plan). As far as Delhi is concerned, Central Government spent Rs. 14,500 lakh in 1993-94. Central Government is expected to make an anticipated expenditure of Rs. 18,000 lakh in 1994-95 and it had approved an outlay amounting to Rs. 21,050 lakh in 1995-96 (Government of India, 1996: 557).

The main source of water supply in Delhi during the olden days was the shallow wells. The wells were found inadequate and untenable on sanitary grounds. Many wells used to go dry during the summer. In 1889, several wells were dug up near Chandrawal and water supplied through a reservoir built at the Ridge. Later with the coming up of New Delhi and Cantonment, this system was changed to direct drawal of raw water from the river Yamuna at Wazirabad which was carried by gravity through masonary conduits to Chandrawal for treatment in sand filters. In 1926, the Delhi Joint Water and Sewage Board was set-up for efficient supply of water and sewage disposal. With the increase in population of Delhi and New Delhi, water works at Wazirabad and Chadrawal were expanded to cope with the demand. A barrage was constructed in 1959 across the river Yamuna near Wazirabad to store water. Additional intake works and treatment plant at Okhla in South Delhi were also constructed. Ranney Wells were sunk in Shahdara and tubewells in South Delhi and West Delhi to augment the supply of water in the city.

Many aspects of water supply become very important. First, it is at the heart of the issue of water supply that the authorities are aware of the quantity of water available from different sources and their reliability and sustainability over a short and long period of time. Second vital concern is the existence of an efficient distribution system with minimum wastage during distribution. Third important aspect is the pricing policy of the authorities controlling water supply networks. Fourth, it is equally important how much, i.e., quantity of water that is actually reaching consumers. Fifthly, what are the techniques used by individuals to augment, the deficit, if any, in the quantity of water required by the consumers. Lastly, it is extremely important that adequate number and capacity treatment plants are available to treat the raw water. These concerns are discussed and analysed in the next section. The last section contains long-term policies for the provision of potable water.

Water Supply and Demand in Delhi

The Delhi Water Supply and Sewage Disposal Undertaking of the Municipal Corporation of Delhi is engaged in providing water and sewerage services to the citizens of Delhi. It provides water in bulk to the New Delhi Municipal Council and Cantonment. In the Municipal Corporation of Delhi area water is supplied through a network of reservoirs, pumping stations and distribution mains. The task is challenging because the city is growing very fast and ever increasing population is showing no signs of abatement.

Quantity, Quality and Sources of Water

A total of over 1,350 MLD of water was achieved by completing water treatment plants of 454 MLD capacity each at Haiderpur in 1981 and thereafter at Gokalpuri, Shahdara by June 1987 and the Second 454 MLD Plant at Haiderpur in 1994 (also refer Table 1).

Table 1. Population and Water Situation, 1951-2001

Year	*Population in lakhs*	*Average Supply in MLD*	*Litres Per Capita Daily*
1951	17.50	190	108
1961	26.50	440	166
1977	41.00	785	190
1981	62.00	1150	185
1991	93.70	2160	231
1995	105.00	2860	272
2001	128.00	3250	275

Source : Delhi Water Supply and Sewage Disposal Undertaking (1996).

In Delhi the sources of raw water include the rivers Yamuna which supplies 65 per cent, river Ganges which contributes 25 per cent, and another 10 per cent is supplied by ground water (Swamy, 1987: 60).

In Delhi in 1981, 98 per cent population was covered by water supply facilities. But this coverage do not reflect either the inadequacy of water supplied or the deprivation of the urban poor (Planning Commission, 1985: 304). In the same year service level was 240 litres per capita daily which is well above the standard of 202.5 LPCD set out by the Zakaria Committee for cities over 5 lakh population.

According to the most recent estimates water supply coverage in Delhi is cent per cent both in terms of area and population. Per capita water supply was 488 LPCD in 1989-90. In Delhi sources of water for the urban poor (see

Table 2), according to the National Institute of Urban Affairs study of 4,073 households are:

Table 2. Sources of Potable Water Supply

Source	*Percentage of Supply*
Tap	62
Handpump	36
Mark II Handpumps	2

National Institute of Urban Affairs (1991: 46).

This means that Delhi's urban poor heavily rely on shallow handpumps. The UNICEF's initiative to launch deep bored handpumps of Mark II type has been restricted only to very few areas.

This study also revealed that out of 4,073 sampled households 78 per cent used community water connections and only 22 per cent had private water connections (National Institute of Urban Affairs, 1991: 49). This points to the fact that government needs to focus on development and maintenance of community water connections. However, a staggering 42 per cent households have to travel as far as more than 100 feet to fetch potable water (see Table 3).

Table 3. Distance from Community Sources of Water Supply

Distance in Feet	*Per cent Households*
> 50	25
50-100	29
> 100	42
No response	4

(National Institute of Urban Affairs, 1991: 51).

Out of 4,073 households surveyed in Delhi, 66 per cent stated that water they get is safe for drinking. Whereas 33 per cent said it was not potable and 1 per cent gave no response (National Institute of Urban Affairs, 1991: 58).

Nationally, 81 per cent say that they get potable water. Therefore, more than one-third of Delhi's urban poor are not satisfied with the quality of water that they get. However, the drinking water supplied by the Undertaking is potable and conforms to the standards laid down by the Ministry of Urban Development. The quality of water is checked at every stage of treatment right from the raw water stage upto storage in service reservoirs and also in the distribution system at the consumer's end. Water supplied from Ranney Wells and tubewells is also tested on regular basis. With a view to ensuring that no contamination takes place during the transmission of water through municipal mains, water samples are lifted daily from the distribution system including individual taps and public hydrants.

Water Supply Distribution System

Since in Delhi the quantity of water supplied through the water distribution system is always less than the quantity of water received by the consumers, it is pertinent to analyse the limitations of the water distribution system. Whether the loss is normal or excessive. We should also know at what stages of the distribution system the wastage or loss take place and why. In most of the households connected with the municipal water pipes, supply is intermittent, viz., two-hour in the morning and two-hour during the evening.

Water is supplied through large service reservoirs and local overhead tanks along with direct boosting in smaller pockets at tail ends. In 1986-87 there were 34 service reservoirs, 55 overhead tanks, 82 booster pumping stations, 168 tubewells, and 10 Ranney Wells. In the same year, the Delhi Water Supply and Sewage Disposal Undertaking had 500 km. length of trunk mains and 3,192 km. length of distribution mains (Swamy, 1987: 61). Most of the funds of the Delhi Water Supply and Sewage Disposal Undertaking are invested in water works outlays. For example, the distribution systems account for as much as

40 per cent to 70 per cent investment in water supply projects in large cities of water works outlay (see table 4).

Table 4. Expenditure on Water Supply in Delhi

Item	*Per cent Expenditure*
Electricity	19.0
Chemicals	5.5
Establishment	20.0
Repair/Maintenance	18.0
Loan repayment	37.0
Miscellaneous	0.5
Total	100.00

Presently, there are 58 underground reservoirs having total capacity of 580 ML and 55 overhead tanks having a total capacity of 82.13 ML. There are also 152 boosting stations spread all over Delhi. To further improve and to rationalise the distribution system, a computer-based study was undertaken by the Undertaking a few years back. The study has indicated the necessity for the construction of 22 ground reservoirs along with the boosting arrangement at different locations and strengthen the trunk transmission system at certain locations. So far 10 ground reservoirs at Khyala, Geeta Colony, Deer Park, Subhash Park, Janak Puri, Bodela, Idgah, Punjabi Bagh, Model Town and Najafgarh have been commissioned. In order to strengthen the distribution system, the work of construction of underground reservoir and booster pumping stations is in progress at Shastri Nagar, Keshopuram, Sanjay Gandhi Transport Nagar, Holambi-Kalan and Rohini Sector XIX. The underground reservoir and booster pumping station at Rohini Sector XI has been taken as a deposit work on behalf of the Delhi Development Authority. The land has been acquired for the construction of underground reservoir and booster pumping station at Malviya Nagar.

But one of the major problems of water supply in

metropolitan cities is the old and obsolete distribution system. The undersized distribution grids need enlargement or replacement. Then the transmission mains (1,050 mm to 1,800 mm diameter) were laid during the early twentieth century. These mains are generally made of steel riveted construction and subject to high degree of corrosion-resulting in frequent bursting or leakage. "Refurbishing of these mains is a great of challenge when one thinks about the narrow, congested roads of the city, bustling with a high density of traffic on the surface and a multiple number of utility services underground, viz., high and low tension electric cables, telephone cables, gas mains, sewers, unfiltered water mains and reserve mains as well as service mains for filtered water supply" (Bhattacharya, 1988: 59). It is estimated that in order to overhaul or replace corroded distribution system in Delhi more than Rs. 26 crore is needed (Swamy, 1987: 62).

This distribution system is further rigged by those colonizers where municipal water connections are not available for development is unauthorised. But due to a criminal nexus between the politicians and municipal officials on one hand and residents of the unauthorised colonies on the other, the distribution system is extended to areas without any consideration, least of all engineering considerations.

Pricing Policy

At present the pricing policy merely includes billing. But the author of this study looks at it from a cohesive point of view which, to begin with, includes the price for the procurement of raw water if the source is not under the jurisdiction of a local authority? What is the cost of transportation of raw water to the treatment plant? What are the losses at this stage? Whether billing of potable water relates to its delivery at a consumption point. This is important not only from the point of view of sustainability of the existing networks but also for augmentation, replacement and further development.

In Delhi payment for water is required to be made by all those who have a municipal water connection. But not all tap owners pay for water. For example out of a sampled 902 households 49 per cent never made any payment for owning a private tap (National Institute of Urban Affairs, 1991: 54). Others who made payments paid less than Rs. 25 per month and only 15 per cent paid more than Rs. 25 per month (National Institute of Urban Affairs, 1991: 54). As far as the pricing policy is concerned, in Delhi, the sliding scale is used for water tariffs :

Domestic :

(a) 35 paise per KL upto 25 KL/month

(b) 70 paise per KL beyond 25 KL/month

Non-domestic :

(c) Rs. 2 per KL per month upto 100 KL/month

(d) Rs. 2.25 KL per mongh beyond 100 KL/month

But the cost of production of water is 46 paise per KL and the distribution cost is 25 paise per KL.

Techniques Used by Individuals to Augment Water Deficit

Water is a precious commodity in the metropolitan cities. What a local authority can provide is not sufficient to meet the drinking, washing, cleaning and other needs. Therefore, individuals turn to other means in order to augment what is being supplied by local authorities.

In Delhi booster pumps (commonly known as motors) are installed almost in all houses including the LIG category households. This effectively means that either the booster draws water quickly from the Municipal Corporation of Delhi pipes or water is drawn from the ground itself. If it is drawn from the Municipal Corporation of Delhi's pipes, some people living at the higher floors in flats receive less water than those who own boosters. Some households may even go without water. As far as urban poor of Delhi are concerned, the situation is dismal to say the least. For instance, in Delhi 59 per cent surveyed households from a total of 4,073 households considered that water supply was inadequate, only 40 per cent said adequate and 1 per cent had no response to offer (National Institute of Urban Affairs, 1991: 56).

Capacity and Number of Water Treatment Plants

At present the Delhi Water Supply and Sewage Disposal Undertaking has the installed capacity of 525 MGD. However, with a population expected to rise to 12.8 million by 2001, Delhi would require at least 1,024 MGD of water. How to get that 499 MGD water will pose a serious threat to the Delhi Water Supply and Sewage Disposal Undertaking (also refer Table 5).

Table 5. Installed Capacity of Various Water Works

(MGD)

Name of the Water Works	*Plan Period* I	*II*	*III*	*IV*	*V*	*VI*	*March 1994*
Chandrawal	60	90	90	90	90	90	90
Wazirabad	—	—	40	80	80	80	120
Ranney Wells and Tubewells	—	—	—	5	20	30	53
Haiderpur	—	—	—	—	50	100	150
Bhagirathi Shahadara	—	—	—	—	—	37	100
Okhla	—	—	—	—	—	—	12
Total	60	90	130	175	240	337	525

Source : Government of the National Capital Territory of Delhi (1995: 266).

Finances Available for Development and Upgradation

The provision of water by the Municipal Corporation of Delhi is still considered as a service rather than a venture which could also become a great source of revenue (see Table 6). This creates serious constraints for the operation, maintenance of the existing distribution system and for undertaking the new development works. In 1986-87, Rs. 23 crore was provided for the capital works and Rs. 45 crore for operation and maintenance. In the Seventh Five Year Plan outlay was Rs. 136.95 crore.

The Delhi Water Supply and Sewage Disposal Undertaking could earn only half of what it spends to supply water (see Table 6).

Tablc 6. Revenue and Expenditure of the Undertaking

Year	*Revenue*	*Expenditure* *(Rupees in lakhs)*
1991	6602.20	12,965.00
1992	7503.39	12,220.76
1993	7681.10	14,200.00
1994 (6 months)	7887.22	7,494.70

Source : Delhi Water Supply and Sewage Disposal Undertaking (1996).

But capital works will be financed by loan from the Ministry of Urban Affairs and Employment at a very high interest rate of 9.25 per cent per annum. Situation is further aggravated by errors in bills. The Delhi Water Supply and Sewage Disposal Undertaking gets more than 50 per cent revenue from non-domestic connections.

Growth of the Personnel

Personnel management including recruitment policy, union activities, inside and outside training facilities and project management need to be considered more seriously. The Delhi Water Supply and Sewage Disposal Undertaking employed 17,620 workers which included 13,250 permanent and 4,370 casual workers in 1987. The Delhi Water Supply and Sewage Disposal Undertaking's major departments include Public Relations, Grievances Cell and Complaint Centres. But all of them are required to be strengthened. To oversee the working of these departments, the Delhi Water Supply and Sewage Disposal Committee has been created which includes 4 elected and 3 nominated members. Commissioner is the chief executive who is assisted by the Deputy Commissioner (Water) in administrative matters. Technical aspects are looked after by the Engineer-in-Chief who is assisted by 4 Chief Engineers and other engineers. Delhi is divided into 11 circles and 42 divisions. Additionally, the bulk supply is made to the New Delhi Municipal Council and Cantonment Board.

After the coming into force of the Delhi Municipal Corporation Act 1957, the Board ceased to exist and its functions were taken over by the Delhi Water Supply and Sewage Disposal Undertaking of the Corporation. The Water Supply and Sewage Disposal Committee is responsible for the conduct and management of the Undertaking.

Conservation of Water

The importance of conservation of potable water is not fully realized by the Delhi Water Supply and Sewage Disposal Undertaking and the residents of Delhi. Firstly, the attitude of authorities must change. Large dia pipes supplying water remain open and/or fractured for days. Water is wasted for it flows into drains. Secondly, unscrupulous elements steal water from the Municipal Corporation's pipes. This phenomenon is becoming ubiquitious in Delhi. As a consequence more often than not water mixes with sewer or other particles of dirt and falls below the standards set out for quality of potable water. Further, people at home do not conserve water because it comes cheaper. Therefore, pricing policy has larger implications. At present one has to pay at a flat rate of only Rs. 25 per month for water if water meter is stolen.

There is unaccounted water to the extent of 35 per cent of total water supplied. Most of the water is wasted due to pilferage of fittings and lack of leak detection by sophisticated electronic instruments. Furthermore, quality of pipes is not good and workmanship is extremely bad. It is estimated that there were as many as 253,977 unauthorised connections in 1992-93.

There are hidden leakages in the distribution system, service pipes, reservoirs etc. which do not come above the surface. The Delhi Water Supply and Sewage Disposal Undertaking has set-up a Leak Detection Cell a few years back. The Cell is equipped with electronic instruments and trained personnel for the detection of hidden leakages.

The Cell has done useful work in detecting many leakages in the distribution system. This has resulted in improvement in water pressure and also helped in reducing wastage and conservation of filtered water. Government attitude towards conservation of water is also beginning to change. For instance, recently, Government has accorded conservation of filtered water in Delhi has been given the highest priority. Use of filtered water in industries and for irrigation of lawns and park is being reduced gradually by sinking more tubewells and using treated effluent. All local bodies and group housing societies have been advised to sink tubewells for gardening of their lawns and parks.

Consumption of Water

For every three metered connections, there existed one unmetered connection in 1992-93. This ratio has continued since 1980-81 (see Table 7).

Table 7. Power Situation in Delhi between 1980-81 and 1992-93

	1980-81	*1990-91*	*1991-92*	*1992-93*
Number of Metered Connections	355157	678461	700923	745029
Number of Unmetered Connections	13143	226960	245451	253977
Water Consumption (in Lakh K. Litres)	1953	4540	4456	4649
Domestic	1542	4013	4049	4082
Commercial/ Industrial	411	527	407	567
Per Capita Consumption of Water	33	—	149	143

Source : Government of the National Capital Territory of Delhi (1995: 268-269).

Policies to Avoid an Avoidable Crisis

Medium and Long Term Proposals for the Augmentation of Water

Special efforts have been made to optimise production of water at the existing plants. Production capacity will be further augmented progressively by taking following measures:

The second Master Plan of Delhi envisages a population of 12.8 million by 2001 AD for which demand of water would be 3,520 MLD at the rate of 275 litres per capita daily. To meet this requirement, the projects finalised for the augmentation of water supply are:

(a) 182 MLD water treatment plant at Nangloi area,

(b) 91 MLD water treatment plant at Bawana and three Ranney Wells in Alipur Block which will give a yield of 45 MLD.

The above proposals are based on the exchange of raw water meant for irrigation purposes with treated effluent from Okhla and Rithala Sewage Plants.

For further augmentation of Delhi's water supply, the following three sources have been identified:

(a) Release of 300 Cusecs of Water from the Tehri Dam

There is a proposal for getting water for Delhi from the proposed Tehri Dam at present under construction in Uttar Pradesh. This 300 cusecs of water from Tehri Dam will become available for Delhi's water supply through the Upper Ganga Canal near Murad Nagar. A conduit between Murad Nagar and Delhi is proposed to be constructed by the Uttar Pradesh Jal Nigam as a deposit work. A new 637 MLD water treatment plant near Wazirabad in Trans-Yamuna area is proposed on the basis of supply of 300 cusecs of water from the Tehri Dam which is scheduled to be completed by 1999. Steps have been taken to acquire land in Trans-Yamuna area for the construction of this water plant. The construction process should be speeded up for timely completion.

(b) Share of Delhi in Yamuna Water

With a view to meeting the increased drinking water requirement of Delhi upto 2001 A.D., the basin states including Uttar Pradesh, Haryana, Himachal Pradesh, Rajasthan and Delhi have agreed sharing of Yamuna water upto Okhla and an agreement was signed on 12 May, 1994 by the Chief Ministers of these states. Under this agreement Delhi has been allocated a share of 0.724 BCM (consumptive) of water in Yamuna on yearly basis. Additional water would become available in the Yamuna river on the completion of two proposed storage dams. However, till the dams are completed, seasonal allocation will be made as an interim arrangement. The above basin states also agreed to constitute the Upper Yamuna Board through an agreement signed on 2 September, 1994 for implementation of the agreement in respect of sharing of Yamuna water amongst the basin states.

Medium to Short Term Policies

1. The distribution problems can be solved by maintaining system records relating to consumer complaints, maintaining service laying, burst mains, burst service pipes, general maintenance of equipment, leakage control, residual pressures, daily demands and night line measurements, service reservoir levels, booster outputs, quality output from source works and in distribution. The above data should be collected for different areas separately so that the effect of climate, soil type, water quality and other local characteristics can be assessed. Trends of this data will help in making considered decisions for the future Lackington (1988: 266).
2. Delhi is dependent for raw water on the states of Uttar Pradesh, Haryana etc. Coordination problem has to be sorted out so that regular supply of raw water is maintained.
3. Fourteen new reservoirs are required to be constructed. Work must begin on all of them in earnest so that the enhanced demand is met.

4. Conservation of water by leak detection and prevention of wastage should be introduced. Non-corrodible pipe material and jointing materials and careful construction of the system and effective hydraulic pressure testing of the pipe system before refilled with earth cover material is urgently needed. The AC pressure pipes or rigid PVC pipes could be used and/or replaced with the CI pipes for small sizes.

5. Graded water tariff rates should be adopted whereby higher rates for industrial, commercial and higher income group domestic users, and lower rates for common people could be practiced. Improvements should also be made in respect of billing cycle and collection efficiency. Computerization of bills at zonal level should be taken up urgently.

6. Tail end of the water distribution system and high-rise and multi-storey constructions generally get less water. Design mechanisms and management strategies should be introduced to enhance supply to such developments.

7. Water accounting is urgently needed. At present 35 per cent of water supplied is unaccounted for.

8. Government has already adopted the policy framework to enhance the water availability. Major policy aspects, as detailed below, should be adopted:

   (a) Surplus water from river Yamuna by construction of storage dams in upper reaches in Himachal Pradesh and Uttar Pradesh at Kisan, Dadau and Renuka dams.

   (b) Surplus water from the Ravi and the Beas rivers—Bhakra Beas Management Board share for Delhi 0.2 MAF.

(c) At the Tehri Dam in Uttar Pradesh on river Bhagirathi, 24 MAF is earmarked for Delhi.

(d) Exchange of sewage effluents for raw water is another possibility. This is also a stated policy contained in the Master Plan for Delhi 2001.

(e) Groundwater is very limited. But still the Ranney Wells can yield upto 53 MGD.

9. The authorities can also use the following tell-tale signs to detect problems (see Table 6).

Table 6. Tell-Tale Signs and Accompanying Causes Problems

Tell-Tale Signs		*Possible Cause*
Burst mains and Service pipes	—	Excessive pressure
	—	Surge problems
	—	Internal corrosion/aggressive water
	—	External corrosion/aggressive soil
	—	Inferior materials
	—	Ground movement
Intermittent Supply	—	Burst mains and service pipes
	—	Hydraulic capacity of mains and/or service pipes
	—	Tuberculated deposits and general main debris
	—	Equipment failures (pumps)
	—	Illegal water usage
	—	Maintenance work
Poor Pressure	—	Hydraulic capacity of mains, service pipes, pumps, etc.
	—	Tuberculated deposits
	—	Illegal demands
	—	Maintenance work
	—	Topography
Discoloured Water	—	Sourcewater treatment
	—	Pipeline materials/linings
	—	Corrosion debris—mains
	—	Corrosion debris—service pipes
	—	Dead ends
	—	Mixing of different source waters
	—	Excessive remedial flushing

Excessive Leakage	—	Excessive residual pressure
	—	Internal-external corrosion
	—	Pipeline materials/linings
	—	Mainlaying techniques
	—	Leakage policy—ACTIVE or PASSIVE
	—	Intrinsic characteristics
	—	Climate and soil type
Taste and Adore	—	Sourcewater quality
	—	Sourcewater treatment
	—	Chemical dosing e.g. excessive chlorine
Animals	—	Treatment inadequacies
	—	Excessive food (mains debris)
	—	Pipeline materials and linings

Source : Lackington (1988 : 268).

10. It may be stipulated that 10 to 15 per cent of the total budgetary support would be attained from the sale of water. As inflation increases or decreases water rates must change.

Priority for the Weaker Sections

The Delhi Water Supply and Sewage Disposal Undertaking has accorded the highest priority to vulnerable areas, viz., resettlement colonies, unauthorised and regularised colonies, Harijan Basties and JJ Clusters inhabited by the weaker sections of the society.

According to the instructions issued by the Secretary (UI), with the approval of the Lt. Governor of Delhi, Slums Department of the Municipal Corporation of Delhi has handed over 820 JJ Clusters to the Delhi Water Supply and Sewage Disposal Undertaking upto June, 1992. As far as water supply system is concerned, 140 additional public water hydrants have been provided. There are 3,236 water hydrants. In addition, 822 deep bore handpumps and 29 tubewells exist in these clusters. To augment the drinking water supply 75 Sintex tanks have also been placed in these JJ Clusters which are filled with water with the help of 12 water tankers and 24 trucks fitted with Sintex tanks. More than 1.57 lakh individual water connections have been provided in the resettlement colonies and 2.53 lakh individual water connections in unauthorised and regularised colonies so far. Out of 567 unauthorised and regularised colonies, water supply has been extended to 541 colonies. It has been decided to make safe drinking water available to residents of all unauthorised colonies and extended abadies of villages through deep bore handpumps, tubewells and also by providing public hydrants wherever feasible. All unauthorised colonies which came into existence before 31 March, 1993 will also be supplied drinking water on regular basis on payment of development charges. Perusal of this policy will go a long way in meeting the water needs of the poor.

Twinning Arrangements with the Seven Trent Authority of UK

Under the twinning arrangements between the Delhi Water Supply and Sewage Disposal Undertaking and the Seven Trent Water Authority of the United Kingdom as approved by the Delhi Water Supply and Sewage Disposal Committee and Ministry of Urban Affairs and Employment, the Undertaking may obtain expert advice on treatment of water and sewage and other allied fields like leakage detection, water testing, etc., from the Seven Trent Water Authority of United Kingdom. For the implementation of the ODA Programme, the United Kingdom's Seven Trent Authority has already taken initiatives whereby the Delhi Water Supply and Sewage Disposal Undertaking's engineers and the Chief Water Analyst have already been trained in the aforesaid areas.

REFERENCES

1. Bhattacharya, S.K., (1988), 'Problems of Water Supply in Congested City Areas—Calcutta, A Case Study', in *Pickford, J. (ed.) Developing World Water*, Grosvenor Press International, Hong Kong.

2. Government of India, (1966), *Annual Plan 1996-97*, Planning Commission, New Delhi.

3. Government of the National Capital Territory of Delhi, (1995), *Delhi*

Statistical Hand Book, Directorate of Economics and Statistics, Government of the National Capital Territory of Delhi, Delhi.

4. Lackington, D., (1988), 'Solving Distribution Problems', in Pickford J. (ed.) Developing World Water, Grosvenor Press International, Hong Kong.

5. National Institute of Urban Affairs, (1986), *Management of Urban Services, Research Study, Series Number 14*, National Institute of Urban Affairs, New Delhi.

6. National Institute of Urban Affairs, (1991), *Basic Services and the Urban Poor, Research Study Series Number 46*, National Institute of Urban Affairs, New Delhi.

7. National Institute of Urban Affairs, (1988), *Upgrading Municipal Services: Norms and Financial Implications*, National Institute of Urban Affairs, New Delhi.

8. Planning Commission, (1985), *Seventh Five Year Plan (1985-90)*, Vol. II, Government of India, New Delhi.

9. Swamy, S.A., (1987), *Delhi Water Supply Schemes—Issues, Problems and Solutions*, A paper prepared for training workshop on "Urban Civic Services and Management" organised by TCPO, New Delhi.

13 SLUMS AND SLUMMING OF URBAN POOR

R.K. WISHWAKARAMA

Most of the developing nations in the world are experiencing rapid growth of population vis-a-vis industrialisation and urbanisation. As a consequence of industrialisation, more jobs and gainful opportunities are expanding in urban areas. This has further given rise to the process of urbanisation, and a large scale migration to urban areas. But the urban infrastructure and services are not growing in proportion to the growth of urban population. Even if the political will is there, the urban authorities are not in a position to house the large influx of migrant population. Consequently, informal housing (the so-called slums and squatters) is perpetuating every city of the world.

To tackle this problem, though efforts have been made and techniques and solutions adopted in many countries of the world ranging from housing control through removal and relocation and self-help housing to sites and services projects, almost none of these programmes could provide adequate housing. The problem of shortage of housing remains. The syndrome of poor, poverty, deprivation and marginalisation of a large section of urban population has thus led to mushrooming growth of urban slums.

In India, urban population has grown from 25.85 million in 1901 to 217.17 million or by 746.7 per cent in 1991 (Table1). This shows an almost eight-fold increase in urban population. But the component of slum population to urban population accounts for 25 to 30 per cent of urban population. It will be quite revealing that of the 159.5 million urban population, as of 1981, 27.92 million (17.5 per cent) was slum population. The slum population has further increased to 46.62 million (21.5 per cent) out of 217.2 million urban population in 1991. The situation in Latin American countries is no better with the population of slum population ranging from 10 to 50 per cent. In Dar-es-Salaam, the slum population accounted for 16 per cent between 1965-69, rising to 24 per cent during 1969-74 but the figures rose to 44 per cent in 1972 and 62 per cent in 1978.[1] In Egypt, 20 per cent of population is living in slums.[2] However, in India, a larger share of slum population is living in million plus cities than in smaller ones. The Table 2 reveals that the estimates of slum population in million plus metrocities vary from a low of 33 per cent to a high of 40 per cent. In metro-cities like Calcutta, Mumbai, Delhi, Chennai, Kanpur over one-third of population live in slums. These visible manifestations of 'poverty' co-exists in India's cities and towns of plenty'.

Table 1. Growth of Urban Population and Level of Urbanisation in India During 1990-91

Year	*Population*		*Decadal Growth Rate*		*Present level*
	Total (millions)	*Total (millions)*	*Total*	*Urban*	*of urbanisation*
1901	238.39	25.85	—	—	10.80
1911	252.09	25.94	5.75	0.35	10.29
1921	251.32	28.08	—0.31	8.27	11.18
1931	278.98	33.45	11.00	19.12	11.99
1941	318.66	44.15	14.22	31.97	13.86
1951	361.09	62.44	13.31	41.42	17.29
1961	439.23	78.93	21.64	26.41	17.97
1971	548.16	109.11	24.80	38.23	19.91
1981	683.32	159.46	24.66	46.14	23.34
1991	844.32	217.17	23.56	36.19	25.72

Source: Censes of India, 1991, Paper 2 of 1991, Population Rural-Urban Distribution.

Table 2. Estimated Slum Population in 1991 and 2001 in Million-Plus Metropolitan Cities as of 1991

(in millions)

Sl. No.	*Metro-City having million plus popul-ation/UAs.*	*Population 1981*	*Population 1991*	*Identified slum population 1991 No.*	*Identified slum population 1991 per-centage*	*Decadal growth percen-tage 1981-91*	*Slum popu-lation 1991*	*Estimated Urban popu-lation 2001*	*Estimated Slum popu-lation 2001*
1	*2*	*3*	*4*	*5*	*6*	*7*	*8*	*9*	*10*
1.	Calcutta	9.20	10.91	3.03	32.9	15.67	3.59	12.94	4.26
2.	Mumbai	8.24	12.57	2.83	34.3	34.45	4.31	19.18	6.59
3.	Delhi	5.73	8.38	1.80	31.4	31.62	2.63	12.26	3.85
4.	Chennai	4.29	5.36	1.36	32.1	19.96	1.72	6.70	2.15
5.	Hyderabad	2.55	4.28	0.50	19.6	40.42	0.84	7.18	1.41
6.	Bangalore	2.92	4.09	0.31	10.4	28.61	0.43	5.73	0.60
7.	Ahmedabad	2.55	3.30	0.54	20.3	22.73	0.67	4.27	0.87
8.	Pune	1.69	2.49	0.27	16.3	32.13	0.41	3.67	0.60
9.	Kanpur	1.64	2.11	0.61	37.5	22.27	0.79	2.71	1.02
10.	Lucknow	1.01	1.64	0.29	28.3	38.41	0.46	2.66	0.75
11.	Nagpur	1.30	1.66	0.42	31.9	21.69	0.53	2.12	0.68
12.	Jaipur	1.02	1.51	0.30	29.1	32.45	0.44	2.24	0.65
13.	Surat	0.91	1.52	0.23	25.4	40.13	0.39	2.54	0.65
14.	Coimbatore	0.92	1.14	—	—	19.30	0.23*	1.41	0.28
15.	Cochin	0.69	1.14	0.17	24.8	39.47	0.28	1.88	0.47
16.	Vadodara	0.75	1.12	0.12	15.8	33.04	0.18	1.67	0.26
17.	Indore	0.83	1.10	0.13	15.2	24.55	0.17	1.46	0.22
18.	Patna	0.91	1.10	0.58	63.5	17.27	0.70	1.32	0.84
19.	Madurai	0.91	1.09	—	—	16.51	0.22*	1.31	0.26*
20.	Bhopal	0.67	1.06	0.06	8.5	36.79	0.09	1.68	0.14
21.	Vishakha-patnam	0.60	1.05	0.15	25.2	42.86	0.26	1.84	0.46
22.	Varanasi	0.80	1.03	0.26	32.6	22.33	0.34	1.33	0.43
23.	Ludhiana	0.61	1.01	0.31	51.1	39.60	0.52	1.67	0.85
	Total	50.74	70.66	14.27	28.12	20.20	99.77	28.29	(28.58%)

* Provisional based on 20 per cent sample urban population.

Sources: 1. Government of India, Town and Country Planning Organisation, New Delhi.

2. Census of India 1991, Provisional Population Totals: Rural-Urban Distribution, Series 1, Paper 2 of 1991.

The rural poverty, while undoubtedly linked to urban poverty, is not its soul cause. This is evident from the fact that rural to urban migration contributes only 32.2 per cent to the decadel increase in urban population, while natural increase 60.2 per cent.

The Case of Delhi

The capital city of Delhi has shown tremendous growth both in population and area. Within nine decades, the population of Delhi has shown more than a four-fold increase in population from 0.208 million in 1901 to 8.427 million in 1991 and in the areas almost fourteen-fold from 43 sq. km. in 1901 to 592 sq. km. in 1991 (Table 3). Although after 1951, the percentage growth of population has shown a declining trend, the absolute population has increased steadily because of (i) healthy economic base, and (ii) diversification of Delhi's economy pulling large scale rural to urban migrants.

Table 3. Growth of Urban Population in Delhi During 1901-91

Year	*Area in sq. kms*	*Population*	*% Growth*
1901	43	2,08,575	—
1911	43	2,32,837	12
1921	168	3,04,420	31
1931	170	4,04,420	47
1941	170	6,95,686	56
1951	196	14,37,134	107
1961	326	23,59,408	64
1971	446	36,47,023	55
1981	592	57,70,000	58
1991	592	84,27,083	46

Source : Census of India 1901 to 1991.

Immigration to Delhi

The healthy economic base of Delhi has been responsible for generating employment both in formal and informal sectors and also in attracting rural to urban migration. During the decade 1981-91, the overall immigration to Delhi was 2.989 million. Of this 27.83 per cent came for employment or in search of grainful employment, 41.36 per cent due to family movement, 14.3 per cent on account of marriage, 2.33 per cent for education and 14.18 per cent for other reasons. Among the rural to urban migrants 67.64 per cent came to urban for economic reasons (in search of grainful employment). The family migration accounted for 23.1 per cent and social migration 8.27 per cent.

The states which have been contributing a lot to the migrant population were Uttar Pradesh (60 per cent), Bihar (16 per cent), Rajasthan (8.5 per cent), Tamil Nadu (6 per cent) and Madhya Pradesh (3 per cent).

Growth of Slums in Delhi

In Delhi, there are four types of slums viz., (i) notified slums; (ii) unauthorised slums; (iii) resettlement colonies; and (iv) JJ Clusters. Notified slums are the areas which have been notified under Slum Areas (Improvement Clearance) Act, of 1956. At the time of formulation of Seventh Plan about 18 lakh people were living in notified slums. The growth of slums and squatter settlements in Delhi showing a remarkable trend has grown more than twenty-fold during a period of four decades i.e. 1951-1991 (Table 4). This squatter families grew from 12,749 in 1951 to 42,814 in 1961 and 62.594 in 1971. Although there has been a steady growth of slums and squatter families, their number remained at 98,709 in 1981 due to relocation of colonies and rehabilitation of a sizeable number of JJ families. Within a period of one decade, their number has increased significantly to 2,59,344. It is estimated that by the end of 1994 Delhi was housing 1089 JJ clusters housing a population of about 2.3 million living 4,85,000 jhuggies and occupying an area of 12,000 hectares. This shows slumming of Delhi at an increasing pace.[3]

Table 4. Growth of Slums in Delhi During 1951-94

Year	*Area in Slums Families*	*Percentage Growth*
1951	12,749	—
1961	42,815	235.8
1971	62,594	46.2
1981	89,709	43.3
1985	1,50,000	67.2
1991	2,59,344	72.9
1994	4,85,000	87.0

Source: Delhi Development Authority, Growth of Slums in Delhi 1994.

As regards the zonal distribution of JJ clusters as of 1991, Central Zone was having 93 clustres, East Zone-123, West Zone-204, North Zone-227 and South Zone-282. The percentage of families living in East and West Zone was almost similar at 16.2 and 16.4, respectively. But the South Zone and North Zone were sharing the highest number of families at 33.6 per cent and 25.4 per cent respectively. Central Zone had only 8.4 per cent families.

Socio-Economic Profile

As regards the age distribution of slum population, 19.0 per cent were in the age-group 0-4, 18.4 per cent in the age-group 10-14. The economically active population was 48.4 per cent and those in the age-group 50 and above constituted 3 per cent. The distribution of slum population by sex indicates 53.15 per cent males and 46.87 per cent females indicating an adverse sex-ratio of 882 females per 1000 males.

The literacy rate has been fairly good at 44.27 per cent but the dependency ratio has been very high as the earner constituted only one-third (29 per cent) of the total population living in JJ Clusters. The dependency ratio expressed in terms of earners and non-earners was 1:2.51. Although the per capita income of Delhi has increased from Rs. 1,199 in 1970-71 to Rs. 5,347 in 1993-94 at

1980-81 prices, the per capita income of urban poor living in JJ Clusters at current prices was Rs. 288 and the household income Rs. 1,338. About 30 per cent of the JJ households were below the poverty line.[4]

The growing population has though been responsible for an informal growth of Delhi constituting an urban belt of poverty, yet they are contributing significantly to the growing demands of the people through their informal sector establishment and informal sector labour.

We have seen the growth of urban population and proliferations of slums, their socio-economic profile and the problems they are facing by living in degraded environment with unsanitary conditions, overcrowding and poverty followed by lack of potable water supply, they are subjecting themselves to epidemics and health hazards which cause ecological changes that favour breeding of vector and spread of diseases. They are also subject to social and political disruption, economic losses on account of increased trauma in emergency settlements. But there has been no political will to enforce laws to arrest the growth of mushrooming JJ Clusters inhabited by different shades of people. Even the thinking of political elites irrespective of their parties has not been positive in respect of slum dwellers. In true sense they do not want to improve their situation and preparing them on enduring basis to make them free from political dependence. The political patronage has been limited only to the extend of using them as their vote banks.

Slum Policy During the Plans

Soon after the partition of the country, the influx of population in many northern towns and cities of India including Delhi provided a beacon for housing policy during the First Plan (1951-56) which continued even during the Second Plan (1956-61).

The Third Plan (1961-66) moved from the narrower focus of housing to urbanisation problem in its own right. The policy of urban development through Master Plan continued even during the Fourth Plan (1966-74) but there was accent on the environmental improvement of slums (with paved lanes, supply of potable water, latrines, storm water drainage and sanitation) due to the adoption of a new scheme of Environmental Improvement of Urban Slums (EIUS). This healthy change in policy over the slum clearance and urban renewal approach of physical planners brought a drastic change in the quality of life of slum dwellers. But this was a transitory phenomenon because of the intervention of urban development authorities into the urban land market and its 'large scale acquisition, sympathetic development and homeopathic disposal' gave a further jolt to the plight of the urban poor. Being priced out of urban land market, urban poor resorted to slums and squatter settlements.

In the Fifth Plan (1974-79) urban development policy took a turn in terms of urban integrated development and urban policy was implemented in three key areas: "the environment, habitat and well being". With this accent in urban planning, the quality of life of urban dwellers though improved, yet considering their magnitude the problems could not be solved. The services provided were outnumbered by the continuous and steady growth of slum population.

In the Sixth Plan (1980-85), the policy of urban integrated development was redesigned in terms of Integrated Development of Small and Medium Towns (IDMST) in order to check (i) the rate of migration to metropolitan areas, and (ii) to make urban development complementary to rural development. But unfortunately none of the two objectives could be achieved and the rural to urban migration continued unabated.

However, during the Seventh Plan (1985-90) a new strategy of Urban Basic Services (UBS) was adopted for the benefit of the people living in slum areas. The idea was to have a targeted development with the involvement of community for participatory approach in the delivery of services to the urban poor living in slums and squatter settlements. After getting a positive feedback from the report of the National Commission on Urbanisation, the programme has since been revised during Eight Plan (1991-95) as Urban Basic Services for the Poor (UBSP). Its strategy is deeply rooted in community participation and empowerment of the community for convergence of various existing services available through various schemes in partnership and cooperation with other agencies. But even this programme meant specifically for the slums could not have its dent as desired, as the Government machinery has been working for them to provide services as 'dole' rather than working with them. This lead to the poor organisation of neighbourhood communities and thus lack of communities participation.

Slums and National Housing Policy

Thanks to the National Housing Policy of 1994 which considered housing as a major economic sector and prescribes the role of state as the facilitator to meet the housing requirements of a majority of the most vulnerable sections of the population. It also recognised slums as a form of informal housing and stressed the need for creating an enabling environment with necessary infrastructural facilities. To this end, the National Commission on Urbanisation recommended for restructuring of parastatal organisation for fulfilment of their new role as facilitators rather than provides of housing. In this present scenario of privatisation, the fate of slum dwellers does not seem to improve in conformity with the goals of housing policy. Depending upon the local politics and political will, some positive measures already existing could be geared to improve the lot of the urban poor at the community level.

Government Schemes to Improve the Quality of Life of Slum Dwellers

The problem of shelter is two-fold. Those having access to shelter even in a rudimentary form, generally get access to the certain level of services and those who have no access to shelter at all, are houseless unfortunate. Their problem needs to be tackled on priority basis. In any shelter policy there is an inherent 'shelter-services' nexus which had been there in our past approaches and it need to be tackled once for all. The Government of India has expressed its concern over the last four decades for the provision of urban basic services to the urban dwellers through one programme or the other. These programmes could be listed as Environmental Improvement of Slum Areas (EIUS), Urban Community Development (UCDP), Low Cost Sanitation (LCS), Sites and Services (S/S), Slum Improvement/Upgradation Programme (SIP/SUP) and Integrated Development of Small and Medium Towns (IDMST) and Urban Basic Services Programme (UBS and UBSP). All these approaches have been varied with a variety of combinations covering land, shelter, basic municipal services, health, education, employment, etc. were targeted at poor and involved the Central Government, State Government, Local Authorities and Non-Governmental Organisations. The close link between shelter and services has been the unique feature of all these programmes and the beneficiaries could avail a house, either a jhuggi, with or without a patta or could buy EWS plots or houses. All these programmes are mostly slum based.[5]

Any policy for providing shelter and liveable environment to the urban poor free from slumming is required to have a policy beyond traditional approach of Master Planning which aims at the creation of regulated development but within defined zonal plans unaffordable by the poor. The political solutions to the problems of urban poverty lies in providing sites and services, upgradation of services and environmental improvement of slum areas granting pattas, etc. But the problem of urban poverty has to have an access between investment in shelter upgradation and employment opportunities. Since much of the business in urban Indian tends to be in the informal sector managed by the poor people and providing about 45 per cent of the total employment, is a pointer in the direction of the policy that should go for infrastructural development bank. In order to tackle the problems of shelter and employment or self-employment in the informal sector of urban economy, the policy should also take into account the distance between the place of work and living environment. The poor cannot afford the time or the money to travel long distances to reach their work places. Therefore, there has to be a proper planning of work and residential areas.

Implementation of Slum Improvement Schemes in Delhi

In Delhi, the services have been provided under three schemes: (i) Urban Improvement of Slum Areas (EIUS); (ii) Urban Basic Services (UBS) and (UBSP); and (iii) IN-SITU programme. The IN-SITU upgradation of JJ Clusters was envisaged in those instances of encroached land sites wherever a no objection certificate (NOC) was obtained from the land owning authority. Generally, these agencies have been reluctant to issue such certificates. There were about 180 JJ Clusters identified by Slums and JJ Departments belonging to various land owning authorities. For implementation of IN-SITU upgradation the L & DO has given concurrence only for 10 such JJ Clusters (till 1992) but Delhi Development Authority's Screening/ Technical Committee did not clear any of the sites from the Master Plan point of view. This is the reason that this scheme could not make any dent on implementation.

The advantage of upgradation programme are three-fold; First, it preserves economic system and opportunities for urban poor. Second, preserves the low cost housing stock already in existence at its present location. Third, it preserves the community structure and the safeguards that already exist for the family and the community group.[6] Considering the advantages of upgradation programme, the then Ministry of Urban Development (now Urban Affairs and Employment) issued directives for the environmental improvement of eligible JJ Clusters and their IN-SITU upgradation to the extent possible, rather than for their resettlement to alternatives sites. Relocation to alternative sites should be undertaken only on case to case basis. On the urgency of requirement of the land for a priority public purpose project, the Land Owning Agency will be required to bear the entire cost of development site in the new location, although, relocation schemes were discouraged to the extent possible.

The Delhi Government approved the scheme of

Environmental Improvement of Urban Slums (EIUS) in 1987 to provide services in all JJ Clusters irrespective of the year of their location, title of land without obtaining NOCs from land owning authorities. The scheme has been implemented in phases. First, it provided Pay and Use Jan Suvidha Complexes, potable water supply through municipal water hydrants and/or India Mark-II deep hand-pumps (depending on the local geographical terrain), street lighting, dustbins/daloos, brick-paved pathways and drains for the outflow of discharged households and rainy water.

The programme of Urban Basic Services (UBS) which aimed at the provision of civic services and amenities and other social inputs through community organisation, covergence and coordination with other agencies is based on community participation and it is being implemented by the Delhi State itself. The schemes has been under implementation in Delhi since 1986, but under the revised Urban Basic Services for the Poor (UBSP) strategy, the schemes of EIUS and Nehru Rojgar Yojana (NRY) have been merged with UBSP, and the services are being provided on the basis of "national norms". These norms are as follows:

(i) Water supply— one tap for 150 persons or 30 households;

(ii) Open drains with the normal outflow of water to avoid accumulation and stagnation;

(iii) Storm water drains to drain out the water quickly;

(iv) Community bath— one bath for 50 persons or 10 households;

(v) One community toilet/Pay and Use Jan Suvidha Complex for 50 persons or 10 households;

(vi) Widening and paving of existing lanes to make room for easy flow of pedestrians, bicycles, hand carts, etc.;

(vii) Provision of street lights;

(viii) One community centre for 1000 households;

(ix) Garbage disposal facilities (daloo/dustbins) one for 200 households;

(x) Maintenance of all facilities mentioned above @ 10 per cent of the per capita outlay; and

(xi) Balwadi/Anganwadi— one for 25 children.

On an average, the national per capita norm of Rs. 525 is not in conformity with the requirements of Delhi.

Policy Implementation Evaluation

These services in the community have been provided as 'deposit works' (through the concerned municipal and other agencies) without bothering for their maintenance and their linkages to city services and community facilities. This system has led to mounting of corruption and dissatisfaction with the provision services.

Although a reasonable amount of services and infrastructure is existing in JJ Clusters, it does not imply that issue of access has been completely resolved. Still a lot more needs to be done. The existing gaps and inadequacies of services and their poor utilisation indicates that their access and maintenance have not been commensurate with the public investment of Rs. 540.25 million during (1985-94) that has undergone in laying down the infrastructure and services. Moreover, the scheme implemented has suffered heavily on account of impending factors of coordination and lack of convergence of services through a suitable administrative structure, on the one hand, and due to bureaucratic, indifference, and mismatch of resources with people centred implementation, on the other.

The thinking of political elites irrespective of their party has not been positive in respect of slum dwellers. In true sense they did not want to improve their situation and preparing them on an enduring basis to make them free from political dependence. The political patronage has been limited only to the extent of using them as their vote banks. The genuine interest has been lacking in empowering the community, an essential element for seeking peoples participation which already existed in the community.

Though a plethora of organisation and institutions have been involved in the delivery of services, there has been little contact between them as only 19 meetings of the Steering Committee could be held till September 1992 since the inception of the UBS programme in 1985. This shows there has been little contact between them.

Since different shades of people are living in slum community, the programme benefits do not reach the needy poor because of non-involvement of community and partly because they are being grabbed by those who are not poor. A solution to their problems requires a look into socio-political dimensions of their problems.

Although there is a law to stop the growth and proliferation of slum areas, yet the government has not been able to enforce it for want of political and bureaucratic will (stated S.C. Vajpeyi former Chief Secretary, Delhi Administration). Delhi Assembly have been passing resolutions for regularising unauthorised constructions and the courts have been giving stay orders on the demolition of these constructions. It may look paradoxical, yet this aspect cannot be completely lost sight of.[7]

A Delhi High Court bench of Justices R.C. Lahoti and S.N. Kapoor observed that "Delhi's policy on slums exists only in theory—it can never be implemented". Slumming is continuing affair in which police and politicians both are involved and the bureaucracy is inert to enforce the court decisions. Having learnt the non-enforcement of a twice repeated direction to remove slums from footpaths the Honoured bench gave the verdict that "this could be the last chance" and directed the complaining counsel to get at the next hearing, a list of places where the order hadn't been implemented—we shall then see "was Justice Lahoti's ominous warning".[8] This shows the deep rooted interest of the vested parties in non-implementation of slum policies.

REFERENCES

1. Mosha, A.C. 'Squatter and Slum Settlements in Tanzania' in Housing the Urban Poor (eds.) Brian C. Aldrich and Ravinder S. Somdhee, Sage Publications, 1995, p. 342.

2. Ahmed, M. Soliman, Informal Housing in Egypt in Housing the Urban Poor, *op. cit.*, p. 300.

3. Proceedings of the Seminar on Organisational Effectiveness of Urban Basic Services in Selected Slum Areas of Delhi, (ed.) R.K. Wishwakarma and Rakesh Gupta, Indian Institute of Public Administration, New Delhi, p. 29.

4. *Ibid.*

5. P.S.N. Rao, Urban Basic Services—Need for Emphasis on Houseless Poor, NAGARLOK, Vol. XXVII, No. 4, Oct.-Dec. 1995, p. 94.

6. Martin, R.J. (1983), Upgrading, People, Poverty and Shelter : Problems of Self Housing (eds.), R.J. Skinner and N.J. Rodli, London, Methuen, p. 52.

7. R.K. Wishwakarma and Rakesh Gupta, Proceedings of the Seminar, *ibid.*, p. 20.

8. *The Times of India*, August 28, 1996.

14 A NETWORK OF INDUSTRIES IN DELHI: CAPITAL ON THE PATH OF INDUSTRIAL PROGRESS

R.K. GUPTA

Historical Delhi has been wellknown as the home of Master Craftsmen for their aesthetic quality of work. Yet unlike the most other metropolitan cities of India it never was considered an industrial town. Delhi has been known to be a Government city and when expressed in relationship to all working forms the role of Government employment has been strikingly high. After the attainment of independence employment in the Central Government as well as in the local and State Governments received fresh impetus. Delhi being called 'The City of Babus' (White-Collar Workers) was not a misnomer.

Historically a lot of developments in physical terms have taken place because Delhi has been the capital of India. With a limitation of employment in Government sector, trade, commerce and industry have provided unlimited resource for employment motivating migration of people from various States and Union Territories to Delhi.

It is a fact that the external economies available in an urban centre such as the improved communications, higher level of education, transport, availability of materials and services all have greatly facilitated, the process of a large proportion of India's industry veering around the urban centres. The rapid increase in population of metropolitan cities has created demands for goods and services resulting in continued growth of manufacturing activities. Delhi has been no exception.

A historical study of the growth pattern of industries revealed that industries in Delhi had their beginning towards the end of the last century. In a span of almost four decades from 1900 to 1939 there was a sporadic growth of industries here and there in Delhi. Quite a few firms were born in this period and came to be localted in widely scattered pattern so that by the beginning of the World War II nearly all the city areas had some industrial concerns. Most of these pre-1939 factories employed 250 workers average.

The World War II gave fresh impetus to the process of industrialization. The number of registered factories increased from 111 in 1939 to 227 in 1945 with a corresponding increase in the number of workers from 17,400 to 37,000 respectively. The following table indicates the true picture of the progress of four decades.

Table 1. Population and Number of Workers Engaged in Industries in Delhi State : 1921-1951

Year	*Population*	*No. of persons engaged in industries*	*Percentage of total working force*	*Est: No. of workers in registered factories*
1921	4,88,452	43,577	21.5	8,000
1931	6,36,246	54,036	20.1	11,000
1941	9,17,939	81,448	23.2	25,000
1951	17,44,072	116,585	18.2	42,635

However, a rapid growth of industries in Delhi was prompted by the influx of refugees who brought with them not only the mechanical skills but also the spirit of enterprise. Between 1951 and 1957 registered sectors of industry expanded with workers from 42,600 to 45,700.

The bulk of organized sector was in not more than half a dozen cloth mills which have long been established in Delhi. The largest single heterogeneous industry was in the light engineering group.

The industries in the organized sector started coming up along highways such as Najafgarh Road, Mathura Road, South of the Ring Road, Shahdara and Subzi Mandi on G.T. Road and at Rohtak Road. On the whole the manufacturing activities were scattered. A limited number of manufacturing-cum-service units got located in better buildings along the highways whereas most of the others accommodated in skeleton makeshift structure due to urgent economic needs of setting up of these establishments. Most of them started operating under conditions of over crowding and inadequate infrastructure.

The urbanised land—use survey of the Delhi conducted in 1958-59 indicated that the industrialization in Delhi covered approximately 636 acres out of a total of 39471 acres of urban land. Even at that time it was observed that nuisance industries were covering 301.87 acres as compared to 334.97 acres being occupied by non-nuisance industries. The impetus provided by the Govt. for encouraging self-employment as a career gave boost to setting up of industries in Delhi.

The economic needs of the ever growing population was another contributing factor. The various incentives by the Government of India to increase the manufacturing base of the country as a whole was the added motivating force in this direction. By 1980 Delhi had a population of more than 5.5 million. It was three times of 1951. Population had a significant impact on the economy as a whole. This meant not only large scale increase in physical development but also provided opportunities for creation of enough jobs to sustain the economy.

This led to haphazard and sub-standard development of the metropolis at a rapid pace especially on the highways leading to the capital. The wide disparity in residential density led further mushrooming growth of industries without the congested areas. There was an unobserved growth almost everywhere in the city of establishing an industry and wholesale business with service industry.

The Master Plan for Delhi 1962 prepared for the first time a land use plan which in a sense was to translate the physical form of planning policies and principles on to the ground.

The whole city was divided into eight planning divisions which were thought to be self-contained in the matter of employment, residences, recreational, shopping and other needs. The plan located land for industry, commerce, leaving play and other major types of urban land use with proper interrelation to each other for an organized development of the city. The details of various industrial areas which have been developed as a result of Planned Development of Delhi by various agencies are described lucidly in the four sections of Table 2.

Table 2. (A) Industrial Areas Developed by DDA

Name of Scheme	*Total Area (Acres)*	*Total No. of Plots/Units*
Okhla Industrial Area Phase-1	368.00	1097
Okhla Industrial Area Phase-2	336.00	884
Lawrence Road Industrial Area	196.20	312
Wazirpur Industrial Area	210.00	784
Wazirpur Group Industries	23.40	175
G.T. Karnal Road Industrial Area	125.00	332
Kirti Nagar Industrial Area	140.00	312
Naraina Industrial Area Phase-1	34.80	151
Naraina Industrial Area Phase-2	114.56	452
Mangolpuri Industrial Area Phase-1	212.00	223
Mangolpuri Industrial Area Phase-2	78.00	1354
Najafgarh Road Industrial Area	329.00	250
Rewari Line Mayapuri Industrial Area Phase-1	147.60	376
Rewari Line Mayapuri Industrial Area Phase-2	166.40	1337
Jhilmil Tahirpur Industrial Area	108.90	238

Table 2. (B) Industrial Area Developed by Co-operative Societies

Name of Scheme	*Total Area (Acres)*	*Total No. of Plots/Units*
Mohan Co-operative Industrial Estate	196.16	292
Rajasthan Co-operative Industrial Area and SMA Industrial Area	140.00	250
Udyog Nagar at Rohtak Road	194.00	250

Table 2. (C) Industrial Area Developed by Directorate of Industries

Name of Scheme	*Total Area (Acres)*	*Total No. of Plots/Units*
Okhla Industrial Area Phase-3	120.00	250
Badli Industrial Area	76.00	280
Patparganj Industrial Area	100.00	500
Jhandewalan Flatted Factories	06.00	570
Flatted Factories for leather goods at Wazirpur	5.00	250
and Bharat Nagar	5.00	120

Table 2. (D) Industrial Area Developed by DSIDC

Name of Scheme	*Total Area (Acres)*	*Total No. of Plots/Units*
1. Work centres		
(a) Jahangirpuri	2.5	88
(b) Shakurpur	1.0	43
(c) Wazirpur	0.73	24
(d) Sangam Park	3.0	126
(e) Kabir Basti	2.0	96
(f) Mangolpuri	13.0	376
(g) Madipur	5.0	188

Table Contd. on Next Page

Table Contd.

Name of Scheme	*Total Area (Acres)*	*Total No. of Plots/Units*
(h) Sultanpuri	10.5	386
(i) Nangloi	6.0	222
(j) Hastal	1.0	44
(k) Naraina	1.2	45
(l) Raghubir Nagar	1.0	33
(m) Khyala	1.3	41
(n) Jawalapuri	6.0	284
(o) Tilak Vihar	5.0	248
(p) Kalkaji	1.2	40
(q) Garhi	0.6	22
(r) Tigri	1.0	42
(s) Madangir	0.6	27
(t) Dakshinpuri	1.0	42
(u) Kotla Mubarakpur	2.5	108
(v) Mata Sundari Road	0.5	77
2. *Industrial Sheds*		
(a) Okhla Phase-I	16.2	232
(b) Okhla Phase-II	20.0	205
(c) Jhilmil Tahirpur	2.5	32
(d) Wazirpur	7.0	102
(e) Lawrence Road	5.0	90
(f) Rohtak Road	26.0	278
(g) Mangolpuri	4.5	94
(h) Kirti Nagar	6.0	216
3. *Industrial Park*		
Narela	600	1800

From the four parts of Table-2 it is evident that so far all the agencies put together have been able to provide only about 20,000 Industrial Work spaces including Industrial Plots and Flatted Factories.

Though the Master Plan of 1962 had outlined a locational policy for industrial growth in the Union Territory of Delhi, with the rapid growth of industries over the last two decades, a fresh look was considered appropriate. It was also necessary to view industrial growth from aspects, other than only locational convenience. Within the various limitations and constraints of running industries in metropolitan areas, it was considered desirable to give industrial growth a positive direction and an attempt was made by the Department of Industries, in consultation with other departments, agencies and local bodies, concerned with industrial matters, such as Delhi Development Authority, Municipal Corporation of Delhi, Bureau of Economics and Statistics, to prepare a policy statement, which considers future industrial growth in the Union Territory of Delhi in comprehensive way. With this aim in view, an Industrial Policy statement was issued in 1982 by the Industries Deptt. of Delhi Administration for the first time.

The industrial policy has the following socio-economic objectives:

1. Optimum utilization of installed industrial capacity;
2. Maximization of production and achieving higher productivity, through modernized and better work techniques and optimum utilization of available resources;
3. Maximizing employment generation, particularly for the local engineers, artisans, educated youth and women;
4. Mobilization of the local entrepreneurial and technical talent for the promotion of industries;
5. Dispersal of industries in all areas of the Union Territory, including rural areas, resettlement colonies and trans-Yamuna areas;

6. Evolve suitable programmes for employment generation in the rural areas, through industrial and territory activities;
7. Promotion of export-oriented and import-substitution industries;
8. Promotion of traditional industries, viz., handicrafts, handlooms, khadi and village industries and leather goods industries, where maximum benefits go to weaker sections of the society;
9. Development of modern sophisticated small-scale industries, to produce a variety of quality consumer and producer goods, with special emphasis on high value-added goods;
10. Encourage modernization, energy conservation and use of renewable sources of energy; and
11. Encourage activities, allied to industries, such as marketing, services, consultancy, etc.

The basic postulates of the industrial policy for Delhi were the promotion of industries, with some of the following characteristics:

1. Can achieve optimum levels of production, within the local constraints on land, power, etc.;
2. Can generate maximum employment, in the minimum space, for local skilled persons, educated youth and women, both in manufacturing and servicing/marketing;
3. Can afford entrepreneurial opportunities to local entrepreneurs, engineers and artisans;
4. Sophisticated industries, with special emphasis on high value-added items, without effluents, smoke, noise and vibration that do not cause pollution and are not obnoxious and hazardous;
5. Belong to traditional group of industries, viz., handicrafts, handlooms, khadi and village

industries, leather goods and household industries;

6. Industries producing goods/services for local consumption/usage, particularly mass consumption goods;
7. Industries touching areas of new technology;
8. Do not cause heavy drain upon local services;
9. Do not attract unskilled labour force form outside; and
10. Do not cause congestion and transportation bottlenecks, by movement of bulky materials/ goods.

When compared with the projections that were made in Master Plan 1962 for a projected population of 1981, the situation is very dismal.

Shortfalls in Master Plan Provisions

1. The Master Plan initiated that in order to decentralize commercial activities it proposed to develop 15 district centres and they were to be set-up within easy travel distance for every 1.5 lakh to 2.5 lakh of population. In order to meet with the need of the society these district centres were also required to provide for work-cum-industrial centres for accommodating repair shops and service industries. An area of forty acres was provided but none of such work-cum-industrial centres could ever come up.

2. In order to further provide work spaces within walking distance of the existing concentration of population in the central areas, it was proposed to have flatted factories in multi-storeyed buildings with high density employment ratio which could house many of these small industries that were operating in residential areas, besides providing for service industries required for the populace. They had provided to follow a unit standard of 200 to 300 workers per acre.

These buildings were to come up in 192 acres of land at various locations of Delhi. Table 3 clearly shows the position of the areas and how many acres they have covered.

Table 3. Areas and Acres of land covered by the Industrial Buildings.

Areas	*Acres*
Ajmere Gate	10
Thompson Road	16
Motia Khan	43
D.C.M. Site	27
Roshanara Road	13
Birla Mill Site on G.T. Road	40
G.B. Road	10
Mori Gate	2
Cannaught Place near Shankar Market	10
Sarai Rohilla	11
Near Gulabi Bagh	10
Total	192

But none of the above sites could be developed resuting there in continued growth of industries in the residential areas.

3. In addition to flatted factories to be located in central areas, there were provision of setting up work centres in outlying residential areas. The idea was to provide for household manufacturing units in such centres which otherwise were to spoil the residential character of the neighbourhood. An area of 168 acres was identified for such industrial-cum-work centres (as detailed in Table 4) which was to provide employment opportunities to 33,000 workers but none of them were set-up for the purpose provided for leading to further concentration of household industrial units in the residential sector.

Table 4. Location and Acres of Industrial-cum-Work Centres

Location	*Acres*
Eleven hundred acres housing scheme	
District centre	10
Kalkaji District Centre	15
West Delhi District Centre (North of Rajouri Garden)	10
Khyber pass District Centre	5
Ranjit Nagar Scheme	10
Ring Road-Mathura Road and Railway line triangle	16
Kotla Mubarakpur	4
Shahdara Central Business District	15
Shahdara between G.T. Road and railway line	18
Okhla	45
Jhilmil	5
North of Tihar Jail	15
Total	168

4. Looking to the special needs of city and to make it grow as a high tech. centre, the Master Plan provided for 103 acres of land to be developed for assembly of precision instruments in South Delhi beside setting up research and development facilities. But land was not made available for such high tech. industries and was instead changed to institutional land use creating a number of such institutions which could have been set-up outside of Delhi. This instead deprived Delhi of High Tech. industrial estate.

5. An area of 106 acres was earmarked for setting up and development of extractive industries including potteries but no such area was either identified or developed.

6. In order to meet the economic needs provisions were made for setting up of light industries and industrial

estates with unit space standard of 30 to 50 persons per acre in an area of 1583 acres of land but only half of this land was developed and made available for industries.

7. Extensive industries with a proposed density of 30 workers per acre were contemplated to be provided in 3600 acres of land but only 4 sites in 1600 acres were developed.

Thus the Master Plan of 1962 till 1993 left an uncovered huge gap uncovered between what has it really planned for the city of Delhi to meet the basic needs of society and population and its achievements of only 20,000 industrial spaces by several agencies resulting thereon an unabated growth of industrial units in non-confirming land use zones.

Reasons for Fast Growth

Main reasons for the rapid growth of tiny and small industries in Delhi with no peripheral official assistance are :

— easy divertibility of physical infrastructure built upon assiduously for residential and allied purposes, to small and allied purposes, to small and tiny industries, particularly in the old city and the 'urbanised' villages in new areas.

— ready availability of unskilled and semi-skilled workers, mostly living in jhuggies and other squatter settlements.

— more favourable rates of sale tax and other local taxes in Delhi than many of the towns in surrounding areas.

— ready market for most of the products in the city itself.

— facilities for packaging and despatch of exportable products.

In spite of the failure on the front of providing industrial infrastructure as was envisaged in the Master

Plan of 1962, the manufacturing activity in the city of Delhi continued to grow all these years. This was mainly because of non-availability of projected industrial land on one hand and continuous growth of population in excess of the estimated projections of the Master Plan on the other. The growing population has its own economic needs and these economic needs led to increase in manufacturing activities since the provision of jobs in the government sector continued to shrink. As a result the industrial growth of Delhi continued unabated over the years as indicated in Table 5.

Table 5. Sketch of Tremendous Industrial Growth of Delhi Since 1951 to 1996

Year	*No. of Units*	*Investment (Rs. crores)*	*Production (Rs. crores)*	*Employment*
1951	8160	18.13	35.35	69266
1961	17000	60.00	121.00	138000
1965	19038	81.00	176.00	159731
1968	23496	129.00	280.00	192711
1978	40000	600.00	1100.00	35000
1990	81000	1580.00	4250.00	729000
1992	89000	1750.00	5000.00	802000
1994	97000	1901.20	5335.00	873000
1996	123000	2370.00	5760.00	110000

Delhi has been leading in country in manufacturing and exports of ready-made garments. After Uttar Pradesh and Maharashtra it is the third state for manufacturing and exports of electronic goods. Similarly, Delhi has become the home town for manufacturing of domestic appliances, electrical devices, automobile parts, sports goods, scientific instruments and host of mass consumption items. It has also been leading in export of various other items. The specific achievements of Delhi in the field of industrial exports are indicated in Table 6.

Table 6. Countable Progress of Delhi in the Field of Industrial Exports

Item	*Amount in million Rs.*
Electronic and Electric Goods	6950
Ready-made Garments	2600
Leather Goods	600
Engg. Goods	370
Chemical and Allied Products	180
Handlooms	153
Gems and Jewellery	88
Handicraft	84
Sports Goods	65
Scientific Instruments	30
Plastic Goods	12
Miscellaneous	240

Provisions of the Second Master Plan

The Second Master Plan for Delhi came into existence in 1993 and it studied for the first time and realised the economic needs of the state and therefore thought of a mixed land use concept and some of the important provisions initiated in the Master Plan are as under:

1. The Walled City contains industrial units using acids, chemical and inflammable material and trades like plastic, rexine, etc., which are noxious and hazardous. The first requirement of the area is that such industries and trades should be shifted on priority to the extensive industrial areas and areas specifically earmarked for the trades. This should be linked with the development of industrial estates and freight complexes proposed in the plan.

2. Hazardous and Noxious Industries

(Refer Annexure-III H(a) of MPD-2001).

(a) The hazardous and noxious industrial units are not permitted in Delhi.

(b) The existing industrial units of this type shall be shifted on priority bases within a maximum period of three years. Project Report to effectuate shifting shall be prepared by the concerned units and submitted to the Delhi Development Authority within a maximum period of one year.

(c) The land which would thus become available on account of shifting as in (b) above, would be used for making up the deficiency, as per the needs of the community; based on norms given in the Master Plan. If any land or part of land, so vacated is not needed for the deficiency of the community services, it will be used as per prescribed land use; however the land shall be used for light and service industries, even if the land use according to the Master Plan/Zonal Development Plan is extensive industry.

(d) Action shall be taken by Delhi Administration to prepare a list of individual noxious and hazardous industrial units to be shifted and depending on the pollution/hazard, administration may force these industrial units to shift within a maximum prescribed period of three years.

3. Heavy and Large Industries

(Refer Annexure III H(b) of MPD-2001)

(a) No new heavy and large industrial units shall be permitted in Delhi.

(b) The existing heavy and large scale industrial units shall shift to Delhi Metropolitan Area and the National Capital Regional keeping in view the National Capital Region plan and National Industrial Policy of the Government of India.

(c) The land which would become available on account of shifting as administered in (b) above, would be used for making up the deficiency, as per the needs of the community-based on norms given in the Master Plan; if any land or part of land so vacated is not needed for the deficiency of the community services, it shall be used as per prescribed land use; however, the land shall be used for light and service industries, even if the land use according to the Master Plan/Zonal Development Plan is extensive industry.

(d) Modernization of heavy and large scale industrial units shall be permitted subject to the following conditions:

— It will reduce pollution and traffic congestion.

— Whenever the unit is asked to shift according to the policies of the Plan, no compensation shall be paid for assets attained because of modernization.

4. Extensive Industries

(Refer Annexure III F of MPD-2001)

(a) No new extensive industrial units shall be permitted, except in existing identified extensive industrial areas.

(b) Existing non-conforming extensive industrial units shall be shifted to the extensive industrial use zone within a maximum period of three years after the allotment of plots by various government agencies.

5. Light and Service Industries

(Refer Annexure III-B, C, D, & E of MPD-2001)

(a) Non-conforming light and service industrial units with 20 or more workers shall be shifted to the industrial use zones within a maximum period of three years after the allotment of plots and by providing necessary incentives by the various government agencies in conforming use zones.

(b) Non-conforming light and service industrial units with 10 to 19 workers, may continue to operate in their present locations but should be reviewed after five years giving them chance during this period for relocation in conforming use zones. Similarly non-conforming light and service industrial units upto 9 workers may continue to operate in their present locations and should be reviewed after 10 years after giving them chance during this period for relocation in conforming use zones.

6. Household Industries

(Refer Annexure III A of MPD-2001)

(a) Household industrial units with maximum 5 workers and one kilowatt power may be allowed to continue in residential areas and new industrial units of this type could be permitted in residential areas. No pollutant industrial unit shall be permitted as household industry.

(b) Household industrial units would be allowed only on ground floor to the extent of the 25 per cent of the floor space or 30 sq. m. whichever is less. These conditions would not apply to the special area and any other area declared as such by the government.

General Conditions

(i) In allocating new industrial plots, which have been recommended for shifting will be given priority by the Authority by offering plots to the industrial units prior to shifting.

(ii) Suitable incentives would be provided to the shifting of industries.

(iii) Ad hoc licensing to industrial units shall be discontinued.

8. Industrial Units to be Permitted by the State Government in Different Use Zones Under the Second Master Plan of 1993.

Table 7. Specific Conditions for Industrial Units

Use zone/ Use premises	*Group permitted (Refer Annexture-III)*	*Max. Worker*	*Max. Power Level KW*
Residential	A	5	1
Residential Rural Areas	A+A1	5	1
Local Shopping	A, B	5	3
Community Centre	A, B, C	9	3
District Centre and CBD	A, B, C	19	5
Service Centres	Repair and Service industries for automobile, electric appliances, buildings, etc.		
Light Industries	A, B, C, D, E	—	30
Flatted Industries	A, B, C, D, E	—	30
Light Industries Food	Food Ind. and G-1	—	30
Extensive			
Industries	A, B, C, D, E, F	—	—
Industrial estates in rural use zone	G	—	30

9. The Master Plan has further provided that in the next two decades to meet the expanding need of industrial units 16 new light industrial areas with a total areas of about 1533 hec. (3,800 acres) would required to be developed in urban extension.

10. Similarly, the Master Plan further provided to have 265 hecs. (660 acres) of land for establishing extensive industrial use zones.

11. It has also provided that industrial area development scheme will be prepared in respect of Anand Parbat, Shahdara and Samaypur Badli areas.

But no action plan was drawn up to implement any

of the provisions of MPO 1993. This left a wide gap in respect of provisions and availability of industrial land forcing industries to continue to exist in non-conforming areas.

In the recent past on a writ petition filed in the Apex Court about such unplanned growth of industries in Delhi, the Apex Court ordered industries to adhere to land use zones prescribed in the Master Plan and rendered over 80,000 industries in the grip of such closure or relocation. But it is a irony of fate that this has been a fall out of failure of Development and Planning process which was to make available land in the conforming use zones. The economic needs of the population of the city continues to exist and grow causing demands of goods and services and the situation, therefore, is of our own making. Even in the industrial areas which have been developed and spaces allotted and provided, there are gross violations of land use pattern, such as areas earmarked for hosiery goods has been converted into stainless steel. Units are bifurcating among themselves thereby increasing the pressure on essential infrastructure services. The different agencies of the administration namely MCD, DESU, DDA, Chief Inspector Factories, Chief Electrical Inspector, Directorate of Industries and Delhi Pollution Control Committee have all continued to depend on each other. With the result an industrialist entitled to use 10 KW of power got a sanction of 90 KW of power and than continued to misuse and sublet and increasing its activity. The change of trade has continued unabatedly. There is no authority to examine justifiable need or quantum of power and water required and observance of safety standards.

Units have continued to look for their profits without bothering productivity and wastages. Low productivity has been responsible for increased wastage and pollution loads. Sewage system continues to chock with extensions and unauthorize constructions permitted with impunity. The industrial areas of yesterday have converted into slums of today which leaves a need for one single unified authority for giving clearance to a project or an industry with all its parameters at one go for providing and proper planning of infrastructure support.

After orders of the Apex Court, the Government of Delhi has initiated a scheme of relocation of industries under the scheme of shifting, about 58,000 industrial units have thus applied for relocation of themselves to new site in confirming land use zones. Some 1,300 acres of land has been identified and more is being identified, so as to make it around 4,000 acres. While looking to this relocation scheme industrial activities seems to be getting clustered in a given direction as lands are now not available for their dispersal.

Master Plan 2001 has provided for a mixed land use so as not to relocate all factories or establishments at areas distant from the Central City. But in contrast to this the overriding provision of 1 kw power per unit as provided in the Master Plan on a unrealistic basis make every other unit to be not permissible under the provisions of mix land use pattern contemplated.

Some of the Important Recommendations of a Seminar on Industries in Delhi New Perspective are Reproduced Below for a Bearing on Industrial Development in Delhi

1. Steps to be taken for development of entrepreneurship answering the potential and prospects of growth even in face of various policies and administrative constraints existing at present.

2. Assistance of academic institutions namely, D.I.T., Indian Institute of Technology, Delhi College of Engg., Industrial Training Institutes may be taken for quick surveys and co-ordination with bodies which organize entrepreneurship development courses.

3. Educated youth could be motivated and guided to set-up small industrial and business ventures

in Delhi which could be environment friendly, less labour intensive, covering hightech fields. Small enterprises of self-employed artisans/ craftsmen in resettlement colonies are also needed to promote, keeping in view their financial limitations.

4. A Lead Institution be nominated to avoid multiplicity of authorities which control industrial growth in Delhi, for identification of entrepreneurs, their training and to assists in establishing their ventures. DSIDC was considered as the most suitable body for this purposes.

5. Having regard to various constraints related to environment pollution, great stress to be given to encourage the growth of service industries.

6. Small industries developed in the past should be diversified and relocated and must be provided latest technology for making them more viable.

7. A new Industrial Policy should be formulated for growth of Lal Dora areas in rural Delhi for gainful self-employment of rural workforce to develop pollution free industries near their habitat.

8. In the context of National Capital Region, the scientific system of dispersion should be followed to shift pollutant industries to insulate the locations against pollution.

9. Present lottery system of allotment of industrial plots/sheds should be replaced by some more scientific system of selection and assistance.

10. No new heavy industry should be promoted in Delhi and the existing large scale industries identified by Master Plan for Delhi should be shifted to National Capital Region.

11. The list of banned industries in Master Plan should be revised.
12. In order to encourage the foreign investment/ entrepreneurs, new industrial estates/township should be developed.
13. Delhi should be developed as a Nerve Centre of International Commerce, Banking Trade Fairs and growth of High Tech Service Industries should be encouraged.
14. Seminars may be timely held and again on the topics such as Management of Technology and Consultancy Services. Also Human Resources Service may be provided and short term courses should be conducted developing video based facility.
15. It was felt to organize a planned growth of Electronic Industry through Hi-Tech Industrial Estate in Delhi in future. This will be possible in Delhi because highly trained/skilled manpower and infrastructural facility are already available in Delhi. It will be more suitable in case Hi-Tech industries are established in Industrial Estate having multistoreyed buildings.
16. It was also emphasized that facilities such as provision of business centre, repair and maintenance, supply of components/equipment, PCB design and fabrication facility, PCB assembly, computer aided design, testing and calibration, tool room and machine shop may be provided at Hi-Tech centre.
17. City authorities were urged to go all out to encourage High-Tech. Industries by eliminating bureaucratic hurdles, locational restrictions so as to provide employment opportunities for highly skilled manpower available in Delhi and other Metro Politant cities. It was also

recommended that green channel treatment and three years grace period may be given to Hi-Tech Units for the compliance of statutory requirements.

18. Facilities available with National Physical Laboratory namely testing of product, consultancy on Production Development and research and development etc. shall be made use of.

19. Fire safety measures vis-a-vis the Technological Development be taken care of at planning stage only. Delhi Fire Service can offer training to industrial force simultaneously.

20. It was suggested that while going for the Hi-Tech Industries, we should not forget that main function of the industries is to provide employment thereby raising the income of workers and their living standard which in term will help to control the pollution in city of Delhi.

21. Adoption of Taiwan model could be more suitable for Delhi by setting up flatted factories and allotting them on affordable cost to the actual entrepreneurs who can reside on upper floor and establish their industrial unit at ground floors. It was suggested that DSIDC can play a leading role in this direction.

22. The role of National Small Industries Corporation was highlighted for supply of machinery on hire-purchase basis and participation in Government Store purchase programme on preferential basis. It was pointed out that NSIC can help in upgradation of technology and substitution of existing machinery.

23. The role of information network for providing access to marketing outlets was stressed, as in present scenario, information has become the

most powerful input of business enterprises. It was also pointed out that DSIDC can render such services to industries in Delhi. The use of computers for business data processing was also stressed.

24. Linkage of manufacturers and market was suggested as managers must know the trends prevailing in the markets and the consumer behaviour pattern. It was also suggested that DSIDC should undertake regular programme of research both product-wise and area-wise of the market potential of various products in India and abroad to fulfil the needs of SSI Units.

25. The need for expansion of ancillarization programme was emphasized with added accent on quality and standard marketing with international standard. The need for a data bank, where other agencies apart from DSIDC, may be involved to pool their information was also felt.

26. It was suggested to limit pollution by carrying out the review existing arrangement for pollution control in industries, weeding out certain absolute machinery and equipment, adopting pollution control measures collectively by industries of a particular area and by utilizing the maximum installed capacity as the country is already power starved.

27. It was suggested that common treatment plant can be established for each type of industrial waste in various industrial complexes by re-cycling and re-using such industrial waste adopting scientific methods. It was also stated that industrial waste from individual industrial units can be collected through pipe-line or in tanks and can be re-cycled for re-use through scientific methods.

28. It was recommended that a cordial relation is to be maintained between enforcing agencies and industrialists to achieve the aim of pollution control.

29. Delhi could be the informational technology city of the country.

30. Social cost is to be accounted for shifting the pollution prone industries.

31. Industrial Advisory Board for Industries may be constituted.

32. Linkage between policy-makers and industrialists was stressed.

33. Linkage between educational institutions and industrialists was also suggested.

34. It was emphasized that SSIs be motivated and subsidies/loans to be provided for modernization with aim for minimization of pollution in the manner, such as

 (a) Change in the raw-material and conservation of input resources;

 (b) Modify the production process, equipment, operational parameters or the technology itself;

 (c) Improvement in production efficiency and procedures;

 (d) Recovery, re-cycle and reuse the wastes within the plant;

 (e) Modify or reformulate the product.

35. Small Industries Development Corporation to be declared as 'Noddle Agency' to undertake pollution prevention and environmental improvement efforts.

36. Provision of environment and pollution

abatement should be incorporated as one of the conditions of allotment of land and lease deed.

37. Industry/Specific Industrial Estates may be developed with supportive infrastructure.

38. Continuous amendments in the rules in various Acts may be made to as to bring in more and more industries under their purview and the rules should be framed according to the needs of the industry.

39. To recycle the existing Industrial Land for its optimum utilization through flatted factory construction.

15 ENVIRONMENTAL CONSERVATION AND SUSTAINABLE DEVELOPMENT

V.K. SHARMA

Delhi today manifests the symptoms of uncontrolled growth—distinct shortfalls in the infrastructural provisions of sewerage and water supply. Public transport facilities are inadequate. Unauthorized and uncontrolled land use, inadequate residential and commercial space, excessive rents, land speculation, unbalanced growth, and social compartmentalization are other problems the city faces. The Master Plan of Delhi 1962 was meant to prevent or contain these problems. Instead, after 31 years of planning, not only have these problems have multiplied, but other major ones have been added, such as—air, water and noise pollution, rapidly dwindling green cover and degradation of the social environment.

Delhi is situated in the northern part of the country, 160 kms south of the Himalayas. Surrounded by the Thar desert of Rajasthan on the west, the central hot plains on the south, and the cooler hilly region to the north and north-east, Delhi has a composite climate with typical features from all these neighbouring regions having an affect on it. Climate and natural sources play an important role in the pollution scenario of Delhi, in addition to the manmade sources. The region, having a semi-arid climate, regularly experiences dust storms in the pre-monsoon period, when westerly winds carry a large concentration of suspended particulate matter from the deserts and deposit it in the city's atmosphere. Alternatively, pre-monsoon calms often lead to increase in pollution loads due to lack of mixing and dilution. Ground based temperature inversions are a regular feature in winter which restrict mixing heights to low levels, limiting pollution dispersal, and thereby adding to the adverse effects of urban pollution.

The resultant scenario presents a condition for Delhi which is fast leading the city to its environmental doom. Administrative measures, coupled with people's action are the only means of saving the city and bringing it back on a sustainable course.

Delhi's Urban Growth

The population of Delhi has increased almost four times from 2.7 million in 1961 to an estimated 10.3 million in 1993. Rural to urban, as well as, inter urban migration brings about two hundred thousand people every year to Delhi, and this is the main reason for the city's population growth. The population figures for urban and rural areas of Delhi since 1961 and their growth rates are as given under:

Table 1. Population Growth in Delhi

Year	*Population (million)*			*Percentage Variation*		
	Urban	*Rural*	*Total*	*Urban*	*Rural*	*Total*
1961	2,359,408	299,204	2,658,612	+64.2	-2.52	+52.4
1971	3,647,023	418,675	4,065,698	+54.6	+39.9	+52.9
1981	5,768,200	452,206	6,220,406	+58.2	+8.0	+53.0
1991	8,471,625	949,019	9,420,644	+46.9	+109.9	+51.45

Source: Delhi Statistical Handbook, 1995.

As compared to this, the population assigned to the Delhi Union Territory for the year 2001 according to the National Capital Region Plan is 11.2 million, of which 11 million is to be urban and 0.2 million rural population.

To accommodate this growing population, the availability of land has been under immense pressure. The phenomenal growth of Delhi resulted in a process of annexation of fringe lands for urban development. Large extensions of the Ridge area were first violated in the name of institutional growth. The green belt was the next target to accommodate additional population. Since 1962, over 405 sq. km. of cultivable land has been annexed. Now the urban limits are to be extended by 240 sq. km. (24000 ha.). Another 160 sq. km. (16000 ha.) may have to be acquired, further squeezing Delhi's rural populace into a narrow semi-urban periphery. Officially the urban area of the State has expanded from 173 sq. km. in 1958-59 to 529 sq. km. in 1981, and soon it is to be extended to 832 sq. km.

Quality of Life in Residential Areas

Nearly half of Delhi's resident population live in slums or a slum like environment. Delhi has the third largest slum population in the country, with an estimated 3.2 million people reduced to living in sub-human conditions. While the net addition to Delhi's population between 1981 and 1991 was about 3.2 million, migration alone accounted for 2 million.

With 1,080 slum clusters dotting the sprawling megapolis that Delhi has become, a 1.8 million population has found shelter in them. Another 1.2 million have made their homes in 46 resettlement colonies, which comprise nearly 280,000 small plots of 18 to 40 sq. m. As many as 1,800 unauthorized colonies have a population of 1.7 million. These are residential areas that lack proper civic amenities. A distribution of sub-standard housing in Delhi is given as under:

Table 2. Sub-Standard Housing in Delhi—1991

Type of Settlement	*Population (in millions)*
Shanties/Jhuggi clusters	1.4
Slum Designated Areas	1.8
Unauthorized Regularized Colonies	1.2
Unauthorized Colonies	0.5
Resettlement Colonies/Urban Villages	1.2
Rural Villages	0.5
Urban Villages	0.6
Total	7.2

Source : Delhi Vikas Varta, Vol. 3, No. 3, 1992.

Delhi has a number of farmhouses sprawling over 2 acres of land owned by single families, while in slums 300 families live on one acre. Over 27 per cent of people living in slums do not have access to safedrinking water and over 75 per cent are without access to sanitation.

Industries

The growth of large industries is restricted due to introduction of planning restrictions in Delhi, by small scale industries have grown rapidly. There was more than 500 per cent increase in industrial units from 18,000 in 1961 to 93,000 in 1993. Engineering, textiles, chemicals, electronics and electrical goods are the major categories of industries located in Delhi. Growth of all industries over the past four decades is given in the following table:

Table 3. Growth of Industries in Delhi

Year	*No. of Units*	*Investment (Rs. million)*	*Employment*
1951	8,160	181.3	69,266
1961	17,000	600.0	138,000
1965	19,038	810.0	159,731
1968	23,469	1,290.0	192,711
1978	40,000	6,000.0	350,000
1985	65,000	12,600.0	595,000
1990	81,000	15,800.0	729,000
1992	89,000	17,500.0	802,000

Source : *Pioneer*, Industrial Pollution in the Capital, April 4, 1993.

The issue of greater concern, however, is that the uncontrolled growth in the small scale industries sector has led to a proliferation of industrial pockets in areas where they do not conform to the surrounding land uses, and are in violation of the plans. An indicator of the magnitude of this problem is that while Delhi has 20 conforming industrial areas, it has 37 non-conforming industrial areas.

Box 1 : SC Orders Shifting of Industries

> The Supreme Court on September 6, 1996 ordered shifting of 513 hazardous industries from Delhi to other areas by January 30, 1997, failing which the industries would be closed down. The Apex Court had ordered the shifting of 168 hazardous industries in August too. The court has decided to examine a third list of 822 hazardous industries on October 30 (*The Pioneer*, 07-09-96).
>
> On October 9, 1996, the court made it clear that 39,000 illegal industries located in residential areas of Delhi will have to close down by January '97 if they failed to get necessary permission from MCD. After scrutiny of 43,000 applications, it was found that these 39,000 units did not qualify for grant of permission to operate under the Master Plan (*The Hindustan Times*, 10-10-96).

Increased industrial activities along with rapid urbanization has put a greater demand for energy in Delhi. There are three thermal power plants and one gas turbine plant in Delhi. The capacity of generation has increased from 78 MW in 1961 to 1319 MW in 1993.

Vehicles

Motor vehicles registration rose by 51 times between 1961 and 1991, whereas the population increased by 4 times over the same period. It is estimated that in 1994, 2.2 million vehicles were registered in Delhi. This is more than the total number of vehicles registered in Mumbai,

Calcutta and Chennai, the other 3 mega-cities of India. It is also estimated that about two-thirds of the total motor vehicles registered in Delhi are two-wheelers. This has a major implication on the environmental scenario, since most of these two-wheelers are driven on 2-stroke engines, that are low in efficiency and have high emission rates. The explosive growth of Delhi's vehicular population is as given under:

Table 4. Rise in Vehicular Population over Last Two Decades

Vehicle Type	*1971*	*1981*	*1991*	*1994*
Cars/Jeeps	56,540	119,495	398,479	522,264
Scooters/M.Cycles	93,263	345,109	1,220,640	1,492,201
Autorickshaws	10,221	20,379	63,005	72,102
Taxis	3,842	6,385	10,157	11,846
Buses	3,038	8,044	18,858	24,211
Goods Vehicles	13,620	36,599	101,828	116,379
Total	204,078	536,011	1,812,967	2,239,003

Source: Comprehensive Action Plan on Environment and Pollution Control in Delhi, 1994.

This phenomenal growth in vehicular population has not been matched with an increase in road space, thereby leading to congestion, and increased pollution levels. Whereas the total number of vehicles per km length of road available in Delhi was 26 in 1972, and 40 in 1981, the projected figures till 2001 are as follows:

Table 5. Vehicular Density on Road Network of Delhi

Year	*No. of Vehicles per km. of Road Length*	*Year*	*No. of Vehicles per km. of Road Length*
1991	113	1997	184
1992	125	1998	196
1993	137	1999	208
1994	149	2000	219
1995	160	2001	231
1996	172		

Source: Delhi Environmental Status Report, WWF.

The significance of the growing numbers of vehicles can be seen in the share of pollution being generated due to these vehicles. While in 1970, 23 per cent of the total air pollution was due to vehicles, in 1990 this went up to 63 per cent, and in 2001 it is expected to be 72 per cent. Category-wise pollution sources can be seen in the following table :

Table 6. Sources of Pollution

(in per cent)

Source	*1970-71*	*1980-81*	*1990-91*	*2000-01*
Industrial	56	40	29	20
Vehicular	23	42	63	72
Domestic	21	18	8	8

Source: PHD Chamber of Commerce and Industry, Report—November, 1991.

Water Pollution

The river Yamuna, Delhi's main source of water since ages, enters Delhi at Palla in the north and Exits at Jaitpur in the south. It enters the urban area of Delhi at Wazirabad in the north and leaves at Okhla in the south. The total length of the river segment within urban Delhi is about 25 kms. Water quality of the river Yamuna gets heavily polluted due to heavy industrial and domestic wastewater discharges. The water quality of the river upstream of Delhi, i.e. upto Wazirabad, is fit for human consumption after treatment, but after the confluence of 17 major drains, it heavily polluted. As a result, the quality of water downstream of Delhi, i.e. south of Okhla is not fit for animal consumption even after primary treatment.

The river Yamuna travels through Haryana, Delhi and Uttar Pradesh before confluence with the Ganges at Allahabad. The length and basin area of the river in Delhi is only 2 per cent when compared to Haryana and Uttar Pradesh, yet the pollution loads contributed to the river by Delhi are 71 per cent of total wastewater and 55 per cent of total Biological Oxygen Demand (BOD) discharged into the river everyday.

Daily about 2000 million litres (ML) of wastewater and 132 metric tonnes (MT) of BOD are discharged into the river from Delhi through more than 17 drains. Najafgarh, Sen Nursing Home and Power House drains together contribute 95 per cent of total wastewater and BOD discharged into the river.

Domestic sector is the main source of water pollution in terms of volume. Everyday approx. 1700 million litres of wastewater is discharged from the domestic sector and 300 million litres from the industrial sector. The increase in population has resulted in increase in the generation of domestic wastewater from 967 million litres per day in 1977 to 1700 million litres in 1993. The capacity for treatment of domestic wastewater has increased from 450 million litres per day in 1977 to 1270 in 1993. In terms of percentage of wastewater treated to total generated, the increase is from 46 per cent to 75 per cent.

On the industrial front, Delhi has 20 large, 25 medium and approximately 93,000 small scale industries. Large and medium scale industries constitute less than 0.05 per cent of the total industries located in Delhi, but contribute 50 per cent of the total 300 million litres of industrial wastewater generated everyday. The large and medium scale industries have some facilities for effluent treatment and emission control, but the small scale industries have no such provisions. This is primarily due to the financial constraints of these establishments, combined with the lack of coordination for setting up of common facilities.

Air Pollution

According to the ambient air quality monitoring carried out by the Central Pollution Control Board in Delhi, the concentration of sulphur dioxide (SO_2) and Nitrogen Dioxide (NO_2) has increased considerably since 1987 at most locations. Major sources of air pollution in Delhi are vehicles, thermal power plants, industries and domestic coal burning. An estimated 2000 metric tonnes of pollutants are emitted in the atmosphere in Delhi everyday. Carbon Monoxide (CO) tops the list of pollutants with an estimated emission of 1063 metric tonnes per day followed by nitrogen dioxide at 323 metric tonnes, hydro-carbons at 320 metric tonnes and sulphur dioxide at 179 metric tonnes.

Vehicular sources contribute about 64 per cent of total pollutants emitted followed by thermal power plants at 16 per cent, industry at 12 per cent and domestic sector at 7 per cent.

The steep increase in vehicular population has resulted in corresponding increase in pollutants emitted by these vehicles. Presently more than 1300 metric tonnes of pollutants are emitted by the vehicles plying in Delhi. This is about 50 per cent more than the 870 metric tonnes emitted in 1987. Two-wheelers constitute about two-thirds of the total motor vehicles registered in Delhi and they are one of the major sources of air pollution in the city.

Diesel driven vehicles constitute 6 per cent of the total vehicles, but contribute 19 per cent of the total vehicular pollution. Many a times their high emission levels are due to poor maintenance of commercial vehicles by operators, and poor law enforcement by the pollution control authorities.

Delhi has three thermal power plants, viz., Badarpur, Indraprastha and Rajghat plants. These three power plants emit an estimated 302 metric tonnes of pollutants everyday (inclusive of suspended particulate matter, SO_2, NOx, and hydrocarbons) which is 31 per cent of the 965 metric tonnes per day in 1987. Due to improvement in the efficiency of the electrostatic smoke precipitators (ESPs) installed in these plants, the suspended particulate matter (SPM) emission was reduced from 720 metric tonnes per day in 1987 to less than 30 metric tonnes in 1993.

Besides the power plants, there are about 10,000 polluting industries operating in Delhi, including hot mix plants, chemical, pesticide, cement, and electroplating industries. An estimated 240 metric tonnes of pollutants are emitted from the industrial sector which is 12 per cent of the total pollutant emissions in Delhi.

Noise Pollution

Till recently, noise was considered just an annoyance, but now noise pollution has reached such dimensions that it has been recognized as a definite health hazard. The effect of noise include both direct physiological effects as well as psychological impacts. Continuous exposure to high noise levels results in loss of hearing, acoustic trauma, and cardiovascular problems. Prolonged exposure to high level of sound can cause severe mental disorientation and violent behaviour. Noise levels beyond 80 dB (decibels) are annoying and constant exposure above this level causes severe health problems. A number of major intersections in Delhi have ambient noise levels above 80 dB, and most of them have maximum noise levels above 90 dB. The noise levels in various localities under different land uses is as given under :

Table 7. Ambient Daytime Noise Levels in Different Activity Areas of Delhi in dB

Location	*Equivalent Level dB (A)*	*Minimum*	*Maximum*	*Standard*
Residential				55
Maharani Bagh	73	54	114	
Malviya Nagar	65	46	90	
Lodi Colony	55	45	69	
Palam Colony	60	48	78	
Punjabi Bagh	69	44	114	
Timarpur	70	45	90	
Commercial				65
Connaught Place	80	56	102	

Contd. on the next page

table contd.

Location	*Equivalent Level dB (A)*	*Minimum*	*Maximum*	*Standard*
Karol Bagh	71	50	112	
Nehru Place	66	54	79	
Chandni Chowk	75	63	91	
Shahdara	68	58	85	
Industrial				75
Jhilmil	70	58	84	
Okhla	74	59	94	
Wazirpur	75	64	94	
Anand Parbat	70	64	78	

Source: Central Pollution Control Board Report, 1992.

Sewerage and Solid Waste

Despite a 312 per cent increase in the sewage treatment capacity from 257 MLD in 1961 to 1270 MLD in 1993, the treatment plants of Delhi are battling against pressure from mounting waste water generation. In the past three decades, the total sewage output has jumped from a mere 329 MLD in 1961 to 1616 MLD in 1991, a 391 per cent increase. The untreated sewage registered a colossal increase of 1,099 per cent, up from 72 MLD in 1961 to 863 MLD in 1991. As of 1993, the total capacity of the STPs was 1,270 MLD as against the total sewage generated of 1,700 MLD, leaving a shortfall of untreated sewage to the tune of 430 MLD.

The Yamuna Action Plan Report indicated that about 1,700 MLD of sewage is generated everyday in Delhi. In view of the quantum of sewage generated and the status of sewage treatment, it is evident that almost 40 per cent of sewage is being discharged into the Yamuna everyday without any treatment. Even the 994 MLD of treated effluent is not receiving full secondary level treatment and therefore partially treated sewage is further adding to the pollution load of the river Yamuna. The proposed capacity of 2,270 MLD to be achieved by the year 1997 appears to be unlikely in view of the present situation and reason that even land for the proposed treatment plants has not been made available by the land authorities so far.

Delhi produced 1.46 million tonnes of solid waste in 1993, with a 28 per cent increase expected by 2001. The solid waste generation projections for Delhi for 2001 are as given in the following table:

Table 9. Solid Waste Generation in Delhi

Year	*Population (million)*	*Solid Waste Generated*		
		Per Capita (kg)	*Per Day (MT)*	*Per Year (Mill. MT)*
1981	5.76	.400	2,307	0.842
1988	7.65	.500	3,826	1.396
1993	10.00	.407	4,070	1.460
2001	12.80	.570	7,300	2.620

Source: Delhi's Environmental Status Report, WWF, 1995.

Over 4000 metric tonnes of municipal refuse is generated in Delhi everyday. These are dumped in unhygienic and inadcquately controlled conditions at various low lying dumping areas within the city. Besides this, the three thermal power plants emit about 5600 metric tonnes of flyash daily, most of which is dumped in the Yamuna river-bed. Other types of solid waste include hazardous industrial waste from the approximately 95,000 industries and hospital waste from the 80 hospitals and approximately 400 private nursing homes in Delhi. Most of this also finds its way to the municipal dumping grounds alongwith the domestic waste.

Green Spaces—the City's Lungs

Delhi seems overwhelmingly green as compared to other Indian cities such as Mumbai or Calcutta. The prototype of this greenery was laid during the Mughal period and extensive areas were turned green later by the

British. As of today, Delhi has 7 existing picnic spots and 7 proposed ones. Besides this, there are 26 existing major parks, 4 semi-public parks and 7 private parks.

The Master Plan for Delhi-1962, had demarcated a 1.6 km. wide green belt around Delhi in harmony with other open spaces. This was to act as a buffer as well as a green area for Delhi. However, in the second Master Plan for the year 2001, most of the 24,000 had of land that is to be taken over for urbanization lies in this green belt. The new document does not mention the unviolable green belt at all. Besides the green belt, the other major open space in Delhi is the Ridge, which is an extension of the Aravallis, and is 53 km. in length. The Ridge was declared as a reserved forest by the architect of New Delhi, Sir Edward Lutyens, and this status was recognized by the first Master Plan of Delhi also.

Box 2. Encroachment of the Ridge

The Ridge has been declared as a Reserved Forest through the Lieutenant Governor's notification under the Indian Forest Act on May 24, 1994. This was done on the recommendation of the Lovraj Committee, stating that the entire Ridge needs to be declared a reserved forest, and not different stretches of it.

However, uncontrolled encroachments of the Ridge continue to add to its degradation, and according to TCPO, 40 per cent of the Ridge had already been destroyed by 1982. What is most appalling is the fact that the list of encroachers in the Ridge include, Religious bodies, Schools, the Home Ministry, and Defense Establishments, besides slums. The legal and public efforts of a forum of NGOs as well as other environmentalists still remain to have the desired impact, as in spite the Supreme Court rulings regarding removal of encroachments, and other pending cases, destruction of the Ridge continues.

Environmental Costs of Uncontrolled Development

The environmental costs of uncontrolled developmental activities emerge in terms of the increasing levels of different kinds of pollution that Delhi is witnessing today. However, this is only an intermediate cost. The final manifestation of these effects is in various health problems that the resident population has to face. This can be seen in the number of cases of different pollution related diseases reported from various Government hospitals in the city.

Table 10. Reported Medical Cases from Government Hospitals

Disease	*1991*			*1992*		
	Outdoor	*Indoor*	*Deaths*	*Outdoor*	*Indoor*	*Deaths*
Cholera	—	8	—	800	74	—
Typhoid	2,617	1,664	46	2,225	1,473	53
Amoebiases	18,250	590	9	19,212	417	19
Diarrhoea	—	—	0	—	—	—
Gastroenteritis	18,837	889	31	—	—	—
Tuberculosis	26	2,297	287	12,105	3,383	449
Pulmonary TB	4,450	1,458	122	3,729	1,637	199
Tetanus	2	121	50	—	171	54
Viral Hepatitis	2,413	428	28	760	324	40
Acute Bronchitis	35,408	764	42	92,430	800	98
Chronic Asthma	27,260	1,921	71	43,515	1,849	88

Source: Directorate of Health Services, Delhi Administration.

As can be seen from the table, cases of outdoor patients as well as deaths due to Acute Bronchitis, a disease related with air pollution, have risen dramatically, more than doubling over a short time span of one year only.

Environment Administration

Much as been done nationally to provide an administrative and legislative framework for environmental control. The concern for environment at national level actually grew in early 70's when the Water (Prevention and Control of Pollution) Act was passed and a Central monitoring body was set-up specifically to enforce this Act. The body—Central Pollution Control Board at the national level, and its state subsidiaries have since then been looking issues related to pollution. The subsequent passing of Acts on Air Pollution and a comprehensive legislation on environmental pollution in 1986 have further enhanced their role vis-a-vis increasing degree and complexity of environmental pollution.

The Central and State Pollution Control Boards have been, from time to time, able to intervene and apply considerable pressure against violations of the environmental protection Acts. However, it has been observed that these boards have been successful only to the extent of bringing about control on specific point sources of pollution such as industries. They have been largely unsuccessful in controlling pollution spread over considerable areas and with numerous sources. As a result, the real causes of environmental degradation such as river pollution from the drains and urban air pollution from motor vehicles have continued unabated.

The only limited intervention has been in the area of monitoring of pollution levels over time. This issue has brought into focus the viability of a single institution solely responsible for pollution control everywhere. The issue may be viewed from two standpoints.

Firstly, is it possible to give more powers to the pollution control boards and widen their scope and function so that they are able to intervene more effectively and make their presence felt more comprehensively. Secondly, whether to empower other institutions at grassroot level which represent the larger community and therefore have a direct interest in their environment.

In the current milieu, the latter seems to be a better option. Municipal Bodies, Panchayati Raj Institutions, and most importantly Non-Governmental Organizations (NGOs) can play an effective role in controlling pollution. Sure enough, NGOs have been involved in environment protection activities for some time now, however, somehow the local government institutions, which are the implementing agencies at the lowest level have been left out. These agencies, particularly in urban areas where the threat of pollution is maximum, as discussed earlier, have little or no control with regard to the pollution sources.

There is thus an urgent need to build a framework for environmental administration by entrusting responsibilities to local governments and NGOs which in turn are monitored by the nodal agencies such as the Pollution Control Boards. Such a framework is the only plausible solution to the growing problem of pollution in India.

16 EDUCATIONAL SYSTEM IN DELHI: ACHIEVEMENTS AND FAILURES

M.M. SHARMA AND SATBIR SILAS

Education in the N.C.T. of Delhi because of its location occupies a unique position which makes education in this territory as the centre of activities, growth, programmes and innovative experiments. Whatever is started in this territory reverbrates not only through the length and breadth of this great country but goes beyond the boundaries and is looked at with expectation, guidance and motivation.

Tracing the progress of Educational Administration and the landmarks achieved is indeed a very interesting phase in this part of the country. Just looking at the growth of the schools in Table 1 will show a very interesting upward graph.

Table 1. Number of Schools

	70-71		*80-81*		*90-91*		*93-94*		*96-97*	
	Boys	*Girls*	*B*	*G*	*B*	*G*	*B*	*G*	*B*	*G*
SR. SEC.	305	196	440	264	761	369	885	384	653	341
MIDDLE	264	194	232	94	407	78	459	74	491	68
PRY.	781	574	965	761	947	964	1487	606	2124	—

In a span of 27 years the senior secondary schools in N.C.T. Delhi have grown from 501 to 994 and the primary schools from 1255 to 2124. Compared to this, the growth of number of students is shown in Table 2.

Table 2. Number of Students

		SR. SEC.	*MIDDLE*	*PRY*
70-71	B	203847	53006	203516
	G	147417	44464	173654
80-81	B	344904	59150	304759
	G	266141	89034	267729
90-91	B	574509	77763	354352
	G	479891	51396	344891
93-94	B	529700	80428	419519
	G	439380	60123	356811
96-97	B	200757	253430	600754
	G	250577	286081	545937

To man these schools and to take care of the rising number of students, naturally, there has been a corresponding increase in the number of teachers. Table 3 depicts this position in respect of teachers.

Table 3. Number of Teachers

		SR. SEC.	*MIDDLE*	*PRY*
70-71	M	8889	2222	5752
	F	7283	2332	6138
80-81	M	11536	1692	7296
	F	13881	2373	8975
90-91	M	18726	2063	7190
	F	20612	2530	11538
93-94	M	18976	2342	3309
	F	27019	4436	10925
96-97	M	17412	2627	10543
	F	27437	4914	16583

According to the available census the population of Delhi has grown from 40.66 lakhs in 1971 to 94.20 lakhs in 1991. The current position of the schools and the number of students is given in Table 4.

Table 4. Number of Schools and Students in Delhi

	Number of Schools	*Number of Students in Delhi*
1. Government Schools	970	21,55,269
2. Government Aided Schools	218	1,82,406
3. Private Schools	689	6,14,916

The education system that has been inherited in N.C.T. Delhi has undergone tremendous change and in this process of change there are quite a few landmarks which are worth the mention and these have come about alongwith the changing scenario of the governmental set-up of N.C.T. Delhi. Briefly enumerating them we mention Pattabhi Sitaramaya Committee set-up on July 31, 1947 then setting up of the Legislative Assembly of Delhi. This grinding to a halt the demand of statehood for Delhi in 1956. The coming of the Delhi Administration Act in 1966 thereby creation of Metropolitan Council and then finally granting of statehood because of a report submitted by Sarkaria Committee to the Government of India in December, 1989.

These changes have had their effect on the education in Delhi because prior to the granting of the statehood to Delhi all the matters concerning education were directly under the purview of the Government of India. Naturally most of the schemes that were being implemented in Delhi were the ones which were sanctioned by the Government of India and thus were more of National character than the state character.

In-service Training of Teachers

The in-service training of teachers in education has always been viewed as far more important factor than the pre-service training because here the training imparted was received by those participants who had developed a critical mind and everything given to them had always had a contributory factor plugged in by them. Initially all these activities were handled by the State Institute of Education in respect of Humanities and the Science Branch in respect of science subjects. Another important activity undertaken by the then State Institute was the production of an annual magazine entitled *Delhi Shiksha.* Indeed it provided a very good forum for all the teachers, educators and educational administrators as also the public at large to interact express and share their views for everybody to act and react.

On 27 May 1988, under the Societies Registration Act, State Council of Educational Research & Training was set-up in Delhi. SCERT actually started functioning in 1989. With this came in a dramatic change in the mode of in-service training and other activities which hitherto were being carried out by the State Institute of Education but at the same time, there was a tremendous input, cooperation and involvement of the National Council of Educational Research and Training (NCERT). This is because Delhi, being a Union Territory had been getting the double benefit of their own programmes and also utilising the programmes conducted by the NCERT at the national level. This resulted in greatly enriching of Delhi teachers and educational functionaries. Under these programmes, a number of teachers have had the occasion to travel to other States. Participate in the programmes conducted by the NCERT and reap double harvest of enriching their academic calibre and knowing the other parts of the nation. This scene has now changed because the programmes conducted by the SCERT are mostly localised and that added charm and advantage previously enjoyed by the teachers of Delhi has gone off to quite an extent.

Keeping in pace with the strides at the national level, Delhi introduced the vocational programmes in the seventh Five Year Plan. At present these vocational programmes are running in 230 schools as per details given in Table 5.

Table 5. Vocational Courses and Number of Schools in Delhi

Vocational Courses	*Number of Schools*		*Number of Schools*
Steno (English)	88	Electronics	06
Steno (Hindi)	15	Electrical	03
Banking	09	Computer Application	15
LIC	05	Library Science	02
Textile Designing	25	Tourism	04
Fashion Designing	55	Hotel Management Bakery and Confect.	01 01
Health care and Beauty culture	45	Horticulture	04
Medical Lab. Tech.	02	Railway Commercial	01
X-Ray Tech.	02	Automobile Tech.	02
Food Serving and Management	07	Structure and Fabrication Air-Conditioning Tech.	01 04

The starting of these vocational programmes was with the aim that quite a bulk of the students would leave the academic stream and go into self-employment or gainful employment. In this effort we have succeeded to quite an extent. To mention a few landmarks more than 200 students per year were employed by Life Insurance Corporation and General Insurance Corporation for a period of 3-4 years which stopped in 1994. Thereafter, these students had the privilege of competing for employment with some positive reservation shown towards them and that is why the number of schools where these courses were offered has been reduced to 5 from 12 schools. Another course which may be mentioned is the Railway Commercial Assistants' Course which is having a very good example of cooperation between the Government of Delhi, Railways and the C.B.S.E. Though this course is offered in only one school in Delhi, 35 to 40 students every year are being absorbed by the Railways.

Amongst the Engineering based courses, Air

conditioning and Refrigeration, Electronics, Electrical gadgets and Computer Application are producing students who after fulfilling the basic requirements of successfully completing the course have reserved seats in Polytechniques waiting for them for the taking. Another course is a paramedical course in Ophthalmic Technique. These days we find that the students who have successfully completed this course are running their own optician's business and some of them are usefully employed in the Eye clinics of government and private hospitals. To cut the long story short the efforts of the government have been motivated by these success stories and we are now planning to have another 150 to 180 schools within the gambit of this vocational education.

The era starting with 1996 saw the dawn of another very worthwhile landmark achieved in education by the Government of Delhi through the Department of Education when a concerted scheme was launched to bring back the values, the rich Indian culture and history mainly targetting at the freedom struggle and the associated lessons to be learnt and the examples to be followed. The action programme launched by the Department of Education in all of its schools will amply substantiate the efforts. Copy of the suggested action plan is enclosed.

One of the great innovation introduced in recasting the mould of our young citizens and through them the entire population of Delhi into being value respecting, relation respecting, friendly environment and forward looking citizens is through a self-evaluating and self-motivating calendar.

Our commitment being to the total allround development of the child not only on papers, but in practice as well, we have launched as many as 14 different schemes which include promotion of sports, yoga, positive health education, arresting the drop out rate especially amongst the girls students and value education amongst other programmes.

Always alive to the need of the weaker sections,

Government of Delhi has launched an innovative scheme of starting of Super Ability Schools. The idea being to provide the best possible environment, education and guidance to the potential leaders of the country who otherwise get lost in the crowd because of their economic handicap because they cannot afford to pay the rising cost of education in public schools.

Striving for a literate Delhi the programme of 'Education for All' has been carried out with emaculate precision and planning involving the schools teachers, students and the NGOs.

The will and the means available in the department of education of Government of Delhi is such that we are all the time encouraged to achieve more and higher landmarks and for this we are reviving the old *Delhi Shiksha* in the form of a new magazine which is going to come up by 31st August, 1997. This magazine will be brought out four times in one year, have the participation of personnel at all levels and will be managed and produced by the internal expertise.

Having discussed the historical and statistical scenario of the growth and development of educational system in Delhi, let us pause and ponder here for a moment to assess the achievements and the failures in this area. Although our politicians, administrators and educationists, both at the Central as also the State level, have talked aiming at imparting education through the government system. Somehow there is almost a consensus amongst knowledgeable persons that we have not succeeded so far in generating confidence of the people the government schools can provide quality education as compared to the so-called public schools. Of course, one of the reasons cited is that scarce public resources are available to the government system, taking into account the increasing number of students and the schools to cater to them, as the statistical tables above indicate. Some enthusiastic educationists, however, do say that the available resources are under-utilised and even mis-utilised.

Apart from the scarce resources and our failure to make optimum utilisation thereof there are other major reasons which could account for the admittedly poor results measured by the current system of examinations. These, *inter alia*, could be :

(a) Poor results in government schools, some people say, are due to low motivation level amongst the teachers. The teachers who are employed once in governmental set-up feel secure in their jobs. They tend to seek comfortable postings and fewer working hours. Government schools teachers, in turn blame the first generation learners, unaware and uninterested parents and primary (feeder) school teachers for poor quality of results.

(b) On the other hand there are the public schools which are believed to give quality education but at exhorbitant cost to the parents. This high cost is increasingly becoming an issue of debate, discussion and agitation amongst the masses. The issue is currently under debate amongst educationists, administrators and political leaders. The quest is to find a viable and fair solution. Seemingly it may be difficult to evolve a cut and dried solution to this problem. Nevertheless, the churning out of the discussion may help improve both government and public in general and the public school system in particular and as to whether the government should and could interfere to regulate the cost-benefit syndrome in public school system.

(c) Yet another contributory factor is the mode of recruitment of teachers in the government schools. Of course, the over-riding criteria of any good recruitment system is that it should be based on impartial and objective judgement of the competence and potential of the candidate in relation to the job requirements. But the crucial question is as to how do we finally adjudge such competence and potential and what is the ideal mechanism to achieve proper selection. Two methods of selection for teacher have been tried out in the government system. In one system the candidates are selected solely on the basis of their academic and professional performance as per objective assessment and in the other system, which lasted only for a couple of years all those who had attained a minimum level of achievement in their academic examination were subjected to a common selection test. It will be worthwhile conducting a study to compare the professional performance of the two set of teachers selected through the two systems. The best way out would apparently be a judicious mix of both the approaches of recruitment.

(d) While we are in the process diagnosing the reasons for the malady of low academic achievement, a concern for the quality of human beings sent out to the society and the system is also a major issue. It is being widely discussed and debated that a well informed and educated but low-on-values individual is more dangerous for the society than otherwise. Whereas the education system must improve, the quality of knowledge being provided to the child, the ability to critically analyse, understand and logically debate various available options also need to be developed in a child.

(e) The current examination system undermines the system of school evaluation and the relationship between the teacher and the taught in as much as no subjective or emotional evaluation of the student is available at any level.

These issues which have emerged from the above discussion as also other matters germane to the objective of improvement of education in Delhi, both quantitatively and qualitatively, will need to be discussed not only at the routinised fora of discussions, but in such a debate we would need to secure the active and constructive participation of all those who have concern for improving education system particularly in the government sector which caters (unfortunately though) mainly to the under privileged and those belonging to middle class who cannot muster resources enough to send their wards to public schools.

Finally before we conclude, a word about Academic Audit may not be out of place. Some parameters of academic audit both the government schools and public schools could voluntarily adopt. The concept is new and some would term it as impractical and difficult to operationalise. However, it would be good for the educationists and others to consider this suggestion.

Academic Audit broadly covers the mechanism to find the inputs and the resultant output in schools. Under this audit various factors to be considered are Institutional Planning, its implementation, review, adjustments and modifications especially in regard to the programme drawn out to improve the results quantitatively and qualitatively; human resources (Teachers), their qualifications at the time of entry, orientation programmes attended, implementations of the training in the orientation programmes and the resultant effect on the teachers vis-a-vis their performance in the classroom; Curriculum, distribution in the school for various classes, its transaction and objective evaluation of this transaction; books and periodicals brought into the library, their use by the teachers and the students and the various projects/ assignments based on these books: the Review Meetings within the faculty and with the parents, their content and the effect they had on the Teaching Learning Process: innovations introduced in the schools, their effect on the process of teaching and the training imparted in their use to the members of staff. These are some of the suggested areas, but the Academic Audit will cover the entire gambit of Teaching-Learning process in the school.

This audit carried out internally by the personnel in an institution subject to independent and imbiased supervisory role by an independent body will, surely, enable the principals and supervisory staff to diagnose the areas of failure or poor performance and that will, naturally, result in corrective mechanism to bring about the qualitative and quantitative improvement of the output of schools.

17 TECHNICAL EDUCATION IN UNION TERRITORY OF DELHI

P.B. SHARMA

The National Capital Territory of Delhi occupies a unique position in the technical education arena both because of the location as well as it being at the centre of the activities, programmes, development and growth of technical education in the country for the last 5 to 6 decades. The scene for technical education in the northern region of the country was set-up by the establishment of the School of Civil Engineering at Saharanpur in 1845 which later become Thomson College of Engineering at Roorkee in 1854 and subsequently University of Roorkee in 1949. However, it was the establishment of Delhi Polytechnic in 1940 that provided a hub for the growth and expansion of technical education in Delhi and around. Delhi Polytechnic which later become Delhi College of Engineering played a pivotal role for the growth and development of technical education from the 40s onwards. Its first Principal Prof. W.W. Wood, was the Chairman of Wood and Abbot Committee, of 1937. Delhi College of Engineering, the then erstwhile polytechnic, provided the initial impetus for the setting up of a number of national projects in higher technical education such as the premier IIT, Delhi in 1960, College of Arts in 1962, College of Pharmacy in 1964 and School of Planning and Architecture in 1964. Latest addition has been the establishment of Delhi Institute of Technology.

As of today Delhi has 4 institutions offering graduate and post-graduate degree programmes in engineering and technology DCE, DIT, Jamia Millia Islamia and IIT, Delhi, 22 Polytechnics (8 under government control and the remaining managed by government sponsored/private societies) and 13 ITIs. The current total intake capacity at various levels is as given below:

(1) Degree level engineering 1000,

(2) Post-Graduate Degree level engineering 310,

(3) Diploma level 2642, and

(4) ITIs 8356 seats.

Degree level institutions are presently affiliated with Delhi University, Delhi, a central University in the National Capital Territory of Delhi. The IIT Delhi and School of Planning and Architecture being the institutions of national importance are deemed to be universities offering degree level engineering programmes. Jamia Millia Islamia is a central University having non-affiliating character. Thus the present growth and expansion of the degree level technical educational institutions, is inhabitated because of the lack of a affiliating technical university in the city.

In fact when India became independent, there were 46 institutions in India of which, 42 offered undergraduate degree level programmes while only 4 offered post-graduate programmes. Soon after independence India launched a major programme of expansion and diversification of higher education in all sectors including agriculture, medicine and engineering.

Table 1 depicts the profile of growth of higher education in the country during the period 1950-1992.

Table 1. Growth of Higher Educational Institutions in the Country Over the Period 1950 to 1992

Institutions	*1950*	*1960*	*1970*	*1980*	*1989*	*1992*
Universities	37	65	109	129	179	194
Engineering Colleges	58	118	163	226	283	342

Contd. table

Institutions	*1950*	*1960*	*1970*	*1980*	*1989*	*1992*
Medical Colleges	30	61	100	108	139	150
Dental Colleges	3	6	9	13	35	56
Agricultural Colleges	33	81	108	117	132	150
Total	161	331	489	593	868	892

Table 2 gives the profile of growth of higher technical education in India over the period of 1947-1992.

Table 2. Number of Engineering and Technology Institutions from 1947 to 1992

Year	*Institutions*	*Programme at Different Levels*			
		Doctorate Degree	*Master's Degree*	*P.G. Diploma*	*Bachelor Degree*
1947	46	0	4	0	42
1950	58	1	6	1	53
1955	80	1	14	2	74
1960	118	2	27	5	111
1965	151	7	37	9	114
1970	163	20	62	14	155
1975	179	32	84	22	169
1980	226	41	94	19	216
1985	258	58	115	16	347
1989	283	74	143	17	372
1992	342	74	143	17	372

It is pertinent to note that the growth in higher technical education during the above period is approximately 600 per cent which is significantly higher than that in the agriculture, 500 per cent and medicine, 500 per cent thereby indicating the high priority, accorded to higher technical education in the succesive 5-Year Plans. Engineering and technology educational institutions offering degree and higher degree programmes have grown from 46 in 1947 to 342 in 1992.

The 7-fold increase in the number of institutions till 1992 has resulted into a cumulative turnover of staggering high numbers of highly qualified workforce comprising of 6614 Doctorate degree holders, 71,408 holding Master's degrees and over two lakhs Bachelors' degree holders. Tables 3, 4 and 5 give details of the out-turn of BE/ME and Ph.Ds for the period 1984-92.

Table 3. State and Union Territory wise Total Out-turn of Doctorate Degree Holders in Engineering

Name of State	*Number of Doctorate Degree Holders in Engg.*		
	1950-1983	*1984-1989*	*1950-1992*
Andhra Pradesh	51	89	140
Bihar	18	42	60
Chandigarh	—	20	20
Delhi	423	366	789
Gujarat	41	43	84
Haryana	28	29	57
Karnataka	624	286	910
Kerala	1	9	10
Madhya Pradesh	44	31	72
Maharashtra	590	285	875
Orissa	10	5	15
Punjab	7	18	25
Rajasthan	22	18	40
Tamil Nadu	490	302	792
Uttar Pradesh	832	397	1229
West Bengal	426	388	814
Total	3607	2328	6614

Table 4. State and Union Territory wise Total Out-turn of Master's Degree Holders in Engineering and Technology for the Period 1950-1989

Name of State	Number of Master's Degree Holders in Engg. and Technology		
	1950-1983	1984-1989	1950-1989
Andhra Pradesh	2592	1653	4245
Assam	13	97	110
Bihar	682	538	1220
Chandigarh	919	304	1223
Delhi	2373	2263	4636
Goa	44	54	98
Gujarat	1526	407	1933
Haryana	261	200	461
Karnataka	5032	2641	7673
Kerala	1443	755	2198
Madhya Pradesh	1004	799	1803
Maharashtra	6070	2829	8899
Orissa	143	219	362
Punjab	242	318	560
Rajasthan	707	853	1560
Tamil Nadu	7152	4965	12117
Uttar Pradesh	8075	3871	11946
West Bengal	7364	3000	10364
Total	45642	25766	71408

State and Union Territory wise Annual Out-turn of Post Graduate Diploma Holders during 1984-1992

Name of State	Number of Post-Graduate Degree Holders in Engineering and Technology	
	Number	Percentage
Bihar	120	5
Delhi	137	6

Contd. table

Name of State	*Number of Post-Graduate Degree Holders in Engineering and Technology*	
	Number	*Percentage*
Gujarat	164	7
Karnataka	89	4
Maharashtra	174	8
Rajasthan	135	6
Tamil Nadu	178	8
Uttar Pradesh	1166	52
West Bengal	96	4
Total	2259	100

Table 5. Out-turn of Bachelor's Degree Holders in Engineering and Technology from Different Institutions, having the out-turn of 2000 or more During the Period 1984-1992

Name of Institution	*Out-turn from 1984-1992*	*Percentage of the Out-turn*
Inst. of Engg., Calcutta	16440	7.6
Faculty of Engg. and Tech., Jadavpur	3112	1.4
Delhi College of Engg.	2880	1.3
Govt. College of Engg., Pune	2763	1.2
Faculty of Engg. and Tech., Vadodara	2723	1.2
College of Engg., Trivendram	2585	1.1
Ms. Ramaiah Inst. of Tech., Bangalore	2467	1.1
L.D. College of Engg., Ahmedabad	2379	1.1
Manipal Institute of Technology, Manipal	2214	1.0

Contd. table

Name of Institution	*Out-turn from 1984-1992*	*Percentage of the Out-turn*
Birla Vishvakarma Mahavidhyalaya, V. Vidhya Nagar	2200	1.0
Regional Engg. College, Srinagar	2116	0.97
Institute of Elect. and Telecom Engg., Delhi	2077	0.96
University of Roorkee	2073	0.95
Zakir Hussain College of Engg. and Tech., Aligarh	2054	0.94
Govt. Engg. College, Jabalpur	2037	0.94

*The total contribution is approximately 23.76 per cent of the total outurn from 342 colleges.

The setting up of IITs in the 1960s have provided a major thrust in the direction of post-graduate education and research comparable to the world standards. The IITs alone have produced 6500 Master's degree holders, and 3000 Doctorates besides over 35000 Bachelors in Technology. In fact, the IITs contribution to PG's and Ph.D.'s greatly out numbers the engineering colleges in India. While the out-turn of IITs is undoubtedly high as per the Indian standards, it is important to realise that the students population in IITs is nothing comparable to the reputed universities and institutions in advanced countries.

The IITs, however, have retained their focus on quality of their produce and it is this factor alone which has established them as the centres of excellence in technology education and research. The only other institutions in India which are able to match the IITs in terms of the quality of education and research are IISc Bangalore (formerly Tata Institute of Science) and to some extent the University of Roorkee. The IITs have undoubtedly contributed to brain-drain but the phenomenon is not so much because of the education in the IITs but the attractions which the advanced west provided to the talented bright graduates of these institutions. While the IITs still continue with their focus on quality and are able to attract the very best to join the faculty as well as the academic programmes, the engineering colleges are increasingly becoming least attractive for the young talents to join the faculty positions. This, in turn, has become one of the major impediments for improvement of quality of teaching and research in these colleges and has seriously hampered their quest for excellence.

It is with this background one has to see the manpower support currently being provided by the engineering institutions in the higher technical education sector. The Indian industry is largely dependent upon 330 odd colleges for its manpower needs. The best from the IITs and other pioneering institutions continue to migrate abroad contributing to brain-drain which has assumed alarming proportions lately.

Regional Imbalance—A Formidable Problem

The map of mother India, dotted with the geographical locational points of engineering degree level institutions, depicts a rather sad story, see Figure 1. The regional imbalance is clearly depicted in Table 6.

Table 4. Regional Imbalance in Respect of Location of Engineering Institutions in India

Name of State	*Number of Engg. Institutions*	*Population per million*
Maharashtra	92	1.12
Tamil Nadu	48	0.84
Andhra Pradesh	34	0.49
Delhi	4	0.40
Madhya Pradesh	17	0.25
Bihar	10	0.11
Uttar Pradesh	16	0.11

It may be seen that in two states, namely UP and Bihar, having the highest population, have the least number of engineering degree level institutions whereas, the smaller and less populated states, namely, Tamil Nadu and Andhra Pradesh have 48 and 34 degree level engineering institutions respectively. In fact, based on state population, UP has 0.11 institutions per million whereas, the figures for Tamil Nadu and Andhra Pradesh are 0.84 and 0.49 million respectively. As of today, two-thirds of the total number of engineering colleges are located in the southern part of India whereas, the central, north, west and east combined has only one-third of the total engineering colleges. What is difficult to understand is that while the southern states allowed the privately owned mushroom growth of teaching shops-cum-engineering colleges during the 70s and 80s, the states, beyond Andhra Pradesh in the upper India, played a deaf ear to the emerging needs of manpower developments in engineering and technology. The AICTE has, by now, granted its charter to most of these privately managed engineering colleges with ease and speed! The prime issue is as to what sort of growth of higher technical education can be considered feasible for the states where such a massive expansion of technology has not taken place? The regional imbalance is a problem to be tackled within the constraints of massive unemployment of engineering graduates as at present.

The Professional Societies—Major Contribution to Human Resource Development

Besides the engineering colleges and the IITs, the professional societies such as Institution of Engineers (India), Aeronautical Society of India, Indian Metals Society, Institution of Electronics and Telecommunication Engineers, IETE, etc. have made significant contribution to the continuing education of the serving engineers. Table 3 shows the out-turn from the professional Associateship Examinations to the growth of engineering and technology manpower in India over a period of 1990 to 1992. It is important to realise that the Associateship Examination of these professional societies, approved as equivalent to the degrees of the universities, is of special significance as these examinations are specifically designed for the professional proficiency besides the preparation for the modern requirement for engineering and technology design, manufacturing and managements. The role of these professional societies has, however, so far been supplementary to the higher technical educational institutions but now onwards, these societies are to increasingly meet the requirements of effective linkages between the industries and the institutions. They are to re-design their courses for effectively imparting continuing education to assure a competitive age for the work force in engineering and technology pursuits. These societies have, therefore, to expand their wings to encompass a greater horizon of educational and professional activities than they have catered so far. Besides, the re-orientation in the institutional objectives, it is the management structure of the institutions that needs to undergo drastic changes along the direction of Total Quality Management.

TQM of Technical Education System

Total quality management has recently become highly relevant as a management philosophy for the higher technical institutions. The demand of quality assurance at world standards as per ISO 9000/IS 14000, coupled with the pressure of global competition is causing compulsions, both in the manufacturing as well as in the service sector of the economy to re-orient the management perspective. It is not only the quality of the end product but the quality in everything that has to be the main thrust of this new management initiative. Besides quality, the productivity is the second most important concern in the modern competitive environment.

Higher technical educational institutions are to meet the challenges of human resource development commensurate with the emerging requirements of the industries and the service sector organisations. The management of higher technical education has, therefore, to gear itself to meet these challenges. The idea is to practice TQM as a management philosophy within the four walls of the institutions so that the students gain, besides knowledge, the attitudes and the work ethics vital for the success in today's highly competitive world. They have also to exhibit a greater commitment to the society and the environment to which they rightly belong and to which they aspire to serve.

Further, the role of higher technical education has evidently become highly significant, specially in view of the added constraints of technology upgradation in the industries. This exercise these days is to be carried out more frequently than in the decades of 70s and 80s. The oil crisis of 1974 has undoubtly accelerated the pace of development of energy-efficient systems. The requirements of R&D, energy audit and environmental considerations have thrown new challenges to engineers and these have been to some extent met in both the developing as well as the developed countries. However, with the beginning of the era of globalisation of economy, the engineers have been brought face to face with many new challenges. These include quality assurance at world levels, productivity to remain cost competitive, highly innovative product designs to ensure conservation of energy and environment and expert maintenance support for trouble free operation. In addition, the engineers of today as well as, the engineers of tomorrow have to exhibit a much greater concern for the society and the environment. The human face of technology has to become more evident in pursuits of engineering excellence from now onwards so as to achieve a greater public appreciation of engineering and technology advances and their impact on the quality of life of people.

The Pressing Problems

Against the above new requirements, the higher technical educational institutions in India are presently facing a number of teething problems arising out of faculty shortage, obsolescence in the laboratories, upgradation of skills of the technicians and above all the resource crunch. The management of these institutions has so far kept itself almost aloof to the management practices prevailing in the industries. As a result these institutions have become highly unproductive besides exhibiting a perpetual divorce with the industry and the society. It is important to realise that it is the pressure of the market competition that keeps the industries on their toes. The lack of competition in the higher technical education sector and easy inflow of funds in the past has made these institutions somewhat complacent. In the emerging economy environment, it is the human resource that will be the most significant ingredient for the success of an organisation. The management of higher technical educational institutions has therefore to gear itself up to the call of total quality management so as to produce the relevant human resource at a competitive investment. These institutions have also to provide the necessary environment for the development of technology and expert knowhow for the industries.

Faculty Development –A Dire Need

India today has around 340 engineering degree level institutions besides 5 IITs and the Indian Institute of Science. Almost half of these institutions are under private management. These institutions as well as those under the government control are facing the problem of lack of motivation and interest in the teaching faculty and technical staff. These problems are to be tackled first if the higher technical education is to remain a vibrant entity in the rapidly changing economy environment.

The IITs, which have enjoyed the benefit of foreign collaborations, have undoubtedly created an excellent infrastructure though at enormously high investment. However, the IITs have not been able to reduce the dependence of Indian industries on technology and knowhow import. The IITs do not have the problem of faculty shortage nor the obsolescence in the laboratories except in emerging areas. It is primarily because of an efficient recruitment policy and attractive environment for R&D in these institutions that the IITs have been able to attract the talented youth to join the faculty positions. Given the present level of expertise and infrastructure, the IITs can serve the nation in the changed economy environment with a much greater contribution to relevant manpower development besides R&D and Technology Transfer. This will, however, significantly depend upon the IIT management, re-orienting its present management philosophy towards TQM so as to nurture excellence alongside with relevance. Gradually, these centres of excellence are to become centres of relevance in higher technical education if the nation is to benefit from their expertise and infrastructure. The support of the IITs in the early 70s to other engineering colleges, through QIP programmes for faculty development and Curriculum Development Cells has gradually declined. There is an urgent need to revitalise these programmes both for the faculty development of the engineering colleges as well as for upgrading the course curriculum and the laboratories.

The regional as well as the other degree level institutions are to concentrate on attracting motivated talented youths to join the faculty positions. Well designed personnel policies providing incentives and rewards for the talented and having the provision of weeding out the dead wood from these institutions are highly called for. It must be realised that there is no lack of talent in India; after all, we are exporting talented youths to the advanced countries of the West. It is only the lack of appreciation of teaching profession and the unattractive work environment that deters the talented youth to opt for a teaching career in India. Compared to this the teaching career is highly attractive and rewarding in the advanced countries. If the nation has to succeed in the today's economic environment, it is absolutely essential that a much greater attention is paid to make teaching career in engineering institutions highly attractive. For, if we fail to re-vitalise the HRD in higher technical education, we shall not be able to turn the threats of globalisation into the opportunities for growth and development.

Attracting Motivated Faculty—A Monumental Task

Engineering institutions continues to receive the very best highly motivated school leavers who come to the engineering colleges with the expectations of catching up with the state of art in science and technology and to receive training in design, manufacturing and managerial functions which will be required from them four years from the date of their entry to a college. It is in this respect that the role of the engineering institutions and the engineering teachers in particular is important. The teachers in engineering institutions have to keep themselves fully informed of the latest developments in engineering science and engineering technology. They themselves have to be seekers of more and more knowledge and must be able to assimilate the growth of knowledge in their teaching scheme. A high degree of commitment and calibre is called for from the teachers in engineering institutions. The task before the management of technical institutions of attracting the motivated ones to join the faculty is truly monumental.

The faculty shortage is not easy to explain given the fact that the turnout of post-graduates and Ph.D. degree holders in engineering and technology in India has been phenomenal over the last two decades. The IITs, alone have produced over 3000 Ph.Ds and 4000 Master's degree holders over the last fifteen years. Why such a highly qualified work force does not turn toward teaching is something worth researching in India. Compared to this in US there is a mad rush for the teaching positions!

Seen from the salaries and promotional avenues teaching profession has been made highly attractive by the last pay revision by AICTE. It has even lowered the recruitment qualification from Master's degree to Bachelor's degree for inducting at the lecturer's level. It is worth noting that the minimum qualification in universities in US is Ph.D and so has it become in the case of the IITs where the lecturers and now inducted at a scale higher than that prevailing in other engineering institutions. The lowering of recruitment qualification of Bachelor's degree, the revision of scales and the provision of three-tier (Lecturer/Assistant Professor and Professor) system is not enough attraction to the Indian skilled and highly qualified manpower to join the engineering colleges. This matter needs a detailed study as the success of our technical education system hinges around the faculty, the teachers in engineering educational institutions.

The highly motivated and qualified professional will be attracted to teaching only if the educational institutions provide an environment to enable them to flourish as expert technologists alongside with teaching. Afterall America, England, Japan and other developed countries have been successful in attracting the very best to teaching by giving a high priority to this profession as its quality and commitment directly affects the industrial advancement and the quality of human resource. In India the reluctance to join teaching is also because of the value system of our society which does not acknowledge or recognise the value of those who create wealth while it fully acknowledges and recognises the role of the managers and administrators of the wealth of the nation.

The Role of an Engineering Teacher—Clear Perspective Needed

There can be no two opinions that the role of a teacher is vital in the growth of technical education and in upholding the quality of human resource development. What is, however, not unanimously upheld is the view that the teacher in an engineering institution should devote not only to teaching but also the R&D and Industrial consultancy. Teaching activity should be given top priority is well understood but what is not acceptable that the teacher teaches from the books and notes alone. With the explosion of knowledge in S&T the books and notes become fast out dated. The new techniques of mathematical analysis, computation, design and drafting and above all manufacturing and management technology which flood the academic world each year require teaching minds to engage themselves into an active research beyond literature surveys. After all what is to be taught is to become relevant four years later. The teaching process has, therefore, to dynamically assimilate the growth of knowledge into its teaching methodology. If done at the level of America or Japan, the teachers in engineering institution will be the peers of knowledge and the institutions will be the centres of not mere learning but centres of technology innovation and research. The teacher will then simultaneously perform triple role; role of a teacher, scientist and expert practicing technologist. The ultimate beneficiary will be the students, the human resources for tomorrow. The industries will be highly benefited as they shall lean with confidence on the expertise available in the Indian institutions, and above all the Government shall be relieved from the fiscal contribution to R&D as the bulk of R&D in the engineering institutions will then be largely funded from sponsored research and industrial consultancy. Technical education will then in the true sense become "Education for wealth creation".

R&D in Educational Institutions—A Vital Component for Nurturing Excellence

Alone teaching alone or both teaching and research as the responsibilities and job functions of teachers in engineering institutions is a matter still being debated in our country. There is a feeling which persists in academic circles that diversion of efforts of a teacher towards R&D usually sacrifices teaching interest. There are teachers who are highly devoted to teaching and spent much of their spare time for preparation of teaching material and innovate in teaching to sustain interest in the class. They obviously do not have much interest in research and development which besides being time consuming deprive them of the intellectual freedom which they enjoy as teachers. R&D being time bound and result oriented demands that the teacher devotes his considerable time to the success of the work which often involves managerial functions besides expert guidance. Being financially rewarding and a means of recognition in the profession, R&D acts as a catalyst to sustain one's interest in innovation and creative research. It also helps a faculty member aspire for a greater original contribution to the growth of knowledge and brings added satisfaction from the application of the knowledge to solve the real life problems. The teaching style of such teachers has a strong element of professional bias, highly relevant to the students who are to take up challenges in their professional career, once they leave the college. It must, however, be realised that there is a basic difference between teaching and research. Teaching unlike research requires excellent communication skills. The interest in teaching stems from one's desire to benefit the pupils from the depth of knowledge which the teacher possesses. This interest is further enhanced if those taught respond to learning. A researcher on the other hand works himself or at the most with his team on a challenging problem and his interest in R&D is basically from the satisfaction he derives from the outcome of his research. He creates the necessary facilities for his research from sponsored research and development projects and the hard work pays in the long run as his research establishes him in the profession. Further, the recognition of research is worldwide while a motivated teacher is at best recognised and rewarded within his university.

The students in engineering institutions are to be taught by those who take pains in sustaining the interest of the students by constantly updating their teaching material while at the same time commanding a high reputation as practicing technologists, something similar to what is done in medical colleges.

Another point of interest here is in respect of funding of R&D in India. The government is the major financer of R&D expenditure. The private industries only contribute per cent to this vital component of economy. In any case, the R&D expenditure in India is only 0 per cent of GNP while the developed nations spend up to 6 per cent of GNP on R&D. The poor spending on R&D speaks for the miserable position in respect of intellectual property generation in India. While, a higher allocation on R&D is essential, the higher technical educational institutions must perform a lot better in respect of effectiveness of their R&D activities.

Institution Industry Linkages—Vital Component of Excellence in Education

The academic environment in an engineering institution is to be enriched both by the analytical as well as practical aptitude. Such an environment can be effectively created if the linkages between institution and the industries are strengthened. Such linkages should provide a dynamic environment in which the expertise from the R&D could be effectively utilised by the industries and the real life problems and prospects of the industries are taken as challenges both by the expert faculty and the students. Presently there is a limited scope of practical experience in technical education system. This is through the laboratory exercises and vocational training in the industries. This is not adequate as the laboratory exercises are basically aimed at illustrating the basic concepts and the vocational training by and large remains observational in nature.

The effective linkages between industry and the institution could take the form of MOUs allowing each other to take advantage of and to support each others activities. Greater participation of students in solving the industrial problems can be ensured by designing project work in consultation with the industries. Such projects will provide a meaningful opportunity for the students to express their innovative and creative skills. The project work will thus induct the students into the research methodology even at the undergraduate level where the mind is often highly innovative and creative. It is also highly desirable that the students are provided much greater contact hours with the experts from the industries and R&D organisations so that they can effectively interact and perceive the value of their studies. Such visits can become more meaningful if a more direct linkage is established with the selected industries and organisation. The idea should be to involve the students in the real-life situations while they are still at the studies. Special courses with a committed intake designed specifically for the industries can also help develop the relevant human resource. The training and re-training of engineers can also be ensured through such linkages.

The linkages between the institutions and the professional societies are also highly important. Such linkages shall help inculcate an attitude of professionalism in the young minds and will help the student community aspire for a contribution to the profession to which they shall rightly belong to take up on leaving the college.

The strength and weaknesses of the present technical education system are required to be analysed in the context of the success or otherwise of the Indian industries and other related organisation. The problem of poor quality and remarkably high price of Indian products is perhaps an outcome of unenthusiastic technical human resource working in an uninspiring industry environment. While the technical education system has a strong bias for analysis and tutorial exercises, it has lacked the environment for the pursuit of excellence through innovation and creativity. It has not fully exploited the mental capabilities of its students nor has it given them the orientation necessary to enhance one's commitment to the cause of technology development for the betterment of the quality of life of the people of their country. The curriculam has also missed on educating its learners about the human face of technology.

Style of Management—Need for Re-orientation

The style of management of higher technical education in India has by and large lacked the appreciation of the role of the teachers, its faculty in the overall development of the institutions. It has lacked its emphasis on people's development least it has cared for nurturing an environment for the development of an individual. The quality improvement programme of the 70s and 80s has no doubt, improved the qualifications of the faculty but it has not largely benefited the institutions' academic or research programmes primarily because of lack of peer pressure on such individuals. They also lacked motivation to improve the institutions, laboratories and work environment. The management and the teachers still remain at loggerheads in respect of their expectations and aspirations. There is no meeting of the minds between the objectives of the institution and the growth and advancement of the faculty members.

The global economy scenario requires world class people who besides being globally competitive must practice a quality and productivity linked work culture. The educational institutions in the higher technical education sector have also to ensure that they have in their faculty and staff people who are world class having calibre and competence to remain knowledge workers throughout their working life. To cater for this requirements the style of management has to undergo a clear re-orientation in respect of:

* Recognition of achievements
* Empowerment of an individual
* Identification of talent
* Respect of one's capabilities
* Motivation for continuous upgradation of skills.

The management must also clearly recognise that its responsibility is not only to attract the best to join its faculty and staff positions but also to ensure that they become better and better everyday rather than becoming gradually dull and unproductive as is the case at present. The management of higher technical education must also have a greater faith in performance re-appraisal and feedback from its students besides exerting peer pressure for continuous quality assurance of its faculty and staff.

Curriculum Innovation—Immediate Steps Needed

With rapid advances in Science and Technology, the fast decrease in half-life of knowledge acquired and with the emerging demands for flexible human resource development, it has become absolutely essential to restructure the course curriculum, design course structure to in-built flexibility as also to strengthen the inter-disciplinary component in engineering and technology courses. At the same time, a sound science base of modern engineering is to be provided. Care and concern for society and environment has to become a core component of the engineering curriculum so that the engineers of today as well as the engineers of tomorrow become more responsible to the society to which they belong. They, then in true sense, will be the pillars of strength of the economy and will be the prime movers of growth and development of a science and technology driven economy.

In order to succeed in our efforts of providing the much needed improvements in the course curriculum, it is absolutely essential that the dons in the educational institutions recognise the need for assessment of skills, aptitudes and knowledge requirements of the industries and organisations which recruit their products. Currently there is a total absence of such a feedback system. The dons overwhelmingly are conscious that it is they who know the best and it is they alone who can decide what is best for the academics. It is this blashphemy which is responsible for the daring obsolescence of the course curriculum and a deadlock on the interaction with the industries. The dons must understand that because of visible compulsions of global competitiveness the industries foresee the technology and human resource requirements faster than the institutions do. In fact the industries are conscious of their requirements and they gear their management to meet the challenges which the market driven economy assigns to them. The dons of the universities and colleges being self-proclaimed experts, these visionaries of growth of knowledge continue to refuse the role of the practitioners of technology in affecting the change in the academic thinking. The Indian dons are undoubtedly more sensitive in this respect than their counterparts in the advanced West where the quality and productivity have percolated in the university circles as much as in the industries. This position needs immediate change lest the universities and colleges are declared places of technology and educational obsolescence.

Funding of Higher Technical Education—Need for Clear Perspective

Higher technical education is highly expensive specially if one has to cater for the needs of the modern day requirements of a quality and productivity linked educational system. The funding of higher technical education is bound to cause a serious concern specially that higher technical education and research is becoming increasing expensive day by day. The cost of the modern day laboratory in polymer technology is of the order of 3 crores. A modern computational laboratory catering for the need of a batch of 40 students will cost around 2 crores; a modern day electron microscope would cost around one crore; a 3-D Laser Doppler Animometer requires an investment of one crore to set-up a laser measurement laboratory, just to give some idea of the cost involved for modern laboratories and equipments. The average expenditure on producing an engineering graduate varies from approximately Rs. 14,000 in institutions like DCE to about Rs. 3,00,000 in the IITs. The Eighth Five Year Plan has provided a total of Rs. 1000 crores on technical education largely being funded by the government exchequer while the out-turn of these institutions are mostly being utilised by the private industries and organisation.

A serious question being asked is why should a common pay for the expenditure of someone who is worth Rs. 10,000 or more per month in the private sector on graduation? The Government of India and the AICTE have had a singular approach in this regard and this thinking has resulted into a single point agenda of increasing the tuition fees to be charged from the students. What the Ministry of HRD and the AICTE have missed is that they have not appreciated the capabilities of the faculty to produce wealth through industrial consultancy and through effective utilisation of the infrastructure in the universities and the colleges. It is painful that while the industry starves for the expensive equipments and instruments for testing and quality certification, the institutions continue to utilise such highly expensive instruments and equipment merely for training and education for a few hours per week. Such equipment, if used for industrial work alongside with teaching, can produce wealth for the institutions. It is this form of resource generation which will offset the pressure on tuition fees besides assuring a greater utilisation and return of investment in modernisation of the laboratories and equipment. The other idea could be to motivate the large business and industry houses to support the cause of laboratory modernisation in the educational institutions, even naming these laboratories in the names of the Tatas, Birlas and others may not be a bad proposition provided they fund the modernisation of the laboratorues and its equipments to relieve the exchequer from the burden of funding a sector of HRD largely to be utilised by private industries and organisations. A clear re-thinking is required in this respect. The increase of fees is not the only solution to the problem of resource crunch. Other avenues of a greater and effective utilisation of in-house talent and infrastructure must be explored so that the talented one's, who cannot pay for their education, can make it to higher technical education in the right earnest.

Concluding Remarks

1. The management of higher technical and management institutions in India has so far lacked its emphasis on quality of the system or monitoring of its productivity. Compared to this, quality culture and productivity movements are the backbone of the success of the modern industries. Time has come when higher technical educational institutions, who contribute one of the most important M'S, i.e. the manpower, adopt and practice TQM, as the management philosophy.
2. Excellence in higher technical education is always talked about. But the excellence alone is not a sufficient condition for the development of quality of human resource. It is the focus on relevance that is equally necessary so that the emergent as well as the long-term needs of the country could be effectively met.
3. The productivity in higher technical educational

institutions is seriously affected by the quality of teachers. Teachers must therefore be highly motivated and committed to the cause of teaching, research and industrial liaison. Attracting talented youth to join the faculty is a monumental challenge to the management of these institutions. There is an urgent need to review the personnel policies in this respect.

4. Teachers in higher technical educational institutions have to enhance their activities beyond teaching. They have to simultaneously perform triple role—the role of a teacher, a scientist and a practising technologist. It is only then their profound wisdom will be an instrument of social change and will undoubtedly be the guiding spirit for the improvement of quality of life of the people at large.

5. Technology development, technology transfer, increased R&D and prototype development are to be given an added impetus in the higher technical educational institutions to meaningful utilise the expertise of the faculty and the infrastructure.

6. Heavy expenditure on modernisation of laboratories, library books and journals, and high speed computational facilities necessarily demands resource sharing among the institutions, R&D organisations and the industries. A part of the solution to resource crisis lies in networking of resources/facilities. A more productive utilisation of infrastructure, laboratories and the talent and skills of the faculty and staff is an essential aspect of resource generation.

7. The management of higher technical education

has, therefore, to adopt TQM as a management system so as to make this sector of economy both competitive and quality conscious while at the same time improving its linkages with the industries and the society.

Acknowledgements

The author wishes to acknowledge the support received from Shri Mohd. Mohsin, Mrs. B. Mattoo and Dr. Aderemi Adekoya in the preparation of the present work.

REFERENCES

1. Qasim, S.Z., *The Role of Technology in the Globalized Indian Economy*, Inaugural Address, Nat. IEEE Sem., DCE, also STAND Vol. VI, pp. 25-27, Feb. 1993.
2. Sharma, P.B. and Gupta P.K., *Quality and Productivity in Technical Education*, Theme Paper, Proc. of EME National Conference, NAFEN, July 1993.
3. Khanna, S.K., *Challenges of Higher Technical Education in India*, Convocation Address, DCE, Sept. 1993.
4. Sharma, P.B., *Excellence in Technical Education—Issues Involved*, Keynote Paper, National Conference on Quality and Productivity in Technical Education, NAFEN, Feb. 1994.
5. *Engineering Manpower Development—A National Perspective*, Report DCE/NC/94 Nodal Centre, Delhi College of Engineering, Sept. 1994.
6. Sharma, P.B., *Management of Engineering Institutions—New Challenges*, International Jr. of Engineering Education, USA. 1994.

18 REDRESSAL OF PUBLIC GRIEVANCES

S.C. VAJPEYI

Effective redressal of public grievances, whether these relate to DESU, DDA, MCD, Police or other departments of the government is the real touch-stone of success of governance. This aspect is being dealt with both at macro and micro levels in this final chapter. This chapter is divided in two parts. In part I the issue of public grievances has been discussed. Part II contains full text of the address of Mr. P.K. Dave, former Lt. Governor of Delhi, at IIPA on 11th August, 1994, on this subject. Action on some of the points raised by him has been updated in the postscript under the Editors' Note following the text.

PART-I

SOME ISSUES REGARDING PUBLIC GRIEVANCES

The question of effective redressal of public grievances has increasingly attracted critical attention at various governmental/non-governmental fora. As the functions of the State multiplied, both in quantitative and qualitative terms, the administration of departments covered in the overall umbrella of 'Welfare State' became complicated and cumbersome. The human element involved in the administrative process and the discretion inherent in the implementation of sophisticated laws, rules and procedures colours the quality of the decisions which could be wrong, partisan, motivated or unfair for reasons which need not be gone into. Hence, the need, for setting-up a machinery exclusively for redressal of public grievances and investigating into the causes of delay and injustice in the disposal of public business and corruption.

The Administrative Reforms Commission[1] initiated several studies[2] to look into this matter and a Committee known as 'Santhanam Committee'[3] had also earlier gone into the causes of corruption in public services. This and various other Committees made various recommendations to improve the administrative system, to rationalise the rules and simplify the procedures, to curb delays, to reduce the element of discretion and to eliminate the chances of corruption in the disposal of work related to the handling of public affairs. It was largely as a result of these recommendations that the Department of Administrative Reforms and Public Grievances came into being in the seventies.[4] Various steps were taken by the Department for ensuring quicker disposal of government business, decentralisation of administrative and financial powers, for undertaking systematic studies of grievance-prone areas, improvement and simplification of cumbersome procedures, identification of the locus of decision-making for enforcing much talked of accountability, involvement of voluntary agencies, attitudinal reorientation and finally by strengthening of monitoring mechanisms and public awareness programmes. Formal instructions issued as a follow-up of these steps and action taken thereon, including the setting-up of institutions like Central Vigilance Commission[5] and those of Lok Ayukta in some of the States[6], have however, failed to make any significant impact, either qualitatively or quantitatively, in redressal of public grievances.

Conscious of the axiom that redressal of public grievances is an inseparable part of the Government, the Estimates Committee of Parliament found it appropriate to examine the whole problem in-depth. Their first report of 1991-92[7] presented to the Lok Sabha on December 10, 1991 and the action taken report presented by its then Chairman Mr. Manoranjan Bhakta in March, 1993[8], have, after a critical analysis of the present scenario, made useful suggestions.

Relevant remarks of the Committee are extracted as follows:

> "The Committee find it distressing that the index of public satisfaction with the activities and services of Government agencies has been so low as to necessitate creation of a separate department under the Ministry of Personnel and Administrative Reforms in order to attend to an exceedingly high volume of over one million grievances/complaints against functioning of Central Government Departments and other related agencies. The Committee are further surprised to find that up to 1985 the Government had not taken due cognizance of mounting public dissatisfaction about the functioning of Government Departments/Agencies. They also depreciate the absence of comprehensive analytical statistics about the nature and dispersal of public grievances" (Page 7 Ist Estimates Committee Report 1991-92)[9].

One must, however, perceive the limitation of the Estimates Committee report—firstly that it looks at the problem only from the point of view of Central Government Departments and agencies, and secondly that too only at the macro level. Two major points which, however, emerge from these reports are that the Committee perceived the attitudinal aspect of officers at middle and cutting edge level in redressing a public grievance to be the core of the whole problem.[10] Attitudinal problem is not so much of a governance or a management problem as it is inspirational in nature. Right attitudes should flow from top downwards so as to inspire and motivate the field level staff to develop positive attitude towards their work. The second point emphasised by the Committee, and accepted by the Government, is that the time lag between making of a complaint and disposal of major public grievances has to be reduced by adopting latest technology for maintenance of records, by setting-up management information systems and commissioning systematic studies in more grievance prone areas. The then Cabinet Secretary during his evidence on January 8, 1993[11] accepted this shortcoming when he said that "I would beseech the indulgence of the Committee that we should, perhaps, take a review after some more time, because I, personally, am not happy by the way in which the redressal is being done. Now, on an average, it takes 155 days. Today, ideally in special cases we should perhaps give a response time of not more than 3 months." This time lag in case of NCT Delhi should be further restricted.

Let us pause here for a moment and look at the problems of the NCT of Delhi. Multiplicity of authorities in Delhi, apart from the other reasons common to delay in disposal of Government business, has given rise to a larger number of grievances and complaints which could not be attended to promptly and properly. Some people hold, and rightly so, that continued absence of an administrative set-up responsive and responsible to Legislature is another contributory factor for non-redressal of genuine grievances to the required extent. A Commitee now known as Balakrishnan Committee[12] was set-up with a view to make recommendations for the future legislative set-up and administrative structure in Delhi. During its deliberations the Committee also looked into how best to alleviate the difficulties experienced by the Delhi citizens and to ensure expeditious settlement of their legitimate grievances. So far as the grievances arising out of the enforcement of law and order are concerned, the Committee went into considerable detail to examine whether the present 'Police Commissioner' system can be continued and if so, whether there is need to have an independent machinery to look into the complaints and grievances connected with administration of law and order. This aspect has been dealt with in next part of this chapter.

The need for setting-up a system for redressal of public grievances in matters dealt with by different departments other than police is long felt and well recognised. Administrators of the Union Territory have in the past, according to their own inclinations, tried various measures but with little success. The existing system theoretically provides for the prompt and proper handling of public complaints and grievances—largely on paper. Ministers and the Chief Minister have set apart fixed hours when they meet members of public and there is a special officer attached to the Chief Minister for attending to public grievances.

For various reasons these measures have not achieved the desired results. Reasons are much too obvious to need scrutiny or elaboration. One of the main causes for dissatisfaction of the general public is the unsympathetic attitude of and non-application of mind by the officers at various levels, delay caused in the disposal of business for various reasons and the hesitation on the part of officers/officials to take a clear cut decision in important matters. Improper motives are also being openly imputed for delay in disposal of cases as also for deciding them not on the basis of merit but otherwise.

The Delhi Branch of the Indian Institute of Public Administration organised three discussions—one in September 1991, the other in July 1992 and the third in November, 1993, to discuss administrative implications of the proposals regarding Delhi set-up and during two of these discussions some former Lt. Governors and former Chief Executive Councillors as also the then Lt. Governor participated. On these occasions it was emphasised that it is the consumer or the citizen who is important, and little does he care for the 'formal administrative set-up' under which he is governed. Therefore, his grievances whether it is vis-a-vis DDA, MCD or Police, must be redressed. Mr. P.K. Dave, the former Lt. Governor, reacted to this in clear and unequivocal terms and it may be worthwhile to quote what he said on July 23, 1992 during these discussions:

> "I am only dealing with major issues. Finally is the grievances. Delhi is full of grievances; everyone is dissatisfied. They are dissatisfied about civil services, transportation, cleanliness, tax structure, property tax; on everything that you can think of they are

dissatisfied. In a growing city, in a city with education spreading, people becoming more and more conscious, with economic activity of a high order—the pace of the Delhi economy is amongst the fastest in the country—this is bound to happen. But I am afraid, the grievance procedures have not got established. We have had somewhat half-hearted attempts at having Adalats. Recently, we started with DESU Adalats. We have the Grievances Day in the DDA. We may have public hearing by the Lt. Governor.

We have to have a system of administrative tribunals. Here I should very much like to put in a thought. The administrative tribunals tend to become legalistic. What we want is someone to go into the grievances examine the paper and give a decision, a short and sweet decision, which is binding on the part of the agency concerned to implement that decision. You will rightly guess, I am referring to the Ombudsman system, probably three or four Ombudsmen, all legal to provide recourse to the public for its grievance, for unfair or unequal treatment. This will cover the entire gamut of services that are rendered by or under the Delhi set-up.

This, I think, is an extremely important measure that ought to receive your attention, may be peripheral here, but in-depth elsewhere".

At this stage it may not be out of place to make a reference to the setting-up of DESU Adalat which consisted of 5 members, including two non-officials and the Chief Engineer, DESU, for the particular zone was the Chairman of the Adalat. Admittedly DESU Adalat, both in this constitution and in its functioning, is not an ideal solution. It needs to be improved in various ways and the working of this institution over the past several years throws up certain ideas which could usefully be adapted for improving this system. That would, however, need deeper study and separate treatment. There were occasions when unanimous decisions of this Adalat were not implemented for months or years. And finally it was the intervention of the High Court in one case which has now enjoined DESU to enforce the decision of the Adalat forthwith. The working of this experiment over the past years is being studied in depth by an independent agency to make it more useful and focused.

The Lt. Governor (former Lt. Governor, Mr. P.K. Dave) was anxious to address himself to this problem. He gave vent to this feeling in the Seminar held on July 23, 1992. The matter was also referred to the Centre for Policy Research for an in-depth study and analysis to enable him to make up his mind on this issue. The Delhi Government has also been equally concerned with the problems of common man and the frustration that he faces at every step. Some of the options which broadly are emerging as an answer to this problem, could briefly be summed up as follows:

(a) A Public Redressal Machinery with senior level functionary be set-up at the Central level as a part of or independent of Delhi Government but under its direct control. It may have authority to register complaints, investigate them, call for records, communicate decisions for implementation to the Heads of the Departments and also direct appropriate effective or remedial action both in an individual case as also for systematic changes as may be necessary.

(b) Unless a statutory authority on the lines of Lok Ayukta with appropriate powers and authority is established, the problem will not be solved. This Authority may look into the complaints/grievances against public officials and pass such orders as may be necessary for rectification of the wrongs done and also for compensating the affected individual. Obviously establishment of this authority is likely to take time although Delhi legislature has passed a legislation to the effect.

While these ideas are laudable and have merit, what is required is a measure which would effectively alleviate public suffering at the hands of various Departments and can be set-up with expedition. Obviously any measure which may be devised cannot be an ideal one and cannot be an adequate answer to all the needs of the situation, but if some system on the lines of DESU Adalat with requisite modifications and changes which have been suggested or which have become necessary taking into account the actual working of such Adalat, could be thought of that would substantially meet the present needs of the situation. The experiment could be tried for a period of 6 months or so and its results could be watched, monitored and adapted and system improved upon with a view to subserve the needs of the citizens.

One must concede that while the internal system has to be reorganized, there is a case for establishing a review system on the lines of Ombudsman (or oversight agencies as in America and in some other countries), the exact nature or constitution thereof has to be clearly delineated. What is proposed is to have an external and independent review or redressal agency. Such a system should have the following elements :

(a) The complaints handling occurs to some degree outside the organisational confines of the department (that is, it is external).

(b) It is accountable to some autonomous official or body (that is, it is independent), and

(c) The staff of the complaint agency is in some measure composed of non-officials.

Perhaps a word of caution needs to be added. These agencies need to go beyond their predominantly ex-post, individual complaint focus to provide a range of information, policy analyses, covering procedural lapses and defects in rules and their implementation which will enable the department to adjust at an organisational level to the aggregated picture of the working of the department provided by citizens' complaints. The role of these agencies is not to supplant departmental involvement in self-regulation, but rather to enhance the self-regulatory potential through what can be termed as interpolable balanced approach. Inadequate internal complaints mechanisms, however, not only undermine public trust and confidence; arguably they are also socially inefficient. Grievances often feed alienation, anomie, frustration, anxiety and kinship friction, and is an enormous waste of money, time and resources for individuals and the economy in general. People never fully relegate disputes to the past, never completely let bygones by bygones... there is always a residue of attitudes, learned techniques, and sensitivities that will, consciously or unconsciously, colour conflict. An inadequate and unresponsive complaints mechanism only compounds the social inefficiencies associated with citizens' grievances. That becomes counter productive. Failing the provision of credible internal mechanisms, external mechanisms are required to deal with these unresolved feelings.

It must, however, be conceded that redressal of individual grievances is an action which at best can be termed as peripheral. Many persons who are dissatisfied do not complain. Others who complain very often do not pursue and even those who pursue the complaint quite often give it up in disgust or frustration due to lukewarm or inadequate or even hostile response. It is, therefore, necessary that the disease must be attacked at its root. In other words, there is need for effecting organisational changes in the departments having public dealings and to effect such other improvement in laws, rules, procedures, as may be necessary, to reduce the discretion and introduce speed in disposal of public business.

REFERENCES

1. Administrative Reforms Commission was set-up by Govt. of India in 1966.

2. The studies covered several areas of administration such as Personnel Administration, Centre-State Relation, Audit and Accounts, Planning Redressal of Citizen Grievances, District Administration, Public Undertakings, etc.

3. Santhanam Committee set-up in 1962 made several recommendations on prevention of corruption in administration in their report submitted in 1964.

4. Department of Administrative Reforms was created in 1964 initially as part of the Ministry of Home Affairs by conversion of the O&M Division on the recommendation of Santhanam Committee. It become Department of Personnel and Administrative Reforms in 1970. In 1985 it became a fullfledged Ministry, viz., Ministry of Personnel, Public Grievances and Pension under the direct charge of Prime Minister.
5. Central Vigilance Commission was set-up through an order of the Govt. of India as follow up of Sanathanam Committee Report in 1964.
6. Creation of Lokayuktas (in States) and Lokpal (in the Centre) was recommended by the Administrative Reforms Commission in their interim report (1966) in 'Redressal of Citizen Grievances. Accordingly several State Governments have set-up Lokeyuktas (1) Maharashtra in 1972, (2) Rajasthan in 1973, (3) Bihar in 1972, (4) U.P. in 1975, (5) Karnataka in 1983, (6) Orissa in 1983, (7) Andhra Pradesh in 1982, (8) Madhya Pradesh in 1979, (9) Gujarat in 1983, (10) Himachal Pradesh in 1975, (11) Punjab in 1995, (12) Chief Minister National Capital Territory of Delhi announced that his Government is in the process of introducing a Bill on the subject.
7. Estimates Committee Report 1991-92.
8. Action Taken Report on Estimates Committee Report (91-92) submitted in March 1993.
9. Estimates Committee Report 1991-92.
10. *Ibid.*
11. Action Taken Report on Estimates Committee (1993).
12. Balakrishnan Committee Report on "Delhi Set-up".
13. Popular elected government under Mr. Madan Lal Khurana as Chief Minister was installed in November, 1993.
14. Seminars on Administrative Implications on Delhi Set-up held in IIPA (by Delhi Chapter) in September, 1991, 23-7-1992 and 26-11-1993.
15. First sitting of DESU Adalat was held on 25-4-1991. Since then this experiment is gathering momentum, but needs to be improved.
16. At the instance of Delhi Electric Supply Undertaking Delhi, an in-depth study of working of DSEU Adalat is to be conducted by IIPA (Delhi Chapter). PA

PART-II

ADDRESS BY MR. P.K. DAVE, THE THEN LT. GOVERNOR, DELHI ON REDRESSAL OF PUBLIC GRIEVANCES ON 11TH AUGUST, 1994 AT IIPA (DELHI CHAPTER)

I am again tempted to talk to you about the harassment of citizens, who have dealings with public agencies. We administrators of all hues, have been unashamed believers in the ad-hoc approach to complaints of citizens. It has been clear for almost three decades or more during which the problem has been much discussed and debated, that this approach has not produced results and is unlikely to do so. One may say that serious harassment of the citizens began with the introduction of the Licence-Permit Raj during the Second World War, and the years of controlled economy that followed independence. Although in this brief discussion I am not looking for root cause, it is believed to be true that controls and regulations have largely contributed to harassment of the public. Even so, that truth does not explain how the problem has assumed such gigantic proportions. Serious harassment, even extortion, have spread through the entire Government machinery, from the political executive through the agencies that direct and control economic and civic activities, and even among those adjudicating upon these matters. And in this process, there are intermediaries of diverse kinds, the professional, the plain or sophisticated touts, those holding elective positions. Virtually every situation that can be used for exploitation and extortion, seems to be so used.

Leaving corruption as such aside, today I would like to concentrate on grievances and complaints of citizens. Grievances and complaints against non-performance of services that a citizen is entitled to, whether from a municipality, a revenue collector's office, a hospital, the sub-registrar of documents or the registrar of births and deaths and, of course, the police and executive magistrate, leaving for the time being the judiciary that must find its own salvation.

It is now fashionable to have departments of public grievances in all major offices. We even have a Secretary to the Government of India in charge of the redressal of public grievances. In a limited way, these have helped, but truth to tell, the impact on the situation is negligible. It is at best the declaration of pious wish.

A number of other institutions have been set-up to deal with this state of affairs, and a lot more has been thought of and not implemented. Those that exist, such as the Consumer Redressal Tribunals have done extremely useful work and as their usefulness becomes choked with cases, what was and is true about the Rent Control Tribunals—I seriously doubt the need for Rent Control at all—has happened with the Consumer Tribunals.

It will happen again with grievance tribunals, if we continue with the unfortunate practice of prescribing formal procedures, and permitting appearance of lawyers.

Even so, there is every reason for firm declaration of intent by governments and all autonomous agencies, including for that matter the highest judiciary. A good example of such a declaration of intent is the Citizen's Charter of the UK presented in the form of a White Paper in 1991 by Prime Minister John Major. Let me quote from that document.

When things go wrong, there must be a swift and simple way of putting them right. People must know how to complain. They must know to whom they should complain. And they must have confidence that their complaint will be dealt with.

It is fundamental to the Citizen's Charter that all public services, including local authorities should have clear and well publicized complaints procedures.

Any Complaints Mechanism Should :

— be open and accessible, and supported by clearly displayed stands at the point of service;

— provide readily available information about how to complain, and clearly identified point of contact for doing so;

provide a code of practice for handling complaints. This should include tight targets for resolving complaints and clear information on further procedures if the customer is not satisfied with the response.

It is usually best to resolve complaints on the spot. The more centralized and remote a complaints procedure is, the likelier it is to be slower, more expensive and less user-friendly.

"The Citizen's Charter commits the Government to an ambitious long-term programme... to raise the standard of public services and make them more responsive to their users".

A system of the kind described above requires a deep sense of motivation flowing down from the highest levels and even more importantly, a commitment on the part of the head of each agency to ensure a diligent and truthful compliance of the schemes in its letter and spirit. If I may confess, in my experience of over two years as Lt. Governor of Delhi I have not witnessed that commitment. Even exhortations to groups of the senior-most officers that their efforts at the redressal of grievances and the cursing of corruption, or the absence of them, would be noticed in the annual confidential reports seem to have brought little result.

Let me take by way of example only three of Delhi's institutions with which the citizen appears to be most dissatisfied. That is a statement based not only reflecting reportage in the press which is, of course, a most useful source of information on such matters, but also borne out by the number of complaints received and public statements made by people's representatives.

First, I would like to take the Delhi Electric Supply Undertaking mainly because it has attempted a grievance procedure of a slightly more open kind than elsewhere. The Bijli Adalat is supposed to be held every month on a fixed day in each zone. The Chief Engineer presides and the Additional Chief Engineer is Member Secretary. There are two outsiders whose association adds to credibility. Grievances can be considered only if they have already been screened, examined and decided at the level of the District Grievance Machinery. The complainant is heard and record inspected and decision announced normally on the spot. A fair amount of satisfaction has resulted from these Adalats. But DESU has not committed itself to implicit acceptance of the recommendations of the Adalat and some important recommendations have not been acted upon. Similarly, if some one has been compelled to go court he is not allowed to come before the Adalat. If he gets redress he would surely be prepared to withdraw his case from the Court before the redress was implemented.

The few Adalats that have been held so far have disclosed not only long delays in creative actions, refunds, reconnections etc. but there has been regrettable reluctance to call defaulting personnel to account. I cannot say, and I am sure people here in the audience will not say that there is a general satisfaction at the services made available by DESU.

The second institution I would mention is the Delhi Development Authority, another much criticized agency, in this case of the Central Government. It works under the Chairmanship of Lt. Governor with a Chief Executive who is the Vice-Chairman. The public complaints against this organization are legion and one would imagine that the whole effect has been such a dismal failure that it had better be wounded up. Sometimes in my despair I think so too.

An organization meant to plan and build a beautiful Delhi and provide accommodation to the millions seems to have done neither. I must say that is by no means a fair assessment. The DDA has achieved a lot in both directions but it has been defeated not only by unchecked growth of population but also by its failure to learn from its experience and adjust. For example, it was only yesterday that at its meeting I remarked that privatization of construction was being thought of in the early 80's and a blueprint was supposed to be ready then. It is not ready till today and the armies of engineers on DDA's strength are opposed to the very idea of privatization.

Let us now talk about the grievances against DDA and what they are doing to redress. In the last two years procedures for meeting people with complainants have been introduced and Heads of Departments meet complaints on two fixed days each week. The Vice-Chairman and Principal Commissioner—the two senior officers—hold public hearings on Fridays. The complaints are generally treated as TBRs, which stands for Time Bound References. I am assured that most of the complaints, "if" the documentation of the complainant is complete, are dealt with in about two weeks. That "if", I am afraid is seldom fulfilled". I have seen files where simple mutations of the name of a lessee when his father has died and every legal aspect is beyond doubt has taken years with sometimes 3, 4 and 5 sets of documentations asked for repeatedly have no understandable reasons. The complaints against DDA are generally of delay, loss of documentations, failure of communications and of course great escalation of cost. The grievance procedure being followed does not appear to be open nor does it involve any impartial outside agency.

Let me quickly cover the third agency the Municipal Corporation of Delhi. Here again there is no particular grievances cell as such though I believe public hearing are given.

As some of you may know, I have been proposing the establishment of Complaints Commissions, one for Delhi Police and another for the remaining departments of Delhi Administration and including in it the DDA. These Commissions, according to me, should be manned by reputed and retired administrators/professionals, and social workers, and should deal with the citizens' grievances and complaints on a summary basis. No formal procedures should be followed, nor lawyers permitted to appear. Heads of departments must be bound to assist the Commissions with the production of all documents necessary for inspection, and they must be bound to carry out the decisions of the Commissions, unless for any special reason, they wish to seek the Government's intervention. If finally, a difference of opinion occurs between the Government and the Commission and the Commission's recommendation is not followed, the case may be mentioned in the annual report to be placed before the Parliament or State Legislature, as the case may be.

While these Complaints Commissions must be established as quickly as possible, that will not take away the essential responsibility of each public agency to have a self-regulatory charter for the performance of its functions to the citizen's satisfaction. Each department should publicize its grievances redressal procedures, have an officer to assist and advise the public and help them to ascertain facts about their cases.

The public perception of the services rendered should be ascertained continuously by inviting them to fill up questionnaire and deposit them in easily accessible boxes. Also through periodic academic studies well publicized.

Post-Script—Editors' Note

The former Lt. Governor's stirring address displays his concern coupled with the anguish and the pain he felt for the common man because the grievance redressal machinery in Delhi is neither prompt nor effective. The Bijli Adalat experiment is, as noted by him, only a partial success. Both the then Lt. Governor P.K. Dave and his predecessor, Markandey Singh, were unable to persuade the DDA and MCD to set-up a redressal machinery in which outsiders could be associated. At his instance DESU has commissioned a study of the functioning of Bijli Adalat so as to learn lessons for future.

Mr. P.K. Dave, former Lt. Governor asked the Centre for Policy Research to make recommendations for redressal of grievances of common people vis-a-vis Police Organization. In June 1994, he made comprehensive recommendations to the Ministry of Home Affairs for setting-up of a Police Complaints Authority on the pattern of the one existing in UK and also some other countries. For more than two years the Ministry of Home Affairs did not respond positively and the proposals remained in cold storage. Analogous social and political systems may and do produce the impetus for change in legal reforms (in this case the setting up of an External Police Complaints Authority) at similar stages but once the demand for change has arisen its priority and results are random. In a social sense randomness is promoted by the centrality of the influence of public scandal or 'expose' criminology. Accident is crucial to scandal; both are random and in that sense arbitrary. The disclosure of police misconduct, be it individual or organizational, the reaction of the public, the media, and the powerful, whether community tolerance. Official tolerance, or the power balance in the given society is high or low for that kind of police deviance and the effects if any, in and beyond the police organization are random and hence, to a significant degree, the system reform which may or may not result is random.

This random factor in catalysing legal reforms or reforms in criminal justice system is illustrated in several studies covering different countries. We need not notice the details of those cases here. Suffice it to say that the random factor is illustrated by the present case of setting-up of the Police Complaints Authority in Delhi. A proposal sent by the then Lt. Governor to the Home Ministry in June, 1994 was lying unattended for more than two years. Suddenly the Home Ministry and the PMO woke up with two cases relating to alleged molestation or rape of an inmate of a Nari Niketan and another relating to the involvement of the nephews of the present Chief Minister were played up by the media and were referred to in the Delhi Legislative Assembly and also in the Rajya Sabha. In the wake of the two controversies, within a day the setting-up of a Police Complaints Authority was approved in principle. The Prime Minister in his statement in the Rajya Sabha on August 2, 1996, indirectly testified to this "random factor". To put it in his own words:

> "...Yesterday, in this House, specific mention was made of two cases, one relating to the alleged molestation/rape of a woman at the residence of a

> VIP and the other relating to the involvement of the nephews of a VIP. Both these cases are under investigation by the Delhi Police at present..."

And finally the P.M. made a policy statement announcing the establishment of a Police Complaints Authority, part of which is reproduced below:

> "There has been a general feeling among the public that complaints against police are investigated by the police themselves and, in most cases, they reach, in their original form, the very officers against whom they are made. Even though there is a Vigilance Cell in the Delhi Police, public confidence in the objectivity and impartiality of the inquiries conducted against police officials seems to be much less than what it should be. It is proposed to create an independent authority, the Police Complaints Authority, for dealing with public complaints against police. These complaints will cover, *inter alia*, police inaction, non-registration of FIRs, partisan attitude on the part of the Police, registration of false cases, corruption and intervention in civil disputes particularly those relating to property and tenancy, custodial torture, rape and other misbehaviour, abuse of police power etc. We would involve eminent public men and women with this Police Complaints Authority".

The setting-up of the Public Complaints Authority has been announced but it is still to take shape. So far as the setting-up of an effective redressal machinery for DDA, MCD and other agencies is concerned, although the Lt. Governor has taken up the matter with the Ministry of Urban Development and the Chief Minister respectively, no positive results are so far visible. Hopefully the setting up of the Police Complaints Authority would act as a catalytic agent for establishment of similar machinery for redressal of public grievances in DDA, Municipal Corporation of Delhi, Cooperative Department and other public dealing departments.

An important step taken by Delhi Government in the area of redressal of grievances and enquiry and investigation into allegations made against a pubic functionary is their proposal for setting-up of Lok Ayukta system in Delhi through "Delhi Lok Ayukta and Up Lok Ayukta Act, 1995. This is likely to serve as a deterrent to indulgence in malpractices by public functionaries.

LIST OF CONTRIBUTORS

1. Prof. Bava, Noorjahan, Department of Political Science, University of Delhi, South Campus.
2. Gaur, M.K., Assistant Editor, IIPA, New Delhi.
3. Dr. Kaur, Inderjeet, Reader, Department of Political Science, Satyawati Co-ed. College, University of Delhi.
4. Dr. Kumar, Ashok, Lecturer, School of Planning and Architecture, New Delhi.
5. Mishra, Yatish, Research Associate, IIPA, New Delhi.
6. Dr. Roy, J. Guha, Sr. Lecturer in Criminal Justice, IIPA, New Delhi.
7. Prof. Sharma, P.B., Principal Delhi College of Engg., Delhi.
8. Dr. Sharma, V.K., Reader in Environmental Studies, IIPA, New Delhi.
9. Dr. Vashisht, K. Rai, Assistant Director, Department of Administrative Reforms, Government of NCT of Delhi.
10. Vajpeyi, S.C., (Former Chief Secretary, Delhi and Pro-Vice-Chancellor, Indira Gandhi National Open University) Hony. Secretary, IIPA, Delhi (Regional Branch).
11. Prof. Verma, S.P., (Former Professor IGNOU and IIPA), Dean and Sr. Director E.M.P.I., New Delhi, Vice-Chairman IIPA, Delhi (Regional Branch).

12. Dr. Wishwakarma, R.K., Reader in Urban Studies, IIPA, New Delhi.

13. Bihari Rakesh, Former Commissioner (Lands), DDA.

— Shrivastava S.K., acted as Research Associate with the Project.

14. Mrs. Silas Satbir, Director of Education N.C.T. of Delhi.

15. Sharma M.M., Assistant Director (Planning), Directorate of Education N.C.T. of Delhi.

16. Gupta R.K., Chief Engineer Delhi State Industrial Development Corporation Limited.

Index